Seven Spies
Who Changed the World

Nigel West is a military historian specialising in security matters and is the European Editor of *Intelligence Quarterly*. He has written several controversial histories of Britain's intelligence organisations, including *A Matter of Trust: MI5 1945–72*, which was banned temporarily, and *Molehunt*. The *Sunday Times* has commented:

> 'His information is often so precise that many people believe that he is the unofficial historian of the secret services. West's sources are undoubtedly excellent. His books are peppered with deliberate clues to potential front-page stories.'

He was voted 'The Experts' Expert' by the *Observer* and the KGB defector Oleg Gordievsky said in the *Evening Standard* that 'Nigel West is generally much better than any other spy writer'.

Also by Nigel West
and available from
Mandarin Paperbacks

The Blue List
Cuban Bluff

SEVEN SPIES WHO CHANGED THE WORLD

NIGEL WEST

Mandarin

A Mandarin Paperback

SEVEN SPIES WHO CHANGED THE WORLD

First published in Great Britain 1991
by Martin Secker & Warburg Ltd
This edition published 1992
by Mandarin Paperbacks
Michelin House, 81 Fulham Road, London SW3 6RB

Mandarin is an imprint of the Octopus Publishing Group,
a division of Reed International Books Limited

A CIP catalogue record for this title
is available from the British Library

ISBN 0 7493 0620 3

Printed and bound in Great Britain
by Cox & Wyman Ltd, Reading, Berks

Contents

Illustrations

The following picture sources are gratefully acknowledged: the Associated Press (8), the author's collection (15, 16, 21), the Hon. Philippe Deane Gigantes (17), the Hulton-Deutsch Collection (19, 22), Marco Popov (1, 2), Popperfoto (6, 10), the Press Association (11, 13, 20), Rex Features (7, 9), James Rusbridger (14), Topham (12), Harry Williamson (4, 5).

Introduction

'Intelligence-gathering' is a polite term for espionage and, according to the universally recognised protocol of the international intelligence community, spies are only employed by one's opponents. But this well-established convention conceals the fact, frequently overlooked or deliberately ignored by historians, that most political decisions of any significance have been strongly influenced by advice supplied by intelligence agencies. All too often, sometimes decades after the event, historians seek other explanations to justify an especially momentous decision, as though the mere acknowledgement of such a dimension somehow implies illegitimacy. Of course, this may indeed be the case, as the process of intelligence collection is often clandestine in nature; but the unpalatable fact remains that the role played by intelligence in the background to a particular event may have been absolutely critical. However, such references as there are will often take the form of mere footnotes.

For years academics have been extraordinarily reluctant to give due recognition to the vital contribution made by the men in the shadows; the unassuming, unsung analysts and case officers who have run agents, interpreted photographs, tapped telephones, intercepted mail and handled agents so that politicians might avoid folly and disaster. Perhaps as often, the decision-makers have ignored *sub rosa* advice and thereby imperilled nations and even whole continents. Yet the history books appear markedly reluctant to take such factors into account when recording these events. The reason, no doubt, is often the confidential nature of the item of intelligence, which may mitigate against premature disclosure. Revelation of the wartime Allied success in the cryptographic field would have eliminated a valuable post-war source of information. Security considerations are entirely valid as motives for omitting certain aspects of history from publication, but the historians who have either submitted to censorship or imposed it upon themselves can hardly blame the public for seeking to learn more about episodes and incidents that have previously been consigned, for the sake of discretion, to locked vaults. However, for them to deride those historiographers who overcome the obstacles and gain access to these previously inaccessible archives as subscribing to an 'airport-bookstall school of history'[1] betrays an intellectual arrogance of breathtaking proportions. Whilst there are plenty of conspiracy theorists perhaps a little too willing to advocate global schemes of labyrinthine complexity, often constructed on foundations of dubious evidence, there is plenty of room in our culture for due recognition to be given to what might be termed 'the secret world'. It is this perspective that has frequently been ignored in the past, often deliberately, by some distinguished historians.

In recent years the unthinkable has happened. Two of Oxbridge's most eminent professorial knights, Harry Hinsley and Michael Howard, have been commissioned by the government to write official accounts of the parts played by Britain's intelligence services during World War II. Suddenly, academic respectability has been given to a subject previously considered taboo.

Even now, when intelligence is at last achieving acceptability, there remains the challenge of identifying all the different factors in the mosaic that add up to the product itself, be it advice proffered or evidence accumulated. They may be in the form of documents or photographs but, as often as not, personalities will be involved, and in all probability their relative insignificance as a cog in the huge administrative bureaucracy of the intelligence machine will prevent them receiving the attention that, in other circumstances, they might expect to receive.

Take, as an example, the case of Wulf Schmidt, a young man from Schleswig-Holstein who parachuted into Cambridgeshire in September 1940. I first met him in 1980 while researching my history of the British Security Service, MI5. At that first encounter I promised never to reveal his new identity without having first obtained his consent, and he has very kindly given permission for the name he now uses to be printed in these pages. He told me, during our many hours of conversation, that he had few expectations of doing anything more than fulfilling his Abwehr assignment of preparing for a Nazi invasion of Britain. He believed his mission would be brief, and he had no reason to suppose that he would stay in England for the rest of his life . . . nor that he would make a considerable contribution to the success of the Allied landings in Normandy during the summer of 1944. His present identity, that of 'Harry Williamson', remains almost completely unknown to the public,[2] although his MI5 code name, TATE, appears in the footnotes of many textbooks on strategic deception. Who was he, what was his motivation, and how does he feel now about having been 'turned' into not just one of a stable of double agents, but a crucial figure in the ambitious Allied plan to persuade the Germans that the long-expected D-Day assault would take place in the Pas-de-Calais region?

Wulf Schmidt's story is one of seven told in the pages that follow. All these men, to a greater or lesser degree, have made a remarkable contribution, either positive or negative, to the course of history, and most have been known to me personally. In the case of Greville Wynne, with whom I was once locked in an epic legal battle, he had little idea at the time of his significance and, even after his eventual release from imprisonment in the Soviet Union, deliberately falsified much of what he had done, thus making the task of historians seeking to piece together his true story all the more difficult, challenging and compelling. Wynne, of course, is virtually a household name, whereas relatively few will have heard of William Buckley, a senior CIA officer and that organisation's Chief of Station in Beirut when he was abducted, supposedly by Muslim fundamentalists, in 1984.

Buckley's clandestine career had taken him to trouble spots across the globe, and he had been present on the presidential podium in Cairo when Anwar Sadat was assassinated in 1977. But not even his kidnapping, as one of numerous other Western hostages taken captive during the period, would have plucked him from the obscurity he had so assiduously cultivated, if it had not been for the loyalty of his DCI, Bill Casey, whom I first met in 1981. Casey's dogged determination to obtain Buckley's release led directly to what became known as the 'Irangate scandal', and a reappraisal of Ronald Reagan's presidency. My reconstruction of the events that led to the arms-for-hostages furore has been helped by Ya'acov Nimrodi, a retired Mossad officer and a key player in the drama, to whom I am exceptionally grateful.

While Buckley's disappearance was to have a profound impact, albeit indirectly, on the American domestic scene, it was the capture of an apparently insignificant pilot, Francis Gary Powers, on 1 May 1960 that was to alter dramatically the US's relationship with the Soviet Union. Powers was not an innocent airman engaged on advanced-weather research for NACA, as was claimed at the time, but a professional CIA pilot. Furthermore, he had not been killed in the crash, as the Soviets first implied. He had failed to use the poison-tipped needle with which he had been issued, and which I examined in the KGB's museum. Instead, Powers was alive and talking to the KGB. Perhaps more significantly, the loss of the U-2 was to be followed by a presidential ban on all further illicit overflights, and this in turn resulted in an end to the prized aerial-reconnaissance photographs that had allowed the CIA to monitor Soviet development of strategic weapons. The sudden removal of this vital source of intelligence meant the Pentagon had to resort to little more than guesswork to quantify the Soviet threat from intercontinental ballistic missiles. The consequent difference between the estimates and the real figures was to become known as the 'missile gap', and set the scene for the arms race which characterised the next three decades. It also helped create the atmosphere of mutual hostility and suspicion that was to mark Soviet-American relations thereafter.

When Powers was finally released from a Soviet prison in 1963, there was pressure from within the CIA for him to be charged with, at the very least, dereliction of duty. However, the calls were resisted because it was widely accepted that the hapless pilot had already suffered enough. Nobody could pretend that Powers had intended to betray his country, as Anthony Blunt had done, but in global terms the consequences of his negligence were infinitely greater.

Blunt's case is also to be examined here, for although he personally may not have changed history, the information he provided in 1964 fundamentally changed the West's understanding of Soviet espionage and the scale of the penetration of the British establishment by the Soviets. Blunt's confession precipitated a massive molehunt; and when the details of his treachery were made public in 1979, stunned the public, which became aware for the first time of the incredible scale of the investigations sparked off on both sides of the Atlantic. On 27 May 1981 he entertained me to tea at his flat in Portsea Hall, the first of a series of meetings. Thereafter we corresponded and, even if he did not always answer my questions, he did display great courtesy and patience, as did his KGB controller, Yuri Modin, with whom I spent several very agreeable hours in Moscow.

One Soviet agent unknown to Blunt was George Blake. Blunt had no personal knowledge of the SIS officer who had volunteered to spy for the KGB, but was keenly interested in his fate. In June 1962 Blake had been sentenced to a record forty-two years of imprisonment, and no doubt this weighed on his mind when, two years later, Blunt was offered an immunity from prosecution. Another couple of years later Blake was to escape from his cell in Wormwood Scrubs and it is only now, after the two individuals who engineered his journey to East Berlin have themselves been prosecuted, and he has published his own controversial memoirs, that the full story can be told. He kindly received me in the flat in which he has lived since his unexpected arrival in Moscow on Christmas Eve, 1966.

Blake, Schmidt, Wynne, Buckley, Powers and Blunt are but six of the spies to be studied here. We start with Dusko Popov, a spy whom I met only once, at his beautiful home in the south of France, and who richly deserves every one of his brief appearances in the annals of espionage. Devastatingly attractive to women, he was unquestionably a man who personified everything that was glamorous and dangerous in what has been termed the world's second-oldest profession.

CHAPTER I

Dusko Popov

As the Wehrmacht swept through northern Europe in 1940, Belgrade was one of several neutral capital cities that metaphorically held their breath. The Nazis had failed to respect the unaligned status of Holland and Belgium, and many anticipated that war would sooner or later come to Yugoslavia. Certainly this calculation had been made by the British Secret Intelligence Service, which concentrated much of its efforts on building the kind of 'stay-behind' network that had been so demonstrably lacking in Poland and France. However, Belgrade had been selected by SIS as its major operating base in the region, and it had established two quite separate clandestine organisations. The first, known as the Sabotage Service in the higher echelons of Whitehall, or Section D to the *cognoscenti*, was run by a local British businessman, Julius Hanau.[1] He headed a hand-picked group of saboteurs who, operating under commercial or journalistic cover, attempted to recruit Yugoslavs who were sympathetic to the Allied cause. The second covert structure was an intelligence-gathering group headed by Clement Hope,[2] an experienced SIS officer who acted as the Passport Control Officer attached to the British Legation. Unfortunately, neither Section D nor Hope's contacts had sufficient time to prepare a well-developed network before the British evacuated in the face of a German invasion.

There was however one individual, a young commercial lawyer whom Hope had cultivated, who was to pay dividends. His name was Dusko Popov, and he was one of three sons of a wealthy Dalmatian family from Dubrovnik. Both he and his elder brother, a doctor named Ivo, approached Hope after the Abwehr had made its own recruitment pitch. Hope's advice was to appear to co-operate with the Germans, but to submit reports discreetly to SIS. Thus a classic double-agent operation got under way with Dusko, code-named SCOUT by Hope, describing how the Abwehr had used a German friend whom he had known at Freiburg University, Johann Jebsen, to recruit and train him for a secret mission. Late in the autumn of 1940 Jebsen revealed his assignment: Dusko was to be sent to England as a spy, leaving Ivo and their youngest brother, Vlado, in Yugoslavia. Once in London Dusko was to make contact with a friend who he claimed would be willing to gather information for the Nazis. In reality, no such person existed outside Dusko's fertile imagination.

SIS persuaded Dusko to fall in with Jebsen's plan and accordingly, in mid-December 1940, he turned up at Lisbon and left a pre-arranged message at the British Passport Control Office at the rua Emenda for Richman Stopford, the local SIS Head of Station and, incidentally, a former MI5 officer. Stopford had been instrumental in identifying and 'turning' the Abwehr's star agent in London, a Welshman named Arthur Owens[3] (known in the Security Service's headquarters by the cryptonym SNOW). As the senior SIS officer in Lisbon, Stopford had been warned to expect Dusko, and knew exactly how to handle him. A signal was sent to London and MI5 was informed that an important enemy agent was about to travel to England carrying a quantity of secret ink and a comprehensive questionnaire on a variety of topics. As well as samples of British ration cards and identity documents, the German military intelligence service, the Abwehr, had requested Dusko to obtain routine military information about coastal installations and anti-aircraft batteries, together with the locations of all headquarter units. He was to investigate a list of sites believed to be constructing aircraft for the RAF and discover their production figures. Of particular interest were the names of ships damaged by mines and torpedoes, and details of the American military aid pouring into the country. Two further instructions intrigued MI5. Dusko was to find out all he could about the British organisation responsible for dealing with enemy parachutists and Fifth-Columnists, and he was to try to penetrate the staff of the Commander-in-Chief Home Fleet, Admiral Sir John Tovey.

Arrangements were made for his safe reception and, by long-established convention, control of Dusko was passed from SIS to MI5. The arrangement whereby the Security Service exercised total control over all espionage activites on British territory throughout the Empire was the cause of constant friction between the two agencies, which often acted as rivals. However, the scope of Dusko's questionnaire, more detailed and potentially more dangerous than any previously found, was to be the catalyst for the creation of a new interdepartmental sub-committee. Early the following year, after a marked deterioration in their relationship, the handling of double agents was formalised by a specialist group, known as the Twenty Committee (after the Roman numerals for double-cross, XX), upon which both MI5 and SIS were represented. Inter-service disputes were to be arbitrated by a highly respected academic, J. C. Masterman from Christ Church, Oxford, who was acknowledged by all sides to be of independent mind. While this sophisticated apparatus was still being negotiated, Dusko was flown from Lisbon with the consent of the director of MI5's counter-espionage division, Guy Liddell. This allowed Dusko to avoid the lengthy screening process that so many refugees and suspect aliens were obliged to endure, and assured him of a warm welcome at Bristol Airport on 20 December 1940 by a suitably briefed MI5 officer, Jock Horsfall, an exhilarating ride to London with the former racing driver, and a room at the Savoy Hotel.

Waiting to meet Dusko at the Savoy was a brilliant MI5 officer, Major T. A. Robertson, the intuitive architect of what was to become known as 'the double-cross system'. Robertson had personally turned SNOW and had run him with great success for the past year. The fact that Dusko's credentials had been confirmed by his former assistant, Richman Stopford, no doubt encouraged the Scot to accept Dusko as another double agent, but the clincher must have been the nugget of information that Dusko had extracted from an Abwehr officer in Lisbon, and retained to prove his bona fides in London. During a briefing session conducted by his German case officer, a certain 'Ludovico von Karstoff', attached to the German Legation, Dusko had also been given the identity of an emergency contact in London, a Czech called Georges Graf. Dusko promptly volunteered the name, and Robertson expressed his gratitude for his help. Although Dusko was not to know it, Graf was already well known to MI5, as was 'von Karstoff', who was listed by MI5 under his true identity of Major Albrecht von Auenrode, from Vienna.

In fact Georges Graf[4] had been 'talent-spotted' for the Abwehr after arriving in Lisbon as a refugee earlier in the summer. He was just twenty-two years old and in 1939 had joined the French Army with a companion, Ivan Spaneil.[5] They had both attended the artillery school at Poitiers, and then had fled across the Pyrenees with the intention of joining the Free French forces in England. While in Portugal they had both accepted von Karstoff's offer to spy for the Germans. In fact, they had never intended to spy, and had hoped to use the Abwehr as a means of facilitating their journey to London. In any event, the person who had recommended their recruitment, a Frenchman named Wiesner, was himself working for Stopford as a double agent under the cryptonym SWEETIE, so the approach was known to SIS almost as soon as von Auenrode had decided to make it. Wiesner said that he had co-operated with the Germans under duress because his family was still in Nazi-occupied territory and therefore vulnerable to reprisals. When Graf and his friend reached England in September they immediately volunteered details of their clandestine roles to the British authorities, and willingly agreed to work as double agents. MI5 assigned them John Bingham as their case officer, the cryptonyms GIRAFFE and SPANEHL respectively, and supervised their correspondence with the Abwehr's postal address in Lisbon. At no time did the Germans show any sign of realising that Wiesner, Graf or Spaneil had fallen under British control.

Dusko, of course, was not allowed to know the more complex background to MI5's clandestine contact with the enemy, for the Security Service deliberately ran each double agent in isolation, taking care to assign a case officer working under a *nom de guerre* to each compartmented individual. The objective was to limit possible exposure to the absolute minimum in the event that a double agent turned sour and betrayed the duplicity to the Abwehr. Accordingly Dusko never knew that Graf had already been enrolled as a double agent. Similarly, when he was introduced to 'Bill Matthews', who was to act as his handler, he did not realise that his true name was William Luke. Dusko's task of creating an import-export firm was assisted by MI5, which installed him in a prestigious office in Imperial House, Regent Street, and a company entitled Tarlair Limited, a name devised by Tommy Robertson with his characteristic sense of humour. His secretary, Gisela Ashley, was also thoughtfully provided by MI5, as was his manager, Mrs Brander; and although Dusko never spotted it, he was kept under constant surveillance. Even his flat in Park Street was fitted with hidden listening devices, just to ensure he did not decide to switch sides. Meanwhile the Security Service distributed copies of Dusko's questionnaires to the relevant departments and tried, unsuccessfully, to extract some reasonable answers that might impress the Germans without compromising security. The eventual solution to MI5's dilemma was the formation of the Twenty Committee.

A month later, in January 1941, Dusko returned to Lisbon to report on his progress to von Auenrode, and then travelled to Madrid where he was met for further debriefing by Jebsen.

He arrived equipped with rather unsatisfactorily vague answers to many of the tasks set by the Abwehr, as the Twenty Committee was still uncertain about its role in supplying the enemy with potentially helpful information. Instead, as compensation, Dusko carried a chart of east-coast minefields which, he claimed, had been given to him by a cowardly Jewish naval officer named Ewen Montagu who was supposedly convinced the Germans would win the war. This ingenious idea, developed with Montagu's enthusiastic consent, was intended to keep the Abwehr occupied until the Twenty Committee could obtain agreement to its plan to concoct a plausible set of answers to Dusko's questionnaire. Between his meetings with the Germans, Dusko kept secret appointments with Colonel Ralph Jarvis, a locally based SIS officer who acted as his link with London.[6] Dusko reported that apparently neither Jebsen nor von Auenrode suspected that they had been deceived, and he received instructions to develop his operation in London a stage further by recruiting two of his contacts, his attractive Austrian girlfriend Friedle Gaertner[7] and a former army officer named Dickie Metcalfe. Both had the best possible credentials for collaborating with the Abwehr. Friedle was already known to the Germans as a Nazi sympathiser who had been a frequent visitor to Ribbentrop's embassy in London before the war. In reality she had acted as an *agent provocateur* for the Security Service, identifying other contacts who were suspected of disloyalty. This had enabled MI5 to arrest and intern a large number of potentially dangerous enemy aliens on the outbreak of war. Code-named GELATINE because Billy Luke thought her 'a jolly little thing', she was to become a key double agent, supplying the Abwehr with political gossip. She was in an especially good position to do this because of her equally beautiful sister, Lisel, had married Ian Menzies, whose elder brother Stewart was Chief of the Secret Intelligence Service. Thus, through Dusko, the Abwehr believed it had achieved access to the very top of the British intelligence structure. In reality, of course, all GELATINE's messages were carefully prepared and vetted by MI5. Dickie Metcalfe was also well positioned to help the Germans, particularly with technical information. His story, partly true, was that he had been obliged to resign his army commission when he had got into financial difficulties after a racehorse deal had failed. He now ran a company based in Piccadilly trading in small arms and had agreed, at MI5's suggestion, to pose as a willing source of technical data regarding weapons. As Dusko acquired his two sub-agents so MI5 gave him a new, more appropriate cryptonym: TRICYCLE.

Dusko's new role as the organiser of an Abwehr network in Britain certainly enhanced his standing with MI5, which continued to prepare answers for the tasks set him by his German controllers. After his return from Lisbon in February 1941 he handed MI5 a questionnaire he had been instructed to complete, which gave the Security Service a useful insight into the enemy's intelligence requirements and revealed the quality of the information already in its possession. For example, one item read:

> Do Vickers Armstrong possess factories at Brighton and Hawarden to the west of the aerodrome? Have the buildings which were near the aerodromes and which were used for army purposes now been taken over by Vickers for manufacturing? How many Wellingtons do Armstrong make each month? Where else are Wellingtons or parts for Wellingtons made? We want sketches showing sites for Vickers at Weybridge and Vickers near Crayford.[8]

In addition, Dusko was requested to complete a detailed study of the defences along a stretch of the English coastline from the Wash in Norfolk to Southampton. He was also specifically asked, 'When are five battleships of *King George V* class ready?',[9] but von Auenrode did not intend Dusko to remain in London. The Abwehr's purpose in recruiting GELATINE and BAL-

LOON was so that they could continue operations in England, leaving Dusko free to undertake a special mission in America.

This new assignment was discussed by von Auenrode and Dusko when they met again in Lisbon at the end of February 1941. Dusko delivered a favourable report on his two new sub-agents and confirmed that they would be perfectly competent to take over his duties in London. During the course of their conversation von Auenrode returned to the topic of a previous talk which had been causing the Abwehr some difficulty, and with which MI5 had expressed itself very eager to help. It seemed that the Abwehr had come up against a number of obstacles in its attempts to establish a permanent, reliable conduit to its agents in England through which they could receive money. Some of the agents had run very low on cash and no acceptable method of transferring funds had been found. Dusko's ingenious solution was to suggest that it might be possible for the Abwehr to make a deposit in a neutral country and arrange for someone already in England to dispense a similar sum to the Abwehr's nominee. The scheme would depend upon finding an individual in England willing to circumvent the strict exchange-control regulations and produce a cash sum in return for a bank credit elsewhere.

Dusko's plan received the backing of Martin Toeppen, the Abwehr's financial supervisor, and von Auenrode was particularly impressed by his suggestion for a nominee, a Jewish theatrical agent who, Dusko asserted, had made a tidy sum in London and was anxious to export his cash to America. The fact that the theatrical agent was Austrian in origin added authenticity to Dusko's proposal, although the person in question, Eric Glass,[10] had absolutely no knowledge of what was being done in his name. Upon his return to London Dusko agreed to obtain the details of an account in New York into which the Abwehr should transfer $100,000, and arrange for the equivalent amount in sterling to be made available at Glass's place of business. In reality, MI5 had placed one of its own staff as a receptionist at

15 Haymarket in anticipation of receiving a request for money from an unknown German spy. When the project eventually got under way, in July 1941, no less than £20,000 was handed over to TATE, thus confirming Wulf Schmidt's standing in German eyes. The arrangement was later abandoned when Martin Toeppen was arrested by the Gestapo for having embezzled some of the Abwehr's foreign currency reserves.

Dusko was to go back to Lisbon in March 1941 to make one last interim report before his American assignment and to finalise the financial transaction, which MI5 aptly dubbed Plan MIDAS. While the Abwehr was keen to proceed with the plan to finance TATE, it showed less enthusiasm for a map which Dusko pretended he had obtained from his acquaintance in the Royal Navy. It supposedly charted the location of minefields along Britain's east coast, but the matter was pursued no further, apparently because the Germans believed the document to be out of date. The remainder of the visit was spent in preparation for Dusko's forthcoming voyage across the Atlantic which was to be made, theoretically at least, on behalf of the Ministry of Information in London to assess the effect of British propaganda on Yugoslavs in America.

Dusko's trip to America has become quite a *cause célèbre*, not least because of his stormy relations with the FBI while he was under their jurisdiction, but chiefly due to the contents of the questionnaire with which he was issued *en route*, early in August 1941. Dusko had travelled to Portugal, for the fourth time that year, on 26 June and received a briefing from von Auenrode concerning the tasks he was to undertake while in the States. In addition he was given a questionnaire which, using microphotography, had been reduced to the size of six full stops concealed on a telegram so as to escape any search Dusko would undergo in Bermuda or New York. This development created great interest in London, because microphotography was then quite a novelty and this was one of the very first examples of its operational use.[11] As for the questionnaire itself, a large part of it related to naval installations in Hawaii, which was to take on a greater significance after the Japanese attack on Pearl Harbor four months later.

Dusko's arrival in Manhattan in mid-August, escorted by an SIS officer, John Pepper, who had met him in Bermuda, proved to be something of an anticlimax. For, whereas MI5 had been delighted by the vote of confidence given to their star double agent by the Abwehr, the FBI was decidedly cool at the prospect of an enemy agent's arrival. J. Edgar Hoover was at that time basking in the glory of having recently broken up a large Nazi spy-ring, and he was ambivalent about allowing a replacement to be built with his co-operation, even if it meant that the enemy's espionage could be kept under tight control. It has also been suggested that Hoover did not much care for Dusko's behaviour, or his morals.[12] Certainly on one occasion the FBI wrecked an amorous weekend and brought Dusko back to New York after he had attempted to take a girlfriend to Florida, thereby crossing state lines for an immoral purpose, contrary to the federal statute known as the Mann Act. While Dusko was in the States, responsibility for liaising with the FBI's local office, headed by Percy J. Foxworth, lay with Pepper, based at British Security Co-ordination, William Stephenson's regional joint headquarters for MI5 and SIS. However, supervision of his day-to-day conduct lay with Charles Lehrman, the Special Agent reluctantly assigned to his case by the FBI.

Dusko's arrival in New York coincided with a major disaster experienced by the Abwehr which decimated its carefully nurtured networks across north America. In June 1941 William G. Sebold, the Abwehr's chief organiser in the States, revealed his long-term collaboration with the FBI, dating back to February 1939, and identified no less than thirty-three separate sub-agents, all of whom were subsequently convicted of espionage. Sebold, a naturalised American citizen and one-time employee of the Consolidated Aircraft Company in California, had been coerced into helping the Abwehr during a visit to his native

Mulheim in Germany before the outbreak of war. Upon his return to New York he had established, with the FBI's help, an illicit wireless transmitter at Centerport, Long Island, and rented a 'front' office in the Knickerbocker Building on Broadway, where he had received messages from other German agents for onward transmission to Hamburg. Each transaction had been filmed by the FBI through a two-way mirror and used to identify the spies involved. It had been a master coup which had almost, but not quite, eliminated the Abwehr from America.

Still reeling from the body-blow delivered by Sebold, the Abwehr suffered a further grievous loss. A few days after Dusko's arrival, Kurt Ludwig was arrested, following a lengthy investigation, together with seven fellow agents. Ludwig had been born in America but brought up in Germany, and had returned to the States in 1940 via Spain. There he had concentrated on recruiting members of the German-American Bund, and mailing letters written in secret ink for another important agent, Dr Paul Borchardt. These had attracted the attention of the BSC postal censors in Bermuda, and prompted the FBI's interest. All received long prison sentences, and the Abwehr was evidently looking to Dusko to start building replacement networks.

Dusko thoroughly enjoyed himself in the States and wasted no time in establishing himself in an apartment on New York's Park Avenue, spending the weekends at a cottage in Locust Valley, Long Island, with his new girlfriend, the French actress Simone Simon. As agreed with the FBI, he did mail a few reports to Portugal but, by October, he had received no acknowledgement of them, which led MI5 to fear that for some inexplicable reason the Abwehr was losing interest in him. The situation was saved by a message from Lisbon ordering Dusko to travel to Brazil and report to the German firm AEG in Rio. This he did, in November, where he was given a large sum in dollars, and instructions to make wireless contact with Lisbon. The FBI produced a suitable transmitter and in February Dusko raised Lisbon, claiming plausibly that the equipment had been procured from a local Croatian. Although Dusko was nominally in charge of his signals, the messages were compiled by the FBI, and this was to lead to further complications: the FBI was far from convinced of the merit of supporting an enemy agent, even if he was a double. The Japanese had attacked Pearl Harbor while Dusko was on a ship between Rio and the US, and the Americans suddenly found themselves embroiled in a world war. As far as J. Edgar Hoover was concerned, double agents should only be used for counter-espionage purposes, to identify other spies, and Dusko had led the FBI to none; this reduced his value to them.

Dusko's activities were monitored by the British, partly though overt liaison with the FBI, but chiefly through the interception of German communications which, after a cryptographic breakthrough in December 1941, had provided a regular and reliable insight into German appreciation of their star agent. Since control of Dusko had been handed back to SIS while he was overseas, it was that organisation's responsibility to check on references to him in the enemy's signals; in March 1942 a decrypt revealed that Berlin had warned the Abwehr in Rio that Dusko was suspected of collaborating with the Allies. This had been followed by a message dated 21 March suggesting a method of testing Dusko's credentials by quizzing him about his salary. A further intercept, this time sent from Abwehr headquarters to Lisbon, stated that the air intelligence section believed Dusko had switched sides in New York. When, after a frustrating delay, SIS eventually imparted this worrying news to MI5, it became evident that the cause of the Abwehr's dissatisfaction was the poor quality of the FBI's messages. This was somewhat understandable, given the sensitivity of some of the topics raised by the Abwehr. The FBI must have been aware that, in retrospect, Dusko's original questionnaire could be seen to have had a terrible relevance to Pearl Harbor, and a request received by Dusko in April 1942,[13] though poorly translated by the FBI, must have set off alarm bells across Washington:

Decay of Uran. According to some information obtained, there is reason to believe that the scientific works for the utilization of the atomic-kernel energy are being driven into a certain direction in the US partly by the use of helium. Continous informations about the tests made on this subject are required and particularly: 1. What process is practised in the US for the sending of heavy uran? 2. Where are being made tests with more important quantities of uran? (Universities, industrial laboratories, etc.) 3. Which other raw materials are being used at these tests? It is to be recommended to entrust only best experts with this test, and if not available, to abstain from it.[14]

The Allied atomic-weapon project was one of the most closely guarded secrets of the war and here, in an early stage of its development, was an example of the Germans entrusting a Yugoslav playboy with the vital task of discovering how much technical progress had been made. No wonder the FBI, already nervous about Dusko's extravagance, became even more anxious.

The situation was further exacerbated by the FBI's reluctance to finance Dusko's exotic lifestyle. SIS made further representations to the FBI which resulted in a perceptible improvement in Dusko's standing with the Abwehr, and an indication that the Germans were attempting to relieve Dusko's financial plight which, by the summer, had become severe. By August the FBI had had enough of Dusko's antics and a formal request was made to SIS for him to be withdrawn.

Thus, just fourteen months after his departure, Dusko returned to Lisbon, having been escorted back across the Atlantic in October 1942 by Ian Wilson, his new MI5 case officer. Hoover's refusal to allow Dusko to travel to Hawaii had handicapped the double agent's ability to carry out his Abwehr assignment, but his return to Europe marked a new, productive phase in the development of his case. He had been warned by Wilson that the Germans had been less than satisfied with his performance in America, but he soon won them round. Not all the thirty-six letters he had mailed from the States had been received at their destination, and there was some dissatisfaction that he had been unable to travel to Hawaii. Dusko defended himself vigorously, claiming that shortage of funds had reduced his efficiency, and gradually won the Abwehr over. They rewarded him with $26,000 and seventy-five thousand escudos, and on 17 October reported to Berlin that Dusko's integrity as a German spy was undiminished.

Dusko spent a week in Lisbon placating his German controllers, and then flew back to London with the seeds of yet another ingenious scheme in mind – this time to free some of his brother's friends from Yugoslavia on the pretext that they could be recruited as agents. The first in this category was Eugn Sostaric,[15] an Air Force officer who had previously been King Peter's aide-de-camp, but was imprisoned after attempting to escape the German occupation via Salonika. On that occasion Sostaric, who had intended to offer his services to the RAF, had been betrayed and sentenced to death. The intervention of Ivo Popov, code-named DREADNOUGHT, saved his life, persuading Jebsen that Sostaric, a strongly anti-Communist Croatian, would make an ideal agent. Eventually the Abwehr authorised Sostaric's release and his journey across Europe to Madrid, where he was received by the British Embassy. Further delays were experienced while Sostaric waited in Gibraltar for transport to England and then, upon his arrival, while he underwent a security screening at the Royal Victoria Patriotic School in Wandsworth, South London. Finally, in April 1943, the airman was enrolled into Dusko's network as METEOR, but there was an unexpected twist to his case. When Sostaric was introduced to MI5 he cheerfully revealed that he had been instructed by the Abwehr to confess his espionage to the British authorities at the first opportunity. He was to admit that he had been provided with an address in Portugal to which he should send apparently innocuous letters, containing messages written in secret ink. Furthermore, the Germans had told him that, having admitted all this, he was to pretend to co-operate with MI5, and then proceed to correspond with another 'postbox', this time in Madrid, in a secret ink made from another formula that was to be withheld from the British. The Abwehr's clear intention was to run Sostaric as that most sophisticated of agents, the so-called 'triple-cross'. Sostaric neatly sabotaged the scheme by disclosing it in its entirety, and it was left to Ian Wilson, who was appointed his case officer, to devise two separate texts for enemy consumption. The first was to contain material that the Germans would perceive to be false, while the second would contain what the Abwehr was calculating would be an authentic report that they could rely on. Astonishingly, this charade was maintained without a hitch until May 1944, when Sostaric was posted to the Mediterranean theatre as a liaison officer to the Allied Commander-in-Chief's staff.

The German attempt at a triple-cross operation generated considerable interest within MI5, because this was only the second known example of the phenomena. Another agent, code-named TEAPOT, who had arrived in England in January 1943 had also declared himself to be a triple, and had been run successfully ever since, communicating with the Abwehr by radio and occasionally meeting his controller. This case had provided MI5 with a rare opportunity to make direct contact with the enemy and give them a demonstration of their relative lack of skill at running double agents. Naturally the object of the exercise had been to persuade the Abwehr that the British were quite untutored in the arcane arts, thereby lulling them into a false sense of security. On the one previous occasion two years earlier that a similar ploy had been tried, with Alphons Timmerman,[16] a Belgian seaman MI5 had code-named SCRUFFY, the Germans had apparently accepted as authentic MI5's deliberately flawed messages. Timmerman had been a genuine Abwehr spy, detected by his interrogators when he had tried to enter Britain posing as a refugee. He had been imprisoned at Wandsworth while an MI5 officer substituted for him, writing in secret ink to his cover address in Portugal. The letters had been drafted to contain mistakes in the hope of proving that MI5 were no match for their opponents but, inexplicably, SCRUFFY's German controllers in Lisbon had continued to maintain the relationship by answering his letters, leaving it to the embarrassed British case officers to terminate the exercise. Timmerman himself had been led to the gallows in July 1942, proving conclusively to the enemy that their agent had never been at liberty to operate, and had always been under MI5's control. The episode, in which Timmerman himself had played no willing part, had forced MI5 to conclude that perhaps the Abwehr did not have the finesse and sophistication it had been credited with. Certainly a very similar experiment undertaken during the First World War had proved much the same point. Correspondence had been maintained by MI5 in the name of Karl Muller,[17] a convicted German spy, *after* his execution had been announced in the newspapers.

During the early part of 1943 Dusko participated in the most ambitious deception scheme yet prepared. He had previously assisted a less sophisticated plan to tempt U-boats into the Mediterranean from the Atlantic which had involved a notional friend, the commander of a naval corvette, whose ship had supposedly been redeployed recently to home waters. Dusko's reports had been intended to imply a reduction of Allied naval strength east of Gibraltar in the hope of luring some of the wolfpacks away from the transatlantic convoy routes. The new plan, code-named COCKADE, was designed to persuade the enemy that the Allies planned to attack northern France and Norway sometime early in September 1943. In fact the authentic military activity was destined to take place in the Mediterranean, but the Abwehr had to be convinced that there were enough troops in Britain to mount COCKADE's two offensives, STARKEY and TINDALL, targeted on Boulogne and Oslo respectively. Dusko's role was to report to the Abwehr on various troop movements in England that suggested an expeditionary force of fifteen divisions had been assembled, with a further twenty-four divisions held in reserve, in addition to the 'Static Home Force' of two million men. The true position was that the British Army had a strength of just twenty-two divisions in total, with a further five Canadian divisions.

From May onwards Dusko sent the Abwehr detailed sightings of Canadian troops on the south coast, Americans (of whom in reality the army had very few) in the west country and a large Allied force concentrating in Scotland. He also claimed that landing craft were being built at secret inland sites, ready to be rushed to the coast and assembled in preparation for a huge amphibious operation. After two months of these observations Dusko was called to Lisbon, where he mentioned that civilian hospitals had been told to prepare for a large number of casualties later in the summer. Theoretically, the Abwehr would process all these items of intelligence and draw the incorrect conclusion that they ought to prepare for an attack in northern Europe, and not in the Mediterranean theatre. Even if there was to be little evidence of STARKEY's success, it did at least have the merit of proving that a convincing large-scale deception was possible, and that the Twenty Committee was competent to co-ordinate all its double agents.

Dusko's return to Portugal, in mid-July 1943, was also an opportunity to try to capitalise on his successs at getting Sostaric to England. This time, instead of travelling under his civilian cover of an international commercial lawyer, he went with a diplomatic passport, having been called up for Yugoslav military service – or so he told Jebsen, who met him in Lisbon. The idea was to persuade the Abwehr to allow a group of Yugoslav officers interned in Switzerland to escape to Spain. As Dusko had anticipated, the Germans seized on the proposal, because it presented them with a useful method of infiltrating agents into the Allied forces. Indeed, the Abwehr had been so taken with the scheme that they asked Ivo Popov, who had now been enrolled into the organisation with officer rank, to supervise the Yugoslav end of the escape route. This was exactly what Dusko wanted, for it left him with an officially sponsored underground route across Europe on which Ivo could send friends with little fear of enemy interference. While Dusko conferred with Jebsen, MI5 was able to monitor the progress of their talks through the interception of the Abwehr's radio link with Berlin. The results were sensational. It seemed that the Abwehr had been highly sceptical of Dusko after his return from America, and suspected that he might have sold out to the Allies. They had been particularly doubtful about a report he had submitted on defences in the Dover area. However, Jebsen's assessment of Dusko had been very favourable and this had proved enough to persuade Berlin to sanction Dusko's proposals.

Dusko remained in Lisbon, shuttling to and from Madrid on his diplomatic passport until mid-September, when he received another old friend, an engineer named Stefan Zeis.[18] His arrival, after a journey via Switzerland lasting more than a year, was to prove critical: he confirmed what Dusko had already come to suspect, that Ivo's principal contact in the Abwehr, Johann Jebsen, was himself a candidate for defection to the Allied side. This extraordinary turn of events required delicate handling, so Dusko flew straight back to England with Jebsen's proposal to co-operate actively with the British. He also brought a wireless transmitter with him, as proof of his acceptance by the Germans, and a large sum of cash. As one might imagine, the prospect of recruiting a genuine Abwehr agent-handler sparked a mixed reaction in London. Whilst it had the superficial attraction of offering a valuable insight into the enemy camp, it was not entirely without risk. If Jebsen either lost his nerve or accidentally did something to betray himself, he would immediately jeopardise the whole of Dusko's ring. Indeed, the consequences might be even more serious, and the Abwehr might be tempted, if conducting a full-scale investigation, to weigh up the loyalties of some of its other agents too. However, to reject Jebsen's offer was not without its hazards either. Such a move might serve to prove to him that all his agents were already under hostile control. The dilemma was deepened by another consideration, known only to a relative handful of senior intelligence officers: most of the Abwehr's wireless traffic was being routinely intercepted and decrypted, and this invaluable source provided such a comprehensive overview of the enemy's activities that there was no operational need to treat with defectors. This debate continued throughout October 1943 while Stefan Zeis was established in MI5's books as THE WORM, a reflection of his unattractive personality, and put to work writing letters in secret ink to a cover address on the Continent.

Jebsen's offer to defect had been spiced with an item of information that the Abwehr officer had calculated would make his proposition extremely attractive to the Allies. He told Dusko that he knew the true identity of the top German agent in England, a man who was exceptionally well placed and was in charge of a whole network of compartmented sub-agents. To Dusko this nugget made Jebsen extremely valuable, but there were a couple of further dimensions to the matter of which he had no knowledge.

Dusko had never been told of the existence of other double agents apart from TATE and the members of his own ring, and he never guessed there was an entire stable run by MI5 until the publication, in 1972, of Sir John Masterman's declassified account, *The Double Cross System*. Some had been handled by MI5 since before the opening of hostilities, while others had been recruited more recently. In the latter category had been Juan Pujol, code-named GARBO,[19] an enterprising Spaniard brought to London in April 1942 and whose network, though entirely fictional, had been run parallel with Dusko's. MI5 had realised, having monitored the Abwehr's wireless traffic, that Pujol was held in high regard by his German controllers, and it was also assumed that Jebsen's 'meal ticket' was probably none other than Juan Pujol. If so, this would have profound consequences for the whole of GARBO's organisation. Indeed, there were much wider ramifications, for Pujol had been selected as one of the key purveyors of deception for the forthcoming Allied invasion of Europe, which was then a few months away.

Dusko's own opinion was that Jebsen could be trusted and that his participation would guarantee the success of his escape line from Switzerland. Although he knew nothing of GARBO, he had been 'absolutely sure'[20] Jebsen had realised that he was secretly working for the British, and in view of that there was little to be lost in bringing him into the fold as well. In addition, there was a further possible benefit in enlisting Jebsen. When he had last seen Dusko, in mid-September, he had warned him to move out of central London because rockets were to be fired at the capital from launch sites along the French coast. This morsel had been received with particular interest in Whitehall, where Duncan Sandys was already chairing a secret committee to investigate similar reports. Finding out more about this weapon had been given a high priority by the War Cabinet, and Jebsen appeared to be a potentially useful source in this regard. The weight of opinion gradually leant in favour of trusting Jebsen, and this was the view that finally prevailed within the Security Service, although a few still had severe reservations. Some of these diminished towards the end of September when, in response to a query from Dusko, Jebsen indicated that he would be willing to remain in place rather than physically defect to England. Accordingly, in November 1943 Dusko returned to the Portuguese resort of Estoril, in the guise of a diplomatic courier, to convey the good news to Jebsen, who had by then taken up residence in a villa there. Thenceforth Jebsen was code-named ARTIST in MI5's files and put in touch with Cecil Gledhill at the local SIS station. This single act of acceptance had suddenly put Jebsen in a position of unprecedented power over a substantial proportion of MI5's double-cross operations. If he had not already done so, he now knew for certain that the

Abwehr's three main agents in Britain, Dusko, Juan Pujol and TATE, were all under MI5's control. For this knowledge to be imparted to any single individual was serious enough. The fact that Jebsen was also an Abwehr officer made the whole matter extraordinarily sensitive and was the subject of many high-level conferences in London. What would happen if Jebsen's loyalties changed again? Might his circumstances change and present him with a chance of betraying everything that MI5 had built up with such care? These questions were to be the cause of constant anxiety over the coming months.

What exacerbated these preoccupations was the very secret fact, withheld from Dusko, that Jebsen was not the only Abwehr officer in the Iberian peninsula to have offered to switch sides. MI5 and SIS had both been aware of another potential defector, codenamed JUNIOR,[21] since February 1941, when a certain Walter Dicketts, one of MI5's many double agents, had held a very profitable rendezvous with Jebsen in Lisbon. Dicketts, known to MI5 as CELERY, had returned to London and given his MI5 case officer a detailed account of his dealings with the Abwehr. He had also reported that one particular Abwehr officer, JUNIOR, had expressed his disenchantment with the Nazis. This had been duly noted and, sure enough, a year later JUNIOR had approached the SIS station in Lisbon with a view to defecting. He had been rebuffed, of course, on MI5's advice, for fear of jeopardising Dusko, known to him because of his meetings with von Auenrode. To MI5's relief, JUNIOR pursued the matter no further, but in January 1943 he had been transferred to the German Embassy in Madrid, where he made another pitch to SIS. On this occasion he had been accepted, but on the condition he remain in place. JUNIOR had agreed to these terms and fortunately this arrangement had worked well, although it presented a definite risk for Dusko: JUNIOR had been able to deduce that Dusko must be operating as a double agent. The unexpected complication arose when, later in the year, JUNIOR was consulted by Jebsen, when the latter visited Madrid, and was put in touch with Colonel W. T. Wren,[22] one of the SIS officers at the local station.

Jebsen's official motive for moving to Madrid during late 1943 had been to facilitate the Spanish end of Dusko's new escape route from Switzerland, but he confided to Wren that his financial dealings had got him into trouble with the Gestapo and he felt he could not return to Germany. He was anxious to know whether SIS would be willing to exfiltrate him if the need arose. Whilst this contact gave Wren a splendid opportunity to conduct a prolonged debriefing of Jebsen and learn more about Germany's new rocket-powered weapons, it placed JUNIOR in much too powerful a position, and he was smuggled to England in November so as to remove him from the scene. In his absence Jebsen moved closer to SIS and finalised the arrangements for Dusko's Yugoslav evaders.

Certainly Dusko's escape route got off to a good start, and among the first to use this method was the Marquis Frano de Bona,[23] an aristocrat from Dubrovnik and an old family friend of the Popovs. De Bona had undergone an Abwehr training course in the use of secret ink and Morse, and had also been provided with a radio transmitter, which he handed over when he was welcomed to Madrid by Dusko. The marquis eventually reached London via Gibraltar in December 1943, where he was assigned the cryptonym FREAK by MI5, and began using his wireless to signal to his German controllers as soon as Dusko returned from Lisbon the following month.

It was at this moment that things began to go wrong for Dusko's spy-ring. During his discussions in Lisbon, Dusko had made various suggestions for expanding BALLOON's dwindling activities, but the Abwehr reaction had been negative. Thus, in mid-November 1943, while Dusko was still in Portugal, Dickie Metcalfe was effectively abandoned by his German controllers, who justified the action by saying that other members of Dusko's network could fulfil his function just as easily. Whilst this was partly true, it was to be interpreted as the first ominous sign that the enemy was not entirely contented with Dusko's ring. Then, after Dusko's return to London in the New Year, there was no response to Stefan Zeis's letters. The information he had conveyed to the Abwehr in earlier correspondence had covered a range of military topics but in January it appeared that his controllers were losing interest in him, too.

Dusko flew back to Lisbon at the end of February 1944 to confer with the Abwehr, and persuaded them to bring his brother Ivo to Lisbon. He stayed there for nearly two months, and when he returned in April he was able to reassure his MI5 case officers of the high standing he still enjoyed. He brought back two Abwehr questionnaires, one from the Sicherheitsdienst, five reports from Jebsen and a message to King Peter from Draza Mihailovic, the Royalist guerrilla leader. But while these were welcomed by MI5 and SIS, the situation in England had altered quite considerably. By now, the Security Service had experienced a perceptible change in its strategic role, and the confidence Dusko expressed was to have exactly the opposite effect to that which he had intended, for two related reasons. The first was Dusko's confirmation that Jebsen was still willing to continue operating as ARTIST. Although there had been some discussion about the possibility of Jebsen slipping away to England, he was dissuaded from doing so. Jebsen had apparently said that his position would continue to be secure so long as the Abwehr protected him from the Gestapo, of whom he lived in understandable dread. The second nagging worry was the perilous position of the Abwehr which, unbeknown to Dusko, was struggling for independence from its arch-rival, the powerful Sicherheitsdienst. The internecine warfare had been watched from afar by the intelligence analysts who had been deciphering the Abwehr's internal wireless traffic, and they reported that a dangerous climax was approaching.

The nub of it was that whereas, up until the New Year of 1944, MI5 had fulfilled what was largely a tactical function by taking and maintaining overall control of the enemy's intelligence networks in Britain, the impending invasion had completely changed the situation and the new priority was not just to exert control, but actually to *manipulate* the spy-rings. Instead of concentrating on the more domestic issue of organising the enemy's espionage, the double-cross system was to be exploited as a conduit of strategic deception. The objective now was to persuade the enemy that the Allied assault was destined for the Pas-de-Calais; both GARBO and TATE had been assigned key parts in the campaign.

The realisation that there was suddenly rather more in the balance than the lives of the families left in enemy-occupied territory had a considerable impact on the case officers charged with responsibility for ensuring the integrity of their agents. Prior to the change in MI5's role, the double-cross game had been played without any great risk. However, entrusting the fate of a wholesale offensive on the intended scale of OVERLORD to a handful of double agents was quite a different matter, especially when it was recognised that they in turn were wholly dependent upon Johann Jebsen, an enemy intelligence officer. Certainly Tomás Harris, GARBO's MI5 case officer, was profoundly uneasy about placing so much reliance on ARTIST, and in February 1944 he recommended that Pujol also should not be used for deception purposes. In justification, Harris pointed out that it was too great a gamble to risk an entire military operation on ARTIST's doubtful loyalty.

Two dramatic developments were to change the situation. One was the removal of Admiral Canaris from his position as Chief of the Abwehr in February 1944, an event quickly followed by the organisation's effective subordination to the Sicherheitsdienst in April. Paradoxically, the decline of the Abwehr that placed Jebsen in greater jeopardy had been hastened by SIS, which had successfully engineered the defection in Istanbul of a senior Abwehr officer, Erich Vermehren. A staunch Anglophile and devout Catholic, Vermehren's decision to switch sides, so soon after JUNIOR's disappearance, had a profound effect in Berlin and acted as the catalyst for the Abwehr's eventual subsumation. MI5 was able to monitor the situation through the medium of the Abwehr's wireless traffic, and was appalled to learn that Jebsen, who had held a meeting with Cecil Gledhill, his SIS contact, on 28 April, had been abducted by the Gestapo later the same day, and driven back to Germany. This was exactly the eventuality that Tomás Harris, for one, had foreseen, but his worst fears were not to materialise. It seemed that Jebsen had been involved in fraudulent currency transactions and the Gestapo had kidnapped him in order to prevent his anticipated defection.

The news that Jebsen had been arrested was devastating in London, and it was little consolation that, as yet, he was not apparently suspected of having already made contact with the British. MI5 decided that Dusko's entire network should be closed down, but opted to continue with GARBO, at least until there was some evidence that Jebsen had been forced to reveal what he knew. Fortunately the Gestapo never suspected Jebsen of the more serious crime, but he was executed at Oranienburg anyway.

The chosen method of winding up Dusko's spy-ring was particularly ingenious, and was intended to allay any lingering doubts the Germans might have had. Dusko wrote a letter to Lisbon stating that the Marquis de Bona's most recent wireless signal, on 19 May, was to be his last, as he had fallen under suspicion following a leak from Mihailovic that he might be a German agent. Surprisingly, the Germans failed to acknowledge Dusko's letter and continued to try and contact de Bona by radio. Eventually, at the end of June, de Bona responded, claiming that he had been ordered to New York in his new capacity as aide-de-camp to King Peter. This excuse was accepted reluctantly by the Germans, and the network came to an end officially when, in August 1944, Ivo was flown out of Yugoslavia by the RAF.

After the war Dusko based himself at Krefeld, and in 1947

he married his first wife, Janine. In 1951 they went to live in Rome, where she still runs an equestrian shop, and where he acquired a taste for politics. This eventually led to his becoming General Secretary of the European Movement in 1955, by which time he had achieved considerable success in business and been responsible for taking the French car giant Peugeot into Germany. Thereafter a business venture in Marseilles, in which SIS had played some murky role, led to his arrest and imprisonment in 1959.

After his release, Dusko was married again, in 1962, to a Swedish student named Jill Jonsson, and over the next few years he worked from Cape Town for a German cocoa company before moving to the south of France, where he bought the Castellaras estate, now developed into a villa complex not far from Grasse.

Dusko eventually published an account of his wartime adventures, entitled *Spy/CounterSpy*, in which he changed the names of the members of his network. However, it got off to a poor start when Dickie Metcalfe pointed out that the first edition incorrectly stated that he had been cashiered from the army. This, of course, was quite untrue, and subsequent editions of the book were altered to reflect what had really happened. During the course of my own research I was able to trace and interview Eugn Sostaric, then living in Switzerland; the Marquis de Bona, residing in exile in Trieste; Friedle Gaertner, who had also moved to Italy; and Dr Ivo Popov, who had retired to the Bahamas; as well, of course, as their respective case officers, Billy Luke and Ian Wilson. Like his younger brother, Ivo had retained his intelligence connections after the war and had collaborated with the CIA in Italy to prevent a Communist takeover. He was also to be active in working against Tito's regime, losing seventeen agents to the Yugoslav secret police.

In December 1980 Ivo Popov died at his home outside Nassau. Eight months later, on 10 August 1981, Dusko died, also at home, in the south of France at Opio.

Chapter II

Wulf Schmidt

In a quiet residential street in Watford lives an elderly, slightly stooped man, now in his eightieth year, who speaks with a trace of a foreign accent. Up until recently he was one of the country's leading breeders of canaries, and he regularly travelled the country as a respected judge at exhibitions of this particular species of bird. He lives alone and is an intensely private individual. What makes Harry Williamson's privacy so unusual is that it is protected by the Security Service, for he is one of the last surviving German double agents of World War II. In fact Harry Williamson does not have the entirely Danish background he sometimes mentions to the inquisitive who ask about his accent. He is a Dane from Abenra[1] in the German territory of Schleswig-Holstein who parachuted into Cambridgeshire soon after midnight on 19/20 September 1940.

Harry's extraordinary story is one of the more remarkable of the Second World War. His mission to England had never been intended to last fifty years, but some members of his family, still in Germany, who know that he received an Iron Cross for his undercover activities believe that he is still on his clandestine assignment.

Harry's work for the Abwehr began in 1939 after his return from working overseas, first as General Manager on a cattle ranch in Argentina, and then growing bananas for a fruit company in the Cameroons. After his service in the Danish Army, stationed in Copenhagen, he had intended to study agriculture at university. Instead he accepted a job accompanying twenty-four head of cattle to Argentina. He then made a second overseas tour, and his return to Germany from Tiko in the Cameroons after the outbreak of war was a long one. He had travelled to Lagos in Nigeria by launch, and then had waited over Christmas 1939 for a neutral ship, the *Duchess d'Aosta*, for a berth to Genoa. Finally he had reached Abenra, and started to look for work. An advertisement for people with a knowledge of foreign languages caught his eye and, after an interview in Hamburg, he was recruited into the Abwehr. He had been sent to Copenhagen on a secret mission, which he executed faultlessly, and then had volunteered for what he believed would be a short stay in England. He spoke good English, albeit with a heavy accent, and his task was to carry out a reconnaissance prior to a German invasion. Although he was to parachute solo, he was in fact one of several agents to be dropped into England during September 1940. Of the others, Goesta Caroli,[2] a Swede by birth who had made two short visits to the Birmingham area just before the outbreak of hostilities, was known to him as they had been trained in Hamburg together: they arranged to meet in England.

Harry was flown to Cambridgeshire by an ace Luftwaffe pilot, Captain Karl Gartenfeld, in one of the Abwehr's special matt-black Heinkel 111 bombers, from an airfield near Brussels. His memory of the flight is still so vivid that he can recall the names of all the crew: Lieutenant Nebel was the co-pilot, Sergeant Wagner the wireless operator, Sergeant Karl-Heinz Suessmann the observer, and Corporal Achtelik the despatcher. After two hours of desperate cold, and with only a word of encouragement from the despatcher as parachute training, Schmidt was dropped over RAF Oakington, close to the village of Willingham. He was perfectly confident when he landed, because he knew that his friend Caroli had been at liberty in England for the past two weeks – or so he had been told before his departure. Not even his sprained ankle, injured when he hit the ground in darkness, undermined his resolve. The truth, however, was somewhat different. Caroli had been taken into custody by the British within a few hours of landing and, in return for a promise that he would be treated as a prisoner of war, had quickly told his interrogators all they wanted to know, including the identity of his Danish friend who was scheduled to follow by the same route. On 17 September, operating from Aylesbury police station, he used his wireless to transmit a safe-arrival signal and report that he had been living rough since his arrival. In reality, of course, he was in MI5's secret detention centre at Latchmere House, Ham Common, Surrey, known within the British Security Service simply as Camp 020.

Harry spent just a few short hours at liberty, for he was challenged by a member of the local Home Guard in Willingham soon after he had finished his breakfast in a café. When he was searched Harry was found to be carrying £132, $160, a genuine Danish passport in the name of Wulf Schmidt, and a forged British identity card bearing the details of 'Harry Williamson'. What made the latter item so interesting was that it contained an address in London that had been suggested to the Abwehr by another of MI5's double agents, Arthur Owens. He had been run since the outbreak of war by Major T. A. Robertson of MI5, the true architect of the famous double-cross system. This instantly betrayed Harry as an enemy agent although, for a while at least, he stuck rigidly to his cover story, that he was a Dane and that he had arrived in England near West Hartlepool by boat some three months earlier. It was only after MI5 had demonstrated that Caroli had been in custody since his arrival, and had already made a very full confession, that Harry began seriously to consider throwing in his hand with his interrogators.

Several factors combined to undermine Harry's confidence. His journey from Cambridgeshire to Scotland Yard, through the heart of the supposedly devastated capital city, was eloquent proof that his Abwehr briefings had contained little more than wishful thinking. Although he did see plenty of bomb damage, there was nothing like the complete breakdown of administration he had been led to expect. He was also somewhat bitter about his lack of preparation and felt he had been misled about the amount of food obviously available to the allegedly beleaguered population. He had little grasp of the strange non-decimal currency and no understanding of how his forged food and clothing coupons should be used. Nor, clearly, was a German invasion imminent. The briefing he had received before his departure, from Major Nikolaus Ritter of the Abwehr, had been wholly inadequate, as had his equipment, which consisted of a pistol with six rounds of ammunition, a packet of twenty Players, a box of Swan Vestas, eight Pervitin stimulant tablets and a short-handled spade for burying his parachute.

Then there was the way in which he was treated. He had anticipated torture and constant physical abuse, but in fact he received nothing but kindness from the police and only once was manhandled, on the second day of his captivity. He was not to know it then, but the Security Service had taken great care to construct a regime at Camp 020 that would encourage co-operation and reduce the incidence of stubborn intransigence. MI5's distinguished psychiatrist Dr Harold Dearden was constantly on hand to assess individual cases and advise on the best approach to particular prisoners so as to obtain maximum results. He had decreed that rough handling was counterproductive, so when Harry was on one occasion beaten, the officer responsible, who happened to be a visitor and not a regular member of the staff, had been severely reprimanded and posted overseas. Harry had been particularly impressed by the reaction of the Camp Commandant, the monocled Colonel 'Tin-eye' Stephens, who dealt swiftly with the offending MI5 officer. Far from administering abuse, the kindly psychiatrist Dearden had perched on the end of his bed and shared a bottle of whisky with him. Whilst Camp 020's regime was harsh, and the interrogations could be very hostile, there was none of the behaviour that so often characterises similar security agencies elsewhere. That is not to say that the rest of Harry's experience was pleasant. As with other suspects, he was kept in solitary confinement and escorted to and from his interrogation sessions by uniformed Intelligence Corps NCOs who were under orders to maintain complete silence. The interviews were also very intimidating and were conducted by a 'board' of four or five uniformed officers who sat at a long desk piled with what appeared to be detailed dossiers containing evidence amassed against the prisoner. The latter stood to attention, sometimes naked, in the centre of the room, answering the questions put to him while a female shorthand note taker maintained a record of everything that was said. This, for him, was probably the most harrowing part of the whole ordeal, having to suffer the humiliation and indignity of responding to questions while completely unclothed, in the presence of an unabashed young secretary.

Harry has given much thought as to exactly why he opted to help MI5. He says that he was never asked what made him change his mind, and his recollection is that it was simply a question of self-preservation. Thereafter he was to develop a strong sense of gratitude and loyalty towards two of the men from MI5 who dealt with him: Major Robertson and his wireless operator, Russell Lee. He agreed to accompany his captors back to Willingham, where he recovered his parachute and radio from their hiding places; at midnight on 16 October he transmitted his call sign, D-F-H, and reported to Hamburg, under the supervision of MI5's wireless expert Ronald Reed, that he had found lodgings near Barnet in Hertfordshire. In reality he had been installed with Major Robertson and his wife at Roundbush House, Radlett. This was to be the first of a thousand wireless signals exchanged with the Abwehr – more than from any other agent, and over a longer period, as Harry was to maintain contact continuously until May 1945.

One thing that persuaded MI5 to accept Harry as a double agent was the transparent candour of his initial statement. In it he identified a dance-band pianist named Pierce as a key member of an existing Abwehr circuit, whose name had been given to Harry in Hamburg in case of emergencies. In reality the pianist was known to MI5 as RAINBOW[3] and had been operating under Robertson's guidance since February. This item provided MI5 with useful confirmation that Harry, now dubbed TATE (because of his resemblance to the music hall comedian Harry Tate) was telling the truth, and that the Abwehr continued to believe RAINBOW was an authentic source.

The fact that Harry and Goesta Caroli (not to mention Pierce and the others) had come under MI5's control at a very early stage was to cause much confusion for post-war historians attempting to document the exploits of Nazi espionage in Britain. Two in particular, Ladislas Farago[4] and David Kahn,[5] depended upon Abwehr archives for their accounts, and were therefore misled into accepting the plausible cover stories invented by MI5 to conceal the period of imprisonment experienced by Caroli (code-named SUMMER) and Harry. For example, Caroli reported that he had been injured on landing, and elaborate arrangements had been made for Owens to meet Caroli in High Wycombe, nurse him back to health, and then install him in a house south of Cambridge. Both Farago and Kahn, using the German records, retailed a version that was entirely fictitious. In fact SUMMER remained at Camp 020 until secure accommodation could be found for him at Hinxton, Cambridgeshire, and was only allowed out, under strict supervision, to work his transmitter.

In contrast, Harry was given rather more freedom to fulfil his mission, which consisted of general reporting and responding to Abwehr questionnaires. A typical one, received in January 1941, gives a flavour of what the Abwehr tasked him to do:

> All information about movement of military units in connection with Greece and the Near East are of interest.[6]

Requests such as these were answered in Harry's own inimitable, though sometimes pungent, style. He expressed an earthy humour and a degree of ill-disciplined independence that must have enraged his German controllers.[7] In February 1941 he travelled to the Midlands, and in his subsequent signal he misspelt RAF Benson and RAF Brize Norton:

> Many bombers are supposed to be stationed in the Oxford area, mainly in Abingdon, Beson, and Breazenorton. Reconnaissance follows.[8]

This was followed on 24 February with a description of Brize Norton:

> New are especially large, grass-covered mounds of earth, supposedly underground hangars, about 200 by 75 metres in size.[9]

Hamburg responded to this message with the information that none of these features were listed in the officially published ordinance survey of the airfield. This prompted Harry to send further details of his scouting mission the following day:

> Further observation of the Brize Norton airfield. The six mounds reported yesterday are in fact underground hangars. I personally saw how two Defiants were pushed into one of these underground hangars on the north-west side. They had the markings N 3446 and N 3479. The exact position of the hangar is as follows: two hangars lie in north-south direction 100 metres west of the village of Brize Norton and north of the road from Brize Norton to Carterton; two further in the same direction but south of the road and 150 metres distant from the road to Bampton; two further lie 1,800 metres south of Carterton and 350 metres west of the road. Observed anti-aircraft positions, one about 700 metres east of Carterton and one 100 metres south of Carterton.[10]

Obviously Harry could not be permitted to continue making detailed studies of this kind for very long, even though they had been screened and subtly altered by the intelligence authorities. Quite how TATE should be exploited was still, three months after his arrival, the subject of some debate within MI5. One project which gained official approval in January 1941 was the provision of a convenient target for the Luftwaffe to bomb. Designated PLAN 1, it called for the building of a fake ammunition dump, the location of which Harry was to report to the Abwehr in the hope that it would attract the enemy's attention. The necessary construction work had been completed by March 1941, and the map co-ordinates duly conveyed to Hamburg, but the expected raid never took place and the idea was eventually abandoned.

Harry's first serious problem concerned money. He had arrived with very little cash and it soon ran out. MI5 was acutely aware that unless he could be supplied with more his mission would have to come to an end. The Germans, of course, were already aware of the difficulty and seemed anxious not to abandon Harry. As a stopgap measure Owens was requested to send Harry £100 by registered mail, but more substantial funds were needed in a hurry. Ironically, it was MI5's determination to monitor Harry's expenditure (so as to keep an authentic-sounding account of his deteriorating financial circumstances) that nearly led to the collapse of his case. MI5 had hoped that Harry's predicament would be solved by cash supplied from some as-yet undiscovered spy, but the Abwehr's decision to nominate Arthur Owens was to have two effects. The first, entirely welcome at that stage, demonstrated that Owens still enjoyed German trust, but the second was less reassuring. It meant that Harry's existence, previously only known to the piano player code-named RAINBOW, had now been disclosed to Owens. Thus the circle indoctrinated into TATE's duplicity had increased by a factor of a hundred per cent and the threat of discovery or betrayal by the same quantity.

Nor was this prospect entirely academic, as events turned out. Owens himself was a highly dubious figure who had worked for SIS and the Abwehr long before he came into contact with the Security Service. His career as a double agent was to come to an end in March 1941, following a visit to Lisbon made in the company of another MI5 nominee, Walter Dicketts (CELERY). Owens had been invited to Portugal in February and been entertained there while Dicketts spent three weeks in Germany undergoing an intensive training course. Exactly what happened next, neither spy could agree on. Owens told his SIS contact in Lisbon that the Germans had charged him with being a double agent, working for the British almost as soon as he had arrived, and he had admitted only to having been in contact with MI5 for the past two or three months. Dicketts, however, told an entirely different story. He insisted that the Germans had never expressed any lack of confidence in him, and produced £10,000 and some sabotage *matériel* as proof of the Abwehr's trust.

These conflicting views placed MI5 in a difficult position which was resolved, on 21 April, by Owen's detention in Dartmoor, where he languished for the remainder of the war. The explanation, relayed over SNOW's wireless link, was that Owens had fallen gravely ill and hidden his transmitter. Whilst this proposition covered Owen's removal from the scene, it was to jeopardise all the other connected double agents, including Harry, whose address had been given to Owens so he could send him some cash. The question was, had the Abwehr swallowed SNOW's slightly lame excuse for his disappearance, or did they suspect the worst? Contact with RAINBOW and TATE was maintained, but MI5 allowed two other agents closely associated with Owens and Dicketts to cease operations. In the months that followed, MI5 subjected all RAINBOW's letters and TATE's wireless signals to intense analysis and it was deduced that the Abwehr had indeed accepted much of what Owens said he had told them, but had mistakenly concluded that Dicketts had denounced Owens to the authorities after their return to England in March 1941. These dramatic events were never imparted to Harry who, characteristically, continued to complain about his deteriorating finances.

At first the Abwehr negotiated with RAINBOW, the piano player from Weston-super-Mare, to get some cash to Harry, and this was interpreted as a sign that at least RAINBOW had escaped falling under suspicion. Then the Germans considered dropping a package containing £500 from a special flight; but eventually they informed Harry that a courier was to be sent carrying money and a new crystal for his transmitter. The arrangements for their meeting were remarkably complicated. The initial rendezvous was to be in the Strand Palace Hotel, with fall-back contacts nominated at the Tate Gallery and the British Museum. Harry attended them all, together with a team of Special Branch detectives, but no one else showed up. The reason was that the Abwehr's courier had been arrested by the Hertfordshire police.

The courier turned out to be Karel Richter, a Sudeten German who arrived with a false identity card in the name of Fred Snyder, bearing an address thoughtfully provided by Arthur Owens, and two passports in his own name. The Czech one was genuine but the Swedish document had been forged. Richter landed near London Colney, Hertfordshire, early on 14 May 1941 but was arrested a few hours later by a suspicious police constable. When searched Richter was found to be carrying $1,000 and £300, some of which was intended for Harry. Under interrogation at Camp 020 Richter admitted that his mission had two objectives, to hand over a crystal and the money to Harry, but also to act independently. In the latter capacity his first task had been to check on Harry and ensure he had not fallen into enemy hands. His conclusions were to be reported to Hamburg either over his own wireless set, or via secret writing to a cover address on the Continent. Oddly, he had not been supplied with the necessary secret ink, but only the chemical formula with which to make it. Its principal ingredient, amidopyrine, was available in England, but only from chemist's shops, where he would have been required by the law to declare his name and address in the poison book.

Richter's arrest, which took place in rather too public circumstances for MI5's liking, placed the Security Service in a very awkward position, and was to lead to the German's execution. The problem arose over the Treachery Act, which had been introduced the previous year to deal with cases of espionage. Until its enactment, enemy agents had been prosecuted under the Official Secrets Act, which had not proved very satisfactory and in any event did not include provision for a death penalty. The terms of the Treachery Act, rushed through Parliament during the summer of 1940, were much more severe, and already three German spies had been convicted under the new law and hanged. In addition, a further five agents had been arrested and were awaiting trial.

MI5's problem arose over its belief that it was empowered to offer inducements to enemy agents in order to obtain their co-operation, and that any promises made would be honoured. This had been the case with Goesta Caroli, who had been assured that if he agreed to help MI5 he would suffer no worse penalty than detention until the end of hostilities, just like any other POW. Similar terms had been agreed with Hans Reysen, a member of the Wehrmacht who had landed by parachute on 3/4 October with instructions to report on defences in the north-west of England in anticipation of an invasion. He had been discovered, sheltering in a barn, by a farmer and had subsequently made a full statement to MI5 in which he identified his unit as the Lehr Brandenburg Regiment. At the time of his capture he had been in civilian clothes but carrying a Wehrmacht paybook and a Luftwaffe uniform. He was accepted as a double agent even though his mission was obviously intended to be very short-term. He had been given just £140 and his radio was found to have no receiver, so he could only transmit messages. Reysen had been enrolled in MI5's books as

GANDER; but it soon became apparent that MI5 possessed no authority whatever to make any such offers.

It subsequently transpired that Churchill had expressed an interest in the very large number of German spies who had been caught during September 1940. As well as Caroli and Williamson, there had been nine others. Four had landed from a boat off Dungeness and been arrested soon after their arrival at the beginning of the month. On 23 September two Abwehr agents, Hugo Jonasson and Gerald Libot, were taken into custody in Plymouth. Both had been on *La Part Bien*, a small French boat escorted into port by a Royal Navy offshore patrol. Under interrogation the Swede and Belgian had admitted having been recruited by the Abwehr for a sabotage mission. Then a week later two more men, Werner Wälti and Karl Drücke, were intercepted in Scotland, together with a woman, Vera von Schalburg.

Although none of these cases was reported by the press until after their trials, the Cabinet had been notified immediately of the arrests, and the Prime Minister had expressed surprise that none of the spies had been shot. This observation had put Lord Swinton, as Chairman of the Home Defence Security Executive, into a quandary, for two reasons. Firstly, he must have assumed, as had everyone else involved with such matters, that the decision to refer espionage cases to the prosecuting authorities had rested with the Director-General of the Security Service who would, no doubt, be guided by operational considerations before handing a suspect over to the police. MI5 might well have objections to certain evidence being presented in court for fear that a particular source of information might be compromised. In the case of the double agents, it was vital that the integrity of the entire double-cross system be protected, because if one were compromised, others might suffer the same fate, perhaps with disastrous consequences. The other point was that the civil law only provided for execution by hanging, and therefore death by firing squad was only available to spies tried by courts martial. Thus the Prime Minister's remark had been wholly inappropriate, but nevertheless led Lord Swinton to decree, on 7 October 1940,[11] that his personal approval had to be obtained before any deal could be made with any spy. The timing of this decision was of special interest to the MI5 officers who had only hours earlier agreed to spare Hans Reysen's life in return for his collaboration.

Swinton's ruling was greeted with universal dismay inside MI5, which raised strong objections. The capacity to offer a suspect his life and eventual liberty was quite the strongest card any interrogator could play when questioning a recalcitrant suspect, and the behaviour of SUMMER, TATE and GANDER proved that as a method of extracting valuable information and future co-operation it was unequalled. The new policy would seriously handicap MI5's ability to get the maximum advantage from enemy agents. After all, why would an agent incriminate himself further unless there was a prospect of saving his life? And how could a case officer assess the potential value of a particular spy unless he had been persuaded into making at least a partial confession? Such a statement, made under caution to a police officer, would amount to a death warrant under the Treachery Act. This also raised some serious ethical problems for those directly involved. Several of the Security Service case officers dealing with German espionage, including John Marriott, Ian Wilson and Christopher Harmer, had been solicitors in peacetime and were therefore sensitive to the needs of the legal system. They had to be satisfied that any inducements offered would be honoured and would not fall victim to political whim or expediency. Following Swinton's ruling, they could have no confidence that their decisions, based on operational need, would not be overturned. This interference was perceived as meddling of the most counter-productive variety, and unanimously deplored. Indeed, the controversy was heightened the following month, when Jose Waldberg, Carl Meier, Charles van den Kieboom and Sjord Pons, the four agents arrested on the beach in Kent, were tried at the Old Bailey. Three were sentenced to hang but Pons was acquitted on the grounds that he had been coerced into working for the Abwehr which, he claimed, had threatened to have him sent to a concentration camp for breaching the Occupation's exchange controls in his native Holland. The conviction of Waldberg, who was German, and Meier, who was naturalised Dutch but German by birth, had been considered entirely reasonable, if not a deplorable waste of an opportunity to turn the tables on the Abwehr, but van den Kieboom's guilt had been less clear-cut. He had deployed much the same defence as Pons, but had been disbelieved by the jury. In any event, the trial ended with three agents being sent to the gallows, and Pons being detained for the duration under the Defence of the Realm regulations. Neither conclusion was considered even remotely satisfactory by those who had argued that enemy agents should be turned and exploited instead of being executed. In short, 'intelligence should have precedence over bloodletting'.

These exchanges, in unusually strong terms, were of rather more than academic interest to MI5, because further Abwehr spies were being caught. On 1 February Josef Jakobs was arrested soon after landing in a potato field in Huntingdonshire. His imminent arrival had been signalled to Arthur Owens who had supplied the Abwehr with his cover name, 'James Rymer', and other information that was found on his forged identity card. MI5 had been confident of catching 'Rymer' because Owens had been instructed to make contact with him, but an unforeseen accident wrecked the scheme. Jakobs had broken his ankle when he hit the ground, and been arrested a few hours later as he lay in agony beside his parachute. The circumstances of his capture near Ramsey were widely known in the neighbourhood, so there was considerable risk in employing him as a double agent, and Jakobs became a prime candidate for prosecution. Indeed, as a member of the Wehrmacht he was entitled to a court martial, which held the promise of satisfying Churchill's demand for a spy to be shot.

But Jakobs's was not the only espionage case pending. At the end of February a thirty-nine-year-old British merchant seaman, George Armstrong, was taken into custody in Cardiff, having been deported from America. He had been arrested in Boston the previous October after deserting his ship and travelling to New York where he had offered his services to the Germans. Motivated by his commitment to Communism, Armstrong had been intercepted before his recruitment by the enemy could be completed so, as far as the Security Service was concerned, he had no value or potential as a double agent. The same, however, could not be said for another merchant seaman, Joseph Laureyssens, who was arrested on 17 February after an investigation lasting less than a fortnight. One of his letters, addressed to an Abwehr postbox in Lisbon, had been detected by the mail censors during a routine chemical test for secret writing. Concealed in an apparently innocuous text was a first-hand description of a German attack on a convoy. Laureyssens was quickly traced as its author, and under interrogation, he admitted that over a period of months he had written sixteen such illicit letters, and made contact with numerous other agents in Britain. His claims about the existence of Abwehr spies unknown to MI5, though causing a flurry of trepidation at the time, were subsequently proved to be fiction, but in the mean time MI5 was particularly anxious to obtain his co-operation. This was yet another reason why Swinton's rigid guidelines were considered impractical by the case officers charged with combating enemy espionage.

Swinton listened to MI5's objections but, in March 1941, rejected them, confirming that 'the Prime Minister has laid it down as a matter of policy that in all suitable cases spies should be brought to trial'.[12] That raised the issue of what constituted a 'suitable' case, and who was to be its arbiter? The matter was of critical importance because, by this date, GANDER's case had come to a conclusion and SUMMER's had gone terribly wrong. Hans Reysen had only ever been intended as a short-term agent and he had been told to expect an invasion within a fortnight after his arrival. He had transmitted daily weather reports and what purported to be assessments of morale in the Midlands, under MI5's supervision, but by November 1940 his money and his mission were exhausted. MI5 had wanted to honour its promise and detain him until the end of the war, but Swinton's ruling suggested that he might be a candidate for a criminal prosecution. This, of course, created some unease within MI5's ranks. A not dissimilar situation had arisen over Goesta Caroli, the Swede who had been lodged at Hinxton and had been transmitting wireless reports on the area around Birmingham. He had inadvertently let slip that an earlier, pre-war visit to England had been undertaken for the Abwehr, a detail that he had omitted from his original statement, so MI5 brought him back to Camp 020 for further interrogation. This had led Caroli, who was already suffering from depression, to attempt suicide by slashing his wrists. MI5 had then returned Caroli to Hinxton and allowed Harry to join him for the Christmas holiday, but instead of being raised his spirits had sunk into an even greater depression. Finally, on 13 January, he had half strangled his lone guard and stolen his motor cycle. Fortunately it broke down, and he was recaptured in Ely whilst *en route* for the east coast. Obviously Caroli could no longer be trusted and he had been transferred to a special detention facility, thereby bringing SUMMER's case to a conclusion. Once again, the question of his future had arisen. Was he to be kept in detention or was he another 'suitable' case, and therefore to be turned over to the prosecuting authorities? MI5 expressed the view that neither GANDER nor SUMMER should be put on trial. Both had co-operated after promises had been made and neither had been a Nazi. Perhaps more importantly, any public disclosure of the circumstances of their capture would be bound to tip off the enemy to MI5's control of their cases, even if it did not actually jeopardise other double agents.

Thus as the debate continued on what was essentially a principle of life and death, and one of direct relevance to at least three of the five spies presently in custody, Karel Richter was arrested. Of course he had no way of knowing that from the moment of his capture his life had been in the balance, with MI5 arguing that he should be spared. The pleas were rejected, and on 17 June Swinton explained:

> I have given my undertaking that any spy or enemy agent whom we no longer require . . . for intelligence purposes shall be brought to justice if the case against him will lie. The right man to decide whether any case can be brought is the DPP, and we should certainly have the insurance of his opinion and advice in every case.[13]

Swinton's decision, regarded as disastrously unprofessional by MI5, had no effect on the trial of George Armstrong, who had been sentenced to hang the previous month. Nor did it have any relevance to Wälti and Drücke, who had been also found guilty under the Treachery Act a few days earlier and now faced execution. Clearly, though, it was the equivalent of a death warrant for Jakobs, who faced a court martial two months later, and for Richter, who went to the Old Bailey at the end of October. Even after the latter's conviction, at a trial held entirely in camera, MI5 reported to the Home Secretary that unless Richter received a reprieve Harry might be exposed as a double agent. Certainly the news of an execution could not be suppressed and the Abwehr, having read the newspaper accounts of the case, might easily conclude that their agent must have betrayed information about Harry whilst under interrogation. For reasons that remain unclear none of these arguments was accepted by Herbert Morrison, and on 10 December 1941 Richter met a grisly death on the scaffold when, at the very last moment and with his head in the noose, he lost his self-control and struggled terribly.

The risk to Harry's security was diminished somewhat by a strictly enforced agreement that MI5 could vet the official bulletin released by the Ministry of Information immediately after the execution had taken place. This measure, theoretically at least, kept the risk to Harry to the minimum, and to MI5's great relief there were no adverse consequences when the Germans learnt of Richter's fate. Paradoxically, Richter's arrest and execution was to have one useful purpose: it provided an added incentive to the Abwehr to urgently devise an alternative method of financing Harry, just when Dusko Popov was proposing Plan MIDAS, his ingenious scheme to extract a very large sum of money from the Germans (See p. 14).

In the mean time, Harry awaited his cash with growing impatience, and on one occasion signalled:

> What is delaying the man with the money you promised? I am beginning to think that you are full of shit.[14]

In response to Harry's demands the Abwehr proposed an interim measure. Harry was to go to the bus terminal at Victoria Station and get on to the Number 11 bus at four o'clock wearing a red tie and carrying a book and a newspaper. At the same time a Japanese, carrying a copy of *The Times*, would also get on the bus. They were not to acknowledge each other, but to alight at the fifth bus stop and wait together there for the next bus on the same route. Then, after an exchange of pre-arranged remarks, the Japanese would hand Harry his paper in which he would find enough money to tide him over until a more satisfactory and permanent conduit could be arranged. Harry responded by pointing out that the Number 11 bus no longer stopped at Victoria, and suggested the Number 16 instead. This was agreed, and when the rendezvous took place, under the watchful eyes of Special Branch detectives, the courier was identified as Lieutenant-Commander Minitory Yosii, an assistant naval attaché at the Japanese Embassy. This episode had the dual merit of getting £200 to Harry, and providing positive proof of Japanese collaboration with the Abwehr.

Harry was to receive a further, more substantial sum through MIDAS, but until that particular route had opened he was kept contented with the news that he was to be decorated with the Iron Cross for his tireless efforts. Since this award could only be received by German nationals, the Abwehr explained that special arrangements had been made to grant him his naturalisation papers at the same time. The medal itself was delivered to his brother, then serving with the Luftwaffe, with instructions that it was to be kept in a place of safety until Harry could return home. Encouraged by this development, Harry continued to undertake routine tasks for the Abwehr. In June, for example, he was instructed to investigate the site of what was suspected to be a Vickers armaments factory:

> Adjoining the aerodrome at Haywarden, west of Chester there is at the south-west corner 1km. north of the village of Broughton, the Vickers factory on the surface. Where is the underground factory? Are the works in operation?[15]

A month later Harry's financial position had been transformed, when he notionally collected the very large sum of £20,000 from Eric Glass, the Jewish theatrical agent. In reality, of course, Glass had played no part in the scheme and MI5's nominee in New York had simply removed the balance of the bank account held in his name. However, with his financial security taken care of, Harry suddenly acquired a new, more dangerous status. Whereas on previous occasions he had been able to decline particularly awkward tasks on the basis that he could not afford the journey, this excuse no longer held any validity. Overnight MI5 realised that, through their own ingenuity, Harry had been transformed from an asset into a potentially very dangerous liability. This embarrassing state of affairs was highlighted in July 1941, when Harry was ordered to Coventry to make an assessment of the bomb damage. The city had been devastated by the huge air raid the previous November which had left more than 550 people dead. Now the Abwehr wanted an on-the-spot eye-witness report of what reconstruction had taken place in the intervening nine months. As was his custom, Harry visited Coventry with his case officer, Ronnie Reed,[16] and then prepared a report which was submitted for MI5's approval before its transmission to the enemy. His original text, which included extraneous material about the condition of roads and installations on the outskirts of Coventry, read:

> The centre of town looks very bad. Many streets completely disappeared. Many roads up. Very many police. Very good food. Barrage balloons over the town. There are many large factories with huge activity a great deal of them undamaged. Thousands of labourers elsewhere.
>
> *Rootes Security Ltd*. Aircraft Division. No. 1 engine factory in Aldermoor Lane. Huge factory, very well camouflaged. Bomb damage not very important. Very great activity.
> Next door in Aldermoor Lane is *Auto Machinery Co Ltd*. Same applies as to *Rootes*.
> In the same street is the *Lucas factory*.
> Behind the houses in Brompton Road is a very large factory which seems to be new. Very well camouflaged.
> In Parkside there are *Maudsley Motor Co Ltd*, and the *Rover Co Ltd* and the *Armstrong Siddeley Motor Co Ltd*. Motor car manufacturers, aircraft dept. offices and motor body works – all in one large factory site. Huge activity – unimportant bomb damage.
> Gulson Road, very large factory. Seems to be *Jurys Crown Electrical Works*. Heavy damage, working full speed.
> Quintin Road – *Maudsley Motor Co Ltd*, and the *British*

Pressed Panels Ltd – slight damage. *Morris Motors* bodies branch – slight damage, much activity.
Little Park Street – Everything completely destroyed, including what seems to have been *Speedwell Gearcase Co.*
Earl Street and West Orchard Street – blown to bits.
Smithford Street – the *Triumph Motor Co Ltd* completely destroyed.
Gosford Street – the *General Electric Co* Whitefriars Works, completely destroyed. Next door, the *Mechanisation and Aero Co Ltd*, practically undamaged, working full speed.
Bell Green Road – *Morris Motor Co*, Courthouse Green Works, badly damaged in parts, but working full speed.
Smith Street – the *Thomas Smith Stamping Works Ltd* as well as the *English Electric Co*, are heavily damaged, but are working full speed.
Lower Ford Street – some damage, but little to factories. The *British Thompson Houston Co Ltd*, is in this street.
Humber Avenue – the *Aeronautical Equipment* (Thomas Smith's Stamping Works) are working full speed.
Aldermoor Green – about three miles north-east from Coventry, power station with three large chimneys and seven Wohl cooling towers – no bomb damage.[17]

A comparison between the first draft, above, and the text that was actually sent to Germany demonstrates the care MI5 exercised in presenting a particular picture to the Abwehr of strict police controls and few clues for the Luftwaffe's aerial-reconnaissance aircraft to pick up. The first version was vetoed by the Home Defence Executive as being far too dangerous, almost to the point of inviting another air raid, which prompted J. C. Masterman to minute on 30 July:

The Germans, whatever we do or say, will choose some targets to bomb. The choice is not between bombing or no bombing, but the bombing of this or that objective. Surely

> therefore it is better to attempt to direct them to places which we consider at least less vulnerable than others, rather than to take no action and let things take their course?[18]

The HDE amended Harry's draft report and slyly inserted a reference to barrage balloons, omitted from the original account, which was intended to deter enemy aircraft from flying low to corroborate Harry's account:

> I have been in Coventry but had to stop operations after my first preliminary run round because I found the Police were conducting an identity card drive and I thought that I should have difficulties clearing myself if picked up.
> In my preliminary survey I found that the centre of town was badly damaged. Many streets completely disappeared, many roads are up. The outskirts seem to have suffered less so far as I could see from the train and from one bus ride. Balloon barrage over the town. This area is interesting to me and seems productive, but I must have a street plan. It may be worthwhile returning when the security drive is over.
> There are many large factories. Some of them are undamaged, but there seems also to have been a great deal of industrial damage. I found much less activity than I had expected even taking into account the extent of the damage, and from such enquiries as I have had time to make the answer seems to be that the authorities were so frightened by the raid of last November that they have put into operation a large-scale dispersal policy. As regards the direction in which this has taken place, I hardly know where to start. For example, GEC, which was badly damaged in November, has transferred operations to a new factory in Lanarkshire. Some of the Morris Motors subsidiaries have

also gone, but I overheard in a bus, it is possible that they have transferred to the outskirts of Manchester.
I was able to get the following detailed information:
Little Park Street – Everything completely destroyed – no activity. Everything burnt out. One factory seems to have been the Gearcase Co Ltd.
Earl Street – Blown to pieces.
Smithford Street – The upper half blown to pieces.
West Orchard – Completely blown to pieces.
Priory Street – Cycle works completely destroyed and burnt out.[19]

The second version has deliberately exaggerated the extent of the damage sustained by Coventry, and suggested that two important strategic targets, Morris Motors and GEC, had been dispersed further afield, shrewdly identifying Lanarkshire as one destination, confident in the knowledge that it was safely out of the Luftwaffe bombers' range.

This kind of censorship, judiciously exercised by a body known as the Wireless Board on the advice of representatives of all the interested services and ministries, allowed Harry to maintain contact with the Abwehr on an extraordinary variety of topics. A month after his visit to Coventry, Harry was cross-examined about retail prices and food stocks. Then, in September, he was requested to find out about the 'many underground food stores'[20] that were supposed to have been built across the country. Later, in November, the Abwehr asked:

Are any parachute troops sent overseas, especially to the Middle East?[21]

Within a year of landing in England, Harry had blossomed into one of the Abwehr's key agents, entrusted with a much wider role than originally intended, and his new financial status not only confirmed his importance to the enemy but gave him a new role, albeit temporarily. He was asked to send some money to John Moe, code-named MUTT by MI5, who had arrived in Scotland by flying boat in April 1941; and in a remarkable reversal of roles Harry was asked to pay his original contact, RAINBOW, a salary of £1,000 per annum to persuade him to give up his job with the band in Weston-super-Mare and move to London. This Pierce agreed to do, and in February 1942 he started work in a factory that enabled him to begin reporting on industrial and economic matters, thus prolonging his life as a double agent by a useful sixteen months.

There was, however, a disadvantage to Harry's apparent success as a uniquely well-funded German spy. MI5 felt that further excuses for Harry's reluctance to answer specific questions might serve to tip off the Abwehr to the fact that he was operating under British control. Furthermore, the Germans now said that as Harry had acquired considerable wealth he ought to be able to move up in the world and make some interesting contacts in a different social circle. This suggestion was ill-received by MI5, and its solution was a report transmitted to Hamburg in September 1941 in which Harry plausibly claimed to have been challenged by the police about his failure to register for national service. This uncomfortable confrontation had led Harry to accept the offer of a job on a farm near Radlett from the father of a girl he had met, which conveniently had the effect of restricting his signals to his regular daily reports on the weather and other equally harmless topics such as crops and rationing. His new occupation, helping to run the estate, did at least exempt him from call-up for military service, but it also meant that he would only be able to travel very occasionally. In order to encourage the Germans to believe that he was not going into a well-heeled retirement, it was explained that he had also found a flat in London which he intended to use at weekends.

The truth, of course, was that Harry was still living with his MI5 wireless operator, Russell Lee, at Roundbush House. Although Harry had initially keyed all his own signals, Lee had taken over for a period when Harry had been hospitalised at St Mary's for treatment for a duodenal ulcer, and after his discharge Lee had continued to transmit for him rather than risk another change in style being spotted in Hamburg. Although Lee had taken over the transmitting, Harry still prepared all his messages, and a fictional life for him on the farm was developed so he could explain his day-to-day activities. Although he was never to recruit sub-agents like TRICYCLE, he did acquire one particularly useful (but imaginary) girlfriend named Mary, who often stayed at the farm at the weekend. She turned out to be a cipher clerk based at the Admiralty in London, and this held out the promise of access to some interesting information in the future.

It was at this stage that Harry's career as a double agent could be said to have reached a plateau, with the Germans acknowledging his daily signals but setting him few specific tasks. This change in attitude, following the euphoria of his award of the Iron Cross, raised the prospect that the Abwehr had become dissatisfied with his performance. Characteristically, Harry tackled the subject head-on:

> You never let me know what you think of my work. An occasional pat on the back would be welcome. After all, I am only human.[22]

Unfortunately there was no independent method available to check on his standing with the enemy because, unlike other double agents who were handled from Madrid or Lisbon, there was no radio relay to Berlin for the wireless interceptors to monitor and decrypt. TRICYCLE's controller, for example, sent regular reports to headquarters charting the spy's progress, but Harry was run from Wohldorf, on the outskirts of Hamburg, and all his signals were sent on via a landline which was, of course, impossible to gain access to.

Up until the end of 1941 Harry's principle value had been in the counter-intelligence field. He had been connected with SNOW and RAINBOW and had played a part in the identification of Karel Richter and Minitory Yosii. However, as events unfolded, it became clear that MI5 had actually taken complete control over the Abwehr's entire network in Britain. During the course of the war about 120 agents were to be drawn into the Security Service's double-cross system, and this was giving it the confidence to move away from the rather defensive role of fending off awkward Abwehr enquiries and fulfilling routine but relatively uncoordinated tasks. Having established a reliable conduit of information straight to the German High Command, MI5 realised that there were tremendous opportunities to indulge in strategic deception on a grand scale. In August 1942 the Director of Naval Intelligence, Admiral John Godfrey, suggested to the other members of the Wireless Board that the entire double-cross organisation ought to be developed for deception purposes. Although not everything in his proposal met with approval, there was an important change in the composition of the Twenty Committee. A representative from the Chief of Combined Operations was invited to attend the regular weekly meetings, as was Colonel John Bevan, the Controlling Officer of Deception.

One consequence of this structural change in the intelligence hierarchy was the decision to use double agents as a means of deceiving the enemy about details of a forthcoming operation of great importance, the Allied invasion of north Africa, scheduled for early November 1942. The intention was to distract the enemy away from the real objective and persuade him that the impending Allied offensive was destined for Norway and the north coast of France. Accordingly, two cover plans, SOLO 1 and OVERTHROW, were developed, which created a framework of individual reports from specified agents that, like a mosaic, would lead the Germans to come to certain conclusions once they had assembled all the separate pieces of intelligence. It was a truly ingenious scheme, and TATE was one of the chief double agents to be assigned a specific role in conveying the cover plan to Berlin.

The deception for TORCH, the invasion of north Africa, was generally believed to have been a success, although judging these matters is not easy. Certainly the Germans never expected such a large landing in the region, although they did believe that an assault on Dakar was probable. In any event, the operation proved conclusively that it was possible to mount a really large military operation and conceal its objective from the enemy. It was also learnt that for the best results, the cover plan ought to relate as closely as practicable to the genuine article. Whatever the belief in Berlin, it did emerge, as the lessons of TORCH were being analysed, that none of the double agents used to convey false information had been damaged by the experience. Indeed, there was good reason to believe that Harry had actually recovered some of his lost ground through contacts he had made through Mary, the fictitious Admiralty cipher clerk. She had been loaned by the Admiralty to the US Naval Mission and had introduced Harry to British and American naval officers who, towards the end of 1942, carelessly left classified documents in Harry's flat. Some of these had revealed details of Allied minefields, information that caused great excitement in Hamburg and led to Harry being instructed to try and obtain specific Admiralty charts, an order Harry declined to follow because it was too risky. Nevertheless he did pass on some of the gossip he overheard from Mary's naval friends, including the news that several convoy escorts had been switched from the Mediterranean to home waters, much to the disappointment of the crews, and the alleged consternation of the US Navy, which had expressed concern about the lack of surface protection for American merchantmen. Although pressed for more detailed material, particularly concerning shipping routes, Harry only ever identified one, and that was after it had been discontinued.

Following TORCH, to which Harry had made a modest contribution, his case again appeared to go into decline. Between March and September 1943 he only received fourteen messages from Germany, although he was on the air every day with his weather reports. At one stage, somewhat disillusioned, MI5 gave serious consideration to bringing the operation to a close, but the Naval Intelligence Division argued that Harry's girlfriend had plenty of scope for development, especially if she could be loaned to the American forces. MI5 gave its consent to his continuation, and to Mary's temporary transfer to the US Navy in Washington as a cipher clerk, only to discover that the Abwehr might have been tipped off about Harry's duplicity.

The problem arose when a group of Germans was repatriated, among their number at least one Abwehr agent. Under normal circumstances this would not have mattered, as they had been isolated from access to anything that might be damaging to Allied interests. Unfortunately, after they had been released, one of MI5's stool pigeons reported the existence of a clandestine signalling system between two internment camps in the Isle of Man. One was Camp L, where large numbers of committed Nazis had been accommodated, and Camp WX, which had once housed Tor Glad, a Norwegian who had been JEFF to Moe's MUTT. Unlike his partner, JEFF had proved uncooperative and been interned, first at Camp WX and then, in September 1942, at Dartmoor. His detention at Camp WX during 1942 had coincided with that of Goesta Caroli, who had been moved there following his escape attempt in January 1941 and, according to MI5's stool pigeon, the link between Camp WX and the Nazis in Camp L had been so complete that there was a good chance that the details of both men had been received by one of the Nazis. MI5 learnt that altogether thirty-three enemy aliens had been in Camp L during the period that JEFF and SUMMER had been held in Camp WX, among them Erich Carl, a suspected Abwehr agent who had been repatriated. Dismayed by the implications of the leak, MI5 launched an inquiry in December 1942 and interrogated several of the detainees at

Dartmoor about their experiences in Camp WX. Gradually it emerged that details of Caroli and Glad had reached the other camp, which implied that John Moe and Harry had also been compromised. MI5 had no choice but to await developments; fortunately there were no repercussions. If upon his return to Germany Erich Carl had indeed reported that Caroli, Harry, John Moe and Tor Glad had fallen under British control, he must have been disbelieved, for there were no adverse consequences for either MUTT or TATE.

The risk of Harry's exposure was a constant source of worry, and as the war progressed and the tide turned against the Axis, more offers to defect were received from disenchanted Abwehr officers, either opportunists who sought to switch sides before it was too late, or authentic dissidents who had always held anti-Nazi sentiments. Harry's vulnerability to betrayal by both was considerable.

The fear that Harry might have come under suspicion meant that he was to play one of the lesser roles in the deception campaign to cover the D-Day landings, but some of his contributions were memorable. For example, he was able to report General Eisenhower's arrival in England in January 1944, to take up his appointment as Supreme Allied Commander, even before the news had been officially released. His farm in Radlett was too far from the coast to make any useful observations so Harry's employer sent him to spend the summer on a friend's farm near Wye in Kent. This was an ideal location from which to monitor troop movements, and he participated in STARKEY, a deception mounted during the summer of 1943 designed to persuade the Germans of an imminent attack in the Pas-de-Calais region, so as to reduce the pressure on the hard-pressed Russian Front. As a precaution, a special GPO landline from London was constructed to the notional remote transmitting site in Kent, so that if the Germans ever decided to use direction-finding equipment to check on the source of Harry's transmissions it would confirm his location in the south-east. In

March 1944 Harry was selected to support the D-Day cover plans. One part, code-named FORTITUDE NORTH, was intended to convey the impression that the forthcoming Allied assault on Europe would take place in Scandinavia, so Harry reported that, by chance, he had learnt that the British Minister in Stockholm, Victor Mallett, had been brought home to London for urgent consultations with the Foreign Office.

Harry was also a player in IRONSIDE, another deception which suggested an amphibious landing was to take place on the French coast in the Bay of Biscay, and FORTITUDE SOUTH, a particularly sophisticated venture to reinforce the German belief in a landing near Calais. This Harry reinforced by reporting the shoulder flashes of American troops, elements of the 83rd Infantry Division, he had noticed billeted near Wye. He described having seen huge numbers of English and Canadian soldiers bivouacking in nearby woods and reported that twenty thousand Canadians had passed through Ashford on their way to Dover. He also mentioned that Mary, having recently returned from Washington, had heard of a huge American expeditionary force gathering on the eastern seaboard.

From other, equally misleading information, the Abwehr concluded that a huge formation, the First United States Army Group, had assembled in Kent in anticipation of a push across the shortest stretch of the Channel. But this was only one half of the deception plan. The really critical part began immediately after the troops had disembarked, when the intention was to persuade the enemy that the Normandy landings were merely a diversionary feint and that the main thrust was still some time away, targeted on the Pas-de-Calais. To support this proposition Harry went to Cambridge, where he saw the US 11th Infantry Division on the move. At the railway station he observed the US XX Corps heading west, and in Norwich the 25th Armoured Division was spotted on its way south. Each item conveyed the impression that a second, more important attack was imminent, and this helped to tie down large numbers of enemy units in

Belgium and northern France while a beach-head was established in Normandy.

After the success of D-Day Harry's services were again in demand, this time to plot the time and location of V–1 explosions. This data was vital for correcting the aim of the weapon and it had been Whitehall's intention to suggest to the enemy that many of the rockets were overflying the capital, or at least impacting north of the centre, so their range would be shortened.

On 21 September 1944 Harry passed a significant milestone, the transmission of his thousandth signal. His message read:

> On the occasion of this, my 1,000th message I beg to ask you to convey to our Fuhrer my humble greetings and ardent wishes for a speedy victorious termination of the war.[23]

Of course the war was moving to its conclusion, but there was still work to be done, this time for the Admiralty, which was facing a shortage of deep-water mines, the only effective deterrent against marauding U-boats operating close to the English coast. Harry had been introduced to an indiscreet Royal Navy officer who was serving aboard HMS *Plover*, one of only two minelayers engaged in these operations, and had generously offered him the use of his flat in London when he was on leave. The result was a quantity of high-quality reports from November 1944 onwards concerning the size and location of new minefields. According to Harry, a new type of deep-water anti-submarine mine had been developed to be moored close to the floor of the sea. Thus it presented a hazard to U-boats but not to surface vessels, which could pass above in perfect safety. To enhance their credibility, Harry was allowed to lace his texts with reference to U-boats that had actually been lost in air attacks in the areas he claimed had been sown with mines. Constant surveillance of the U-boat radio frequencies occasionally identified one of the hapless craft that had sunk without getting off a signal to the Kriegsmarine. In these cases Harry reported the loss, attributing it to a newly laid mine, before U-boat headquarters itself had been notified. Harry's advice was taken seriously and led to an order, issued on 1 January 1945, which warned U-boats to keep away from southern Ireland. This ingenious deception had been all the more convincing when Kapitanleutnant Hubertus Purkhold, the commander of *U260*, an Atlantic-type VIIC U-boat, signalled on 12 March that he had been obliged to scuttle after hitting a mine in an area south-east of the Fastnet Rock that roughly corresponded to Harry's information. Purkhold's crew of forty-four had waded ashore at Clonakilty Bay in Eire, never realising that they had unintentionally confirmed Harry's bona fides. Accordingly the Germans issued a directive the day afterwards which effectively closed four grid squares, amounting to some 3,600 square miles of the Western Approaches, to U-boat traffic.

Harry's last message, about mine-laying in the Kola inlet, was transmitted on 2 May 1945 and was acknowledged only hours before Allied troops entered Hamburg. Harry's Abwehr controller urged him to maintain contact with his sources, and ended the signal by answering Harry's query about a suitcase of his possessions he had left in Hamburg in 1939. The Abwehr confirmed that it had been delivered to his sister in September the previous year, the compromising documents it contained having been destroyed.

Harry subsequently returned home to recover his suitcase, and the Iron Cross that his brother had kept for him; he did not stay long. Instead he was granted British citizenship and became a photographer on a local newspaper in Watford, where he lives in retirement today. Perhaps the last word on him should be left to the late Sir John Masterman, who referred to TATE while preparing an account of the double-cross system for the Security Service archives at the end of the war:

> His work was of great value, first for counter-espionage purposes and later in deception, and he was instrumental in securing large sums of money from the Germans. He was specially naturalised by wireless in order to receive the Iron Cross First and Second class, and was to end regarded by the Germans as a 'pearl' among agents. Here his career was even more remarkable.[24]

Harry married an Englishwoman and had a daughter. He resisted returning to Hamburg for nearly ten years, and then visited his brother, who was a Luftwaffe veteran, and his sister, who had married a surgeon. His other sister had moved to Bogotá after the war. Now, following his retirement and divorce, he lives in Watford, alone except for his memories of his quite extraordinary war.

CHAPTER III

William Buckley

Just after 7.30 a.m. on the morning of Friday 16 March 1984, a slightly stooped, fifty-six-year-old American made himself breakfast in his second-floor apartment and took the elevator to the basement garage in which his car was parked. It was a routine that hundreds of thousands of divorcees the world over engage in every day, but for William Buckley the situation was rather unusual, for two reasons. Firstly, his apartment building was located in the Christian enclave of west Beirut, a virtual war zone following the collapse the previous evening of the truce between the Muslim and Christian militiamen declared only three days earlier; secondly, he was the CIA's Chief of Station in the ravaged capital of Lebanon. Since 6 February, when Druze and Shia militias had taken control of west Beirut from the Lebanese Army, the district had become a battleground. Suddenly the quiet and reserved Buckley, the donnish intelligence analyst who ran an antique shop in Virginia as a hobby, was out of his depth. As Felix Rodriguez, one of his Vietnam colleagues, remarked, 'He was probably brighter than 99.9 percent of the people I have known. But he lacked street smarts [and] never developed the kind of primal instincts that keep field agents alive.'[1]

Exactly what happened when Buckley reached the basement level and emerged from the lift is unknown. He had dismissed his bodyguard the previous evening, saying that he was to meet an informant. Certainly he had started his own car and had begun to drive it out of the cul-de-sac leading to his apartment block when a white Renault blocked his path. According to the subsequent police report which quoted Muhammed Mousaa, Buckley's apartment manager, who witnessed the incident, the American had been assaulted by three masked Shiites who held a pistol to his head and forced him into the Renault's boot. The car had then shot off at high speed, and had last been seen in the southern suburb of Khalde, heading for Syrian-controlled territory.

Buckley was not the first American to be taken hostage that year. On 10 February Frank Regier, the Professor of Engineering at the American University, had been snatched, and on 17 March, the day after the CIA officer was taken, Jeremy Levin, the bureau chief for Cable News Network Television had also been grabbed. Regier had been freed soon afterwards by a rival Shiite militia, and he was later to be replaced as a hostage on 8 May by a Presbyterian clergyman, the Reverend Benjamin Weir, who had lived in the Lebanon for the past thirty years. Thus Buckley was the second American kidnap victim in just over a month, one of four to be seized in the spring of 1984.

News that Buckley had fallen victim to the latest wave of hostage-taking, an ancient practice in the Middle East, was greeted with dismay three-quarters of a mile away at the American Embassy, although his exact status was deliberately withheld. The local CIA station, located on the fifth floor of the main embassy building, had already been the target of terrorist attack. Indeed, Buckley had volunteered for the post following the death of his predecessor, Kenneth Haas, just eleven months earlier on 18 April, when a huge bomb concealed in a delivery van had been detonated inside the embassy compound right beside the front entrance. The entire centre section of the eight-storey building had collapsed in the blast, killing sixty-three people, and all but two of the CIA station's officers. In addition to the loss of the recently married Chief of Station, six other CIA staffers had died in the incident, including Haas's deputy, James Lewis; his wife Monique, who had just started work as a secretary; another secretary named Phyllis Faraci; and Robert C. Ames, one of the Agency's most senior Middle East analysts, who had only just arrived in Beirut. The loss of seven station staff was the worst single incident in the Agency's history, and the DCI William J. Casey had been at Andrews Air Force Base to pay his respects when the seventeen American bodies were returned to Washington.

Once back at Langley, Casey had ordered an investigation into how such an avoidable catastrophe could have been allowed to happen. The Lebanese police, assisted by the CIA, eventually identified three suspects, including a Palestinian employee of the embassy who admitted, under torture, that his role had been to signal confirmation that Ambassador Robert Dillon was in his office. His confession, together with evidence from the three other prisoners, implicated a fifth conspirator who was also detained and who, after interrogation, claimed a Syrian intelligence officer had actually supervised the preparation of the bomb in the van. There the case remained because the prisoner subsequently died. Keith Hall, one of the CIA interrogators from what was left of the embassy, was later fired from the Agency for his participation in the 'overly harsh' interrogation which allegedly included the use of electric shocks.

Casey's decision to replace Haas with Buckley had not been easy; the Agency had been denuded of talent in recent years. When Casey had been appointed DCI in January 1981 it was still reeling from the effects of his predecessors' savage cuts in the Directorate of Operations. Over a three-year period 2,800 experienced intelligence officers had either been axed by Admiral Stansfield Turner or had taken voluntary redundancy, and this had been in addition to the savage cuts made by James R. Schlesinger in 1973. A total of 820 permanent posts had been abolished. In consequence, three-quarters of the Agency's chiefs of overseas stations were approaching retirement age. Fewer than half the analysts spoke the language of the country they had been designated to study, and an even smaller proportion had actually visited the country to which they had been assigned. Thus the loss of Haas, Ames and Lewis was a serious problem for the Agency and, although Buckley was well qualified for the post, he did have some disadvantages too. In Korea he had been decorated with the Silver Star for gallantry after wiping out an enemy machine-gun post. He joined the Agency and served in Vietnam as deputy to Tucker Gougelmann, who had masterminded the highly successful Provincial Reconnaissance Units.[2] After his tour in Saigon he had been assigned to Damascus, where he was attached to the embassy under diplomatic cover, and was exposed. Once 'blown' he had been withdrawn and transferred to Cairo to supervise the training of Anwar Sadat's bodyguards. Then he had been posted to Islamabad, where he had only narrowly escaped a mob of religious fundamentalists during a riot when they stormed the embassy building. On that occasion Buckley had made a dramatic escape and sought refuge in the British Embassy.

The difficulty facing Casey was that Buckley's identity as a CIA officer had been exposed in Syria just four years earlier, and therefore any cover he adopted in the Lebanon would be semi-transparent. The Agency's own rule was that no member of the clandestine service should be deployed in a region where he had been blown for at least five years. In addition, Buckley had been named as a CIA officer in an article contributed by Philip Agee to *CounterSpy*, a radical magazine in Washington.[3] A renegade clandestine service officer, Agee had left the Agency in 1968 and then devoted himself to exposing his former colleagues and their sources. Agee's public denunciation of Buckley should have spelt the end of his covert career, but evidently Casey felt differently, and offered Buckley the post, apparently because he believed him to be quite the best prepared to take on the terrorists. Buckley was by now the Agency's in-house expert on counter-terrorism and he knew the risks involved. He also had a wealth of knowledge concerning American tactics, and according to some reports he had been reluctant to go to

Beirut. He had served as the CIA's representative on the Inter-Agency Group on terrorism, and had been a regular visitor to Fort Bragg to see the much-vaunted Delta Force on manoeuvres. Thus, quite apart from presenting extremists with a prestige assassination target, the data he had accumulated made him an attractive candidate for interrogation.

As soon as the kidnapping became known the Director of Central Intelligence gathered his closest subordinates together to conduct a damage-control exercise, working on a worst-case scenario that everything Buckley knew would become known to his captors sooner or later. Those present at this initial meeting were John N. McMahon, Casey's Deputy Director; John H. Stein, the Deputy Director for Operations and head of the clandestine service; the DCI's executive assistant, Robert Gates; the head of CIA's Office of Security, William J. Kopatish; the head of Near East Division, Charles Cogan; and the director of Near East Operations, Dick Holm. Their response was threefold: a request to undertake a detailed aerial survey of any possible locations where Buckley might be kept hostage; an urgent cable to the FBI for a team, to investigate on the ground the circumstances of the loss in Beirut; and a request to the US Army's crack Intelligence Support Activity to infiltrate its men into the city for an undercover search. In addition the CIA station was ordered to suspend whatever sensitive operations Buckley had been privy to, and to deploy as many of its informants as possible with the task of ascertaining which group had taken Buckley. His capture was a grievous blow for the CIA, not least because, like most intelligence agencies, it was relatively inexperienced in dealing with such situations. Apart from Ken Haas, the Agency had only lost one previous chief of station, Dick Welch, who had been murdered in Athens in 1975. The last kidnap victim, Tom Ahern, had been held hostage with the rest of the US Embassy staff in Tehran in 1979, but he at least had survived his captivity. Nor was the CIA's experience unique in this respect. The British, for example, had only lost two senior officers in the post-war era. One, Desmond Doran, had been assassinated with a grenade thrown by Irgun terrorists in Tel Aviv in September 1946; the other had died in a car accident. In contrast, there are the names of sixty-five Mossad personnel on that organisation's memorial to its dead, located at Glilot, north of Tel Aviv.

As for the identity of the culprits, the weight of opinion was that 'Islamic Jihad' was responsible, which only complicated matters. Very little was known about this shadowy umbrella group which called itself 'Holy War', but there were stories that a particularly militant cell led by Imad Mugniyah, a young well-educated Shiite from southern Lebanon, had been involved. Certainly he was a likely candidate. A known Muslim fanatic, he had commanded the bodyguard of the Shiite religious leader Sheik Mohammed Hussein Fadlallah, and his brother-in-law had been convicted of bombing the French and American embassies in Kuwait with other members of a group called al-Dawa ('The Call') just three months earlier, in December 1983. The CIA believed it significant that the first American to be kidnapped in Beirut that year, Professor Frank Regier, had been seized the day before the al-Dawa trial opened in Kuwait.

Sheik Fadlallah was considered by many to be the architect and principal exploiter of the current religious conflict in the Lebanon. On Sunday 23 October 1983, 241 American servicemen had been killed when a yellow Mercedes truck packed with twelve thousand pounds of TNT had exploded in the Marine compound at Beirut airport. On the same day fifty-eight French soldiers had also been killed in their barracks during a similar attack. The intensive research undertaken following those two incidents had tended to incriminate, but not prove a case against, Sheik Fadlallah's supporters in the Bekaa Valley.

The question of who controlled the Hezbollah ('Party of Allah') fanatics remains a matter of controversy. The Syrians were widely regarded as the most influential power in the area, and had already been implicated in the April 1983 embassy bombing. Nevertheless, President Assad was approached to see whether he would intercede with the kidnappers. This was a bold decision, given the suspected sponsorship of the embassy bombing, and the fact that the Syrian intelligence service was run by Assad's brother, Rifaat. These moves quickly became known to Mossad's Deputy Director, Mark Hessner,[4] who was responsible for liaising with the CIA, and he attempted to persuade the Agency that the Iranians were more likely to hold the key to Buckley's release, and offered to intervene.

Mossad certainly knew of Imad Mugniyah and had two good reasons for wanting him eliminated. Firstly, he was regarded as Sheik Fadlallah's chief of operations and was known to have played a key role in the bombing in November 1985 of the Israeli Border Guards base in Tyre which had been destroyed by a suicide car bomber. A green Chevrolet pick-up truck, packed with half a ton of TNT, had been driven around the dragon's teeth at the main entrance of the compound and detonated. Nineteen Israeli policemen from the 21st Company had been killed, together with thirty-two of their Shiite Palestinian prisoners, all suspected members of Hezbollah. The explosion had wrecked the building and had temporarily crippled the Israelis' anti-terrorist operations in southern Lebanon.[5]

Mossad's second reason for interest in Mugniyah was their suspicion of links between him and George Ibrahim Abdullah, a Palestinian assassin who had been arrested in Paris following the murder in 1982 of Charles Ray, the American deputy military attaché, and Yacov Barsimantov, the local Mossad station chief. On one occasion when Mugniyah was in France trying to obtain Abdullah's release, the French security service, the DST, had actually captured Mugniyah on a tip from Mossad, but instead of being charged he had been quietly deported.

The Israeli offer to assist resulted in a visit to Mossad's headquarters in Tel Aviv, located in a large anonymous office block, known as the Hadar Dafna Building on King Saul Boulevard, by the CIA's station chief and his assistant. They went up to the ninth floor and called on Nahum Admony, who had run Mossad since 1982. According to Mossad agent Victor Ostrovsky, the visit was followed by a formal request from the US Ambassador to Shimon Peres for Mossad's help, and this resulted in a conference held at the Mossad training academy, a secure establishment located at Midrasha, between Tel Aviv and Haifa. Conveniently close to the luxurious Country Club resort hotel, it masqueraded as the Prime Minister's summer residence. There the CIA officers were introduced to Mossad's experts on the PLO who work in a branch known as the Saifanim ('goldfish'). However, when the CIA men returned two days later to clarify one of the items of intelligence mentioned in the briefing, Mossad declined to allow them to meet the actual case officers handling agents in the Lebanon. Called *katsas*, the true identities of these key officers are closely guarded even within Mossad, and the hierarchy was emphatic about refusing the CIA permission to cross-examine them. A visit to Tel Aviv by John McMahon, Casey's DDCI, failed to get the Israelis to budge, and some cynics in the CIA took the view that Mossad had never really had anything of substance to offer anyway.[6] They had simply seized an opportunity to implicate the PLO in Buckley's kidnapping, although in all probability the Palestinians had been entirely innocent of the crime.

The CIA's apparent inability to get to grips with Buckley's kidnappers was not the only slow-moving area within the American intelligence community. Coincidentally, within a fortnight of Buckley's capture President Reagan had signed a document known as 'National Security Decision Directive 138' which was intended to co-ordinate the activities of all the various agencies involved in counter-terrorism. The problem was, there were just too many of them. The Pentagon, Defence Intelligence Agency, National Security Agency, FBI and State Department all ran their own independent units, and only communicated through the bureaucratic mechanism of committee meetings or Casey's own brainchild, a classified computer network code-named FLASHBOARD. Another innovation was the Hostage Locating Task Force, with experts seconded from all the usual organisations and extra help from the Drug Enforcement Agency, the Immigration and Naturalisation Service, and even the US Customs. However, none of these bodies had any success in determining where Buckley was.

Despite all the research undertaken, Buckley's exact location remains unknown to this day. He only came into contact with the other hostages in mid-March 1985, and in the few brief conversations he managed to snatch with them he gave no indication of where he had been taken previously. There are, however, several theories. One is that in July 1984 he was moved to the Saleh-Abad military camp to the south-west of Tehran, where several senior officials participated in his interrogation in September or October, including Mohsen Rafiqdust, then Minister for the Revolutionary Guards. Amir Taheri, once Editor of *Kayhan*, Iran's largest daily newspaper, suggests that a trial was held in Tehran which lasted some forty hours, all of them recorded on a harrowing videotape which was later delivered to the US Embassy in Cairo.[7] Others, including White House staff, cannot recall the tape but agree that Buckley's plight became a dominant issue at the time. That the Iranians were ruthless torturers no one had any doubt. General Ne'ematullah Nassiri, the former head of the Shah's police, who had replaced General Pakravan as chief of the security apparatus SAVAK in 1965, was already in prison, awaiting trial on corruption charges, when the Islamic revolution had occurred in January 1979, and his experience had been given wide circulation. He had been forced to eat razor blades, then been hanged, drawn, and finally shot.

Six months after Buckley's abduction, a second attack on American diplomatic premises in the Lebanon took place, this time on the embassy annexe in Christian East Beirut. On Thursday 20 September 1984, just as the British Ambassador was visiting the building, a suicide bomber in a van displaying diplomatic number plates dodged through the concrete obstacles on the approach road to the main building and crashed into a stationary vehicle. Twenty-four people, including two US servicemen, were killed in the subsequent explosion, and ninety were wounded. However, on this occasion there was clear evidence linking the attack to Hezbollah. An aerial-reconnaissance photograph of the Sheik Abdullah Barracks in the Bekaa Valley, taken within a few hours of the bombing, revealed an identical configuration of the three concrete barriers that had been constructed to protect the embassy annexe. Tyre burns on the road surface showed that the bomber had been practising zigzagging a vehicle around the obstacles at speed. The trace of these rehearsals was considered almost conclusive proof of Hezbollah's complicity.

Just as the CIA appeared to stall on what further measures could be taken to find Buckley, the Beirut kidnappers struck again. On 3 December 1984 a librarian at the American University of Beirut, Peter Kilburn, and a month later on 8 January a Catholic priest, Father Lawrence Jenco, were also grabbed. Jenco shared his captivity with Benjamin Weir, the Presbyterian missionary taken hostage eight months earlier, and the CNN reporter Jeremy Levin. The first news in the West of how the hostages were faring appeared in a video cassette released on 28 January 1985, in which Buckley confirmed that he was well, and was being held with Weir and Levin, who were also still in good health. Buckley's statement, obviously made under duress, was confirmed within a fortnight by Levin, when the television reporter escaped on 14 February 1985, and made his way to a Syrian Army checkpoint in the Bekaa Valley. From there he had been escorted to Damascus where he had been released into American custody. Unfortunately no rescue mission could be launched: although Levin had pinpointed correctly the house where he, Buckley, Weir and Jenco had been held – a villa next to the Sheik Abdullah Barracks in the Bekaa Valley, in the very heart of the Iranian centre of power – a photo-reconnaissance mission showed that the remaining American hostages had already been dispersed. The CIA later determined that they had been moved to somewhere in the Shiite district of Bir Al-Abed in south-west Beirut. However, Levin was able to give the first reliable news of Buckley who, he said, was still alive, but his condition was deteriorating fast.

Levin's escape from Hezbollah proved a turning point for the CIA. Now for the first time there were definite indications that it was the Iranians, and not the Syrians, who were backing the kidnappers. Thus it seemed likely that the truck-bomb attacks on the American Embassy in Kuwait, the embassy and annexe in Beirut and the Marine barracks had all been orchestrated by the same fundamentalist cell, which was itself controlled by the mullahs. This news led to more contact with Mossad for help in establishing contact with Tehran; meanwhile however the situation in the Lebanon was deteriorating.

The first significant attempt on the life of Sheik Fadlallah took place on 8 March 1985, when a car bomb was detonated fifty yards from his modern tower-block headquarters in the Beirut suburbs. Eighty people were killed in the blast, and two hundred wounded, but Fadlallah himself escaped unhurt. Who perpetrated this incident remains uncertain but, according to the *Washington Post* journalist Bob Woodward, the operation had been run by the Lebanese intelligence service with backing from the Saudis, who had been paid $3m by the CIA. Woodward claims that Casey persuaded the Lebanese and Saudis to mount the attack so that later he could deny any direct American involvement. Allegedly the Saudis approached a former SAS soldier to plan the operation, but it was the Lebanese who hired the participants.[8] Whether true or not, the CIA was certainly keen to eliminate Sheik Fadlallah, rightly regarded as an intransigent obstacle to any kind of negotiated settlement to the hostage crisis. However, the timing of the attack, so soon after Levin's confirmation that Buckley was still alive, is probably significant. Unfortunately, the affair proved counter-productive.

Hezbollah's response, on 16 March, was to kidnap Terry Anderson, an Associated Press correspondent who was seized off the street after a game of tennis and taken to the old Basta Prison, in southern Beirut, where the other hostages had been accommodated. In the following fortnight more hostages were taken: on 22 March two French diplomats, Marcel Fontaine and Marcel Carton, were grabbed; four days later the British journalist Alec Collett was snatched. Then, on 17 May, six poor-quality photographs were released by Islamic Jihad of a haggard Buckley, Anderson, Jenco, Weir, Carton and Fontaine. Five days later, on 22 May, two more Frenchmen, Seurat and Jean-Paul Kaufmann, were grabbed.

On 28 May the five American hostages, Buckley, Weir, Anderson, Jenco and Kilburn, were joined by David Jacobsen, the Administrator of the American University Hospital. On 9/10 June another American from the university was taken. He was Thomas Sutherland, the Dean of Agriculture, but by this date Buckley is believed to have died. Testimony from the surviving hostages suggests that Buckley, in a state of delirium and without any medical attention, finally expired on the night of 3/4 June 1985. Weir and Jacobsen were both in the basement room at the time, blindfolded and shackled to the wall in their underclothes, and heard what they described as Buckley's 'death rattle' when he expired, ravaged by pneumonia and beatings. Weir is certain of the date as he stole a look from under his blindfold as their captors carried out Buckley's body. Whether his death prompted the kidnapping of Sutherland, or the hijacking of TWA's flight 847 from Athens to Rome, cannot be determined, but there is unquestionably a link between the three events in the person of Imad Mugniyah.

On 14 June 1985 TWA's flight to Rome, carrying 135 US citizens, was diverted to Beirut by two hijackers. There the Boeing 727 was refuelled and the hijackers made their demands: the release of seven hundred Lebanese Shiites from Atlit prison, south of Haifa in Israel, and of seventeen Shiite prisoners from

Kuwait. They also identified four other convicts, two in Spain and two in Cyprus. Clearly Imad Mugniyah had struck again. Once the fuel tanks had been filled to capacity the plane took off for Algiers and, having off-loaded some of the passengers, returned to Beirut. There Mugniyah supervised the removal of thirty-nine hostages in two groups, leaving the aircraft for the second time to depart Beirut destined for Algiers. Twenty-five hours after landing, the Boeing was on its way back to Beirut, where the remaining passengers were taken under guard to different locations in the city.

This extraordinary sequence of events had only one interpretation: that William Buckley had been forced to disclose in precise detail exactly how the Americans would react to a hijacking. Of course, the PLO had learnt many lessons about how *not* to hijack aircraft, at Entebbe in June 1976 and at Mogadishu in October 1977, where rescue missions had been successfully mounted against two different Palestinian factions. Yet on this occasion it was evident that the hijackers had taken every precaution to avoid being caught on the ground by a specialist anti-terrorist unit. Several had been deployed, but the Boeing 727 had not remained in one place long enough for the necessary preparations to be made. Instead the team from Delta Force, the Pentagon's specialist counter-terrorist unit despatched to the area, was obliged to stay in Cyprus for the duration, inoperative. In the end, on 29 June, the Israelis reluctantly agreed to a deal which allowed seven hundred Shiites to be freed from Atlit in return for the release of the TWA Flight 847 hostages into the care of the Red Cross, which delivered them to Damascus. All survived the experience except a young US Navy diver, Robert Stetham, who had been shot on the aircraft in Beirut and his body dumped on the tarmac.

Buckley, of course, was already dead, but this was not announced until 4 October 1985, apparently as retaliation for the Israeli air raid on the PLO headquarters in Tunis carried out three days earlier. Hezbollah's statement had been accompanied by a Polaroid colour photograph of the CIA officer gazing sorrowfully into the camera lens. Thus, after the release of the TWA passengers at the end of June, the American authorities believed there were still seven Americans detained in the Lebanon – Buckley, Jenco, Kilburn, Jacobsen, Weir, Anderson and Sutherland – and it was determination to free them that led to a sequence of events that was to change completely the political scene in America, jeopardise Vice-President George Bush's political future and destroy the international credibility of the administration's stated foreign policy.

One incident which may have encouraged the CIA to take the initiative was the kidnapping at the end of September of three Soviet diplomats. Arkadi Katkov, Oleg Spirine, Valeri Kornev plus the embassy doctor Nikolai Versky were all taken the same day by Islamic Jihad and threatened with execution. This was an extraordinary development, because no Russian had ever been seized during the whole ten-year history of Lebanon's bloody civil war. The statement issued by Islamic Jihad demanded that Syrian troops suspended their siege of Tripoli, where fundamentalist Sunni gunmen were holding off pro-Syrian irregulars, in return for the release of the Soviets. In one of the inexplicable changes in allegiance that had marked the conflict. Hezbollah had suddenly announced its support of the besieged Sunnis in the north of the country, and turned on the Russians. The twisted logic behind this move was to target the Soviets because of their undisguised sponsorship of Syria.

At first the Soviets took little action over the disappearance of the four men, relying on their Syrian allies to find them; but then on 2 October the body of Arkady Katkov was found, riddled with 7.62mm bullets, on a rubbish tip close to the Avenue Camille Chamoun, near to the ruins of Beirut's old sports stadium. However, Islamic Jihad had not reckoned on Katkov's special significance. For as well as being a first secretary in the embassy's consular section and the father of two children, Katkov was also a popular KGB officer. The murder infuriated the KGB, which sent a team to find a relative of one of those thought to have been involved in the kidnapping. The man was tortured, and allegedly his penis was delivered to Hezbollah in a parcel also containing an ultimatum: Release the three remaining Soviets or a similar fate will befall the families of all those responsible for the abduction. Simultaneously 120 Soviet citizens, escorted by Syrian troops, were evacuated from Beirut, leaving just thirty diplomats and journalists in the city. This move was interpreted as a preliminary to an all-out covert offensive, and the three Russian hostages were promptly freed.

Such effective tactics were never even contemplated by the CIA, which instead opted for an Israeli solution. The first step in the scandal that was later to be called Irangate was taken by the Israelis when David Kimche, previously Deputy Director of Mossad and currently the Israeli Foreign Ministry's most senior civil servant, began to put out feelers to see if negotiations could be opened with the Iranians. The British-born Kimche was in touch with Ya'acov Nimrodi, another Mossad veteran then living in London, who boasted unrivalled connections in the expatriate Iranian community. He had served as Mossad's station chief in Tehran continuously between 1956 and 1970 and had helped create SAVAK, the Shah's secret police. A Jew born in Iraq, Nimrodi spoke Farsi as his first language and rightly regarded Iran as his own country. In 1976 he had retired from Mossad and set up a contracting company to build desalination plants in Iran. After Khomeini's revolution Nimrodi had kept in touch with Tehran and had already been instrumental in ensuring that some embargoed *matériel*, such as Hawk anti-aircraft missiles and Copperhead bazookas, had reached Iran. He was enthusiastic about his assignment and wasted no time in contacting Adnan Khashoggi, the Saudi arms dealer who had come to prominence during the Congressional investigations into Lockheed's corrupt overseas contracts, and Manucher Ghorbanifar, a self-styled entrepreneur who, coincidentally, had been a source of information (not all of it accurate) for the CIA for a decade, and for SAVAK even longer. Another key figure was SAVAK's former head of Department VIII, the counter-espionage branch, Brigadier-General Manuchehr Hashemi, who also happened to be in close touch with Theodore G. Shackley,[9] a retired CIA officer with experience in south-east Asia where he had been Chief of Station in Vientiane and Saigon, and who had left the Agency in 1979 having been transferred out of the DDO in Admiral Turner's 1977 purge, after a career lasting twenty-eight years. During that period he had also served as the CIA's station chief in Tehran.

Between 19 and 21 November Hashemi and Ghorbanifar held a series of meetings in Hamburg with Ted Shackley, who reported to Langley that both men boasted good contacts in Tehran and had set a deadline of 7 December for an exchange. The Iranians were offering Buckley and three other American hostages, together with items of Soviet military hardware captured from the Iraqis, including a T-72 tank, in return for a quantity of the lethal TOW anti-tank missiles manufactured by Hughes in California and a sum of cash.

What Nimrodi, Ghorbanifar and Kimche were suggesting was not really so novel, although the arms embargo imposed by the US government in November 1979 was still in force. Even when many of the trade restrictions had been lifted in January 1981, following the release of the American Embassy hostages, the administration had maintained a ban on weapon sales, and had urged other countries to remain neutral in the Iran–Iraq War. The Iranians had been disadvantaged during their struggle with Iraq because of their shortage of weapons, and were desperate to acquire new equipment. They were also sensitive to the continuing Iraqi high-altitude overflights of Iranian territory, about which they could do nothing unless they acquired a missile that was effective above sixty thousand feet. Soviet aerial-reconnaissance planes were also suspected of operating even higher, at above seventy-five thousand feet, and intruding up to forty miles into Iranian airspace. Two senior Iranian officers had already been released from detention in Tehran and sent to London in a bid to buy new supplies: their co-operation had been secured by preventing the rest of their families from joining them. In addition, the mullahs had been persuaded to change their attitude to members of the previous regime. In October 1982 a senior KGB officer in Tehran, Vladimir Kuzichkin, had defected to the British and revealed the scale of Soviet-inspired espionage and subversion inside the Islamic Republic.[10] The British had shared this data with the CIA and had deliberately allowed much of it to filter back to Tehran. A ruthless purge of the Tudeh Party had followed, in which almost the entire leadership, amounting to more than a hundred people, had been detained, tortured and executed. Once alerted to Soviet mischief in Iran, the mullahs had decided to rebuild their country's shattered counter-espionage capability and had begun approaching former SAVAK personnel including, coincidentally, Hashemi, then living in London. Thus, as events unfolded, all the components were present for a successful deal: a willing buyer, a willing seller and some wealthy middlemen. However, when Shackley's proposal reached the State Department's Bureau of Research and Intelligence, it was rejected by its head, Hugh Montgomery.

The brush-off was in part due to advice from the CIA's Operations Directorate. Tom Twetton, the Chief of the Near East Division was later to state that, at the time:

> We have in the DDO probably 30 to 40 requests per year from Iranians and Iranian exiles to provide us with very fancy intelligence, very important internal political insights, if we in return can arrange for the sale of a dozen Bell helicopter gunships or 1,000 TOW missiles or something else that is on the contraband list.[11]

In fact the CIA had already given serious consideration to the idea of developing contacts with the Khomeini regime in the hope of furthering American interests. One of the first proposals had come from Graham Fuller, the CIA's National Intelligence Officer for Near East affairs, who had already suggested the sale of weapons as one of several possible options in a policy discussion document. He worked in the overt side of the agency, but his brief was wider than just Iran, and the idea withered on the vine. Indeed, even if this particular proposal had achieved a wider audience, or found favour elsewhere in the administration, there were still the legal obstacles to arms sales to be overcome. It was technically illegal for the US to supply arms to Iran.

Considering the CIA's scepticism about the past approaches it is not surprising that the State Department had been unimpressed by Shackley's proposals. However, early in the New Year of 1985, the National Security Council (NSC) began to play an active role in the crisis and opened up discussions with Tel Aviv. Meanwhile, Shackley's contacts were suspended, but by June 1985 he was in touch with Oliver North, the US Marine lieutenant-colonel seconded to the National Security Council as the staff officer with responsibility for counter-terrorism policy. North had his own ideas about a solution to the crisis. One was a straight swap, the release of the hostages in return for the deportation from Kuwait of the Al-Dawa prisoners. The second, which seemed more promising, was the payment of a ransom for Buckley's release. Federal funds were out of the question but H. Ross Perot, an American billionaire and super-patriot, had pledged some $2m in cash for the purpose.[12] The plan called for two experienced agents from the US Drug Enforcement Agency to handle the negotiations and supervise the transfer of money, but the exchange never took place. Instead the Israelis now looked like achieving the long-awaited breakthrough.

The conclusion of Nimrodi's efforts was a meeting in London in May 1985, at which Ghorbanifar indicated that he might be able to secure the release of the American hostages if arrangements could be made for Iran to circumvent the United Nations ban on arms shipments to the region. The proposal was for a total of 508 TOW anti-tank missiles to be sold to Iran by the Israeli government, with Khashoggi putting up $5m to broker the deal. On paper there would be two separate sales: one to Khashoggi by the Israelis, the second to Tehran. This avoided direct American involvement although, of course, the Israelis expected the Americans to replenish their reduced stock of anti-tank weaponry. Kimche gave his approval to the scheme and outlined it to Robert C. McFarlane, a retired US Marine lieutenant-colonel and President Reagan's Deputy National Security Advisor. McFarlane conveyed the message to a select group in Washington, and gave Kimche the go-ahead. This single act was to bring Reagan's presidency into disrepute and, when the transaction eventually became public more than a year later, raise the question of who was running America's foreign policy – whether a secret government, consisting of Casey's cronies, had taken matters into their own hands so as to circumvent Congress.

The financial arrangements were complicated. Khashoggi made two separate deposits into an Israeli bank account in Geneva and Ghorbanifar gave him two post-dated drafts drawn on his own account at Credit Suisse, on the understanding that Khashoggi would present them for payment upon delivery of the weapons. Thus Khashoggi provided the bridge between buyer and seller and avoided the necessity of the two opposing parties doing business with each other. Khashoggi expected to make a twenty per cent commission on the arrangement, which put a price of $10,000 on each TOW, but in the event he never achieved this because the Iranians returned part of the first consignment as being sub-standard.

This first deal resulted in a successful delivery on 20 August of ninety-six TOW missiles, packed on eight pallets and loaded on to a DC-8 in the military section of Ben Gurion Airport. In order to eliminate any direct American involvement in the transaction, the US-registered aircraft was sold to a Nigerian company, International Air Tours, based in Brussels. The pilot,

Herman Duran, and his engineer were Colombian, and the co-pilot was a Portuguese American, so they were all issued with false papers identifying them as Argentinians. They flew the plane, with Ghorbanifar on board, west towards Cyprus and then headed over Turkey to Tabriz, having registered a false flight plan with the air-traffic controllers in Nicosia. After this mission had been completed came the encouraging news from David Kimche that the Iranians had asked the Americans to nominate the hostage they wanted released. McFarlane offered Buckley's name, and it seemed that his release was imminent. Although Ghorbanifar was arrested on his arrival in Tabriz, his detention by SAVAMA (SAVAK's even more ruthless successor) proved temporary and the Iranians not only repaid Khashoggi, but authorised the release of a hostage. Word was circulated in Washington that Buckley was about to be freed, perhaps within days.

This first shipment was followed a fortnight later by a second consignment of 408 TOW missiles on thirty-four pallets, flown to Tabriz on the same chartered aircraft. However, to the dismay of those involved, the Iranians told Ghorbanifar that Buckley was 'too ill' to be moved, and the captive to be released would instead be the Reverend Ben Weir, who was freed the following day, 15 September, just outside the British Embassy into the custody of Terry Waite, the Archbishop of Canterbury's special envoy. Waite had a background of mediating in complex international disputes, and had achieved some success with Colonel Gadaffi of Libya where others had failed. He had arrived in Beirut for the first time ten months earlier, equipped with a walkie-talkie set to a pre-arranged frequency, supplied by Associated Press, with which to establish contact with the Hezbollah kidnappers. During his subsequent debriefing in Wiesbaden Weir disclosed that he had been held in the Bekaa Valley, and that he believed William Buckley had died the previous June. Weir's release proved a dreadful disappointment, not least because the minister was himself virulently anti-American and, despite his sixteen months' imprisonment, of which twelve had been in solitary confinement, a passionate advocate of the Shiites. He proved such an embarrassment to the American administration that one adviser to the National Security Council, Michael Ledeen, joked that perhaps Hezbollah could be persuaded to take him back.

It is a sign of Casey's persistence that, despite Weir's belief that Buckley was probably dead, he was prepared to pursue the negotiations. Weir's opinion did not carry complete conviction with the American authorities, as was made clear by the State Department on 13 October when it released a statement saying it did not regard the poor-quality snapshot of Buckley delivered earlier in the month as proof that Buckley was really dead. Conversely, Oliver North reported in a memorandum dated 5 December 1985 that he was 'relatively confident' that Buckley was dead. There was also the implication of Weir's release, which suggested Buckley was no longer available. But none of this amounted to firm evidence, and was not good enough for Casey, so the contact was maintained. Indeed, the fact that no further hostages had been taken during the negotiating period throughout September was regarded as a good sign that progress was being made. The CIA also learnt – as a result of Terry Waite's visit to Beirut on 14 November, through another channel also thought to be reliable, this time Canadian – that Anderson, Jacobsen, Jenco, Sutherland and Kilburn were definitely still alive. The negative aspect to this was Waite's opinion

> that those who hold the hostages are under immense political and military pressure from the Syrians, Druze, Phalange, and Amal and that there is the distinct possibility that our hostages as well as the French and British could be killed in the near future.[13]

Almost simultaneously reports circulated in Washington that Buckley had died 'last April in Tehran of a heart attack', and that Peter Kilburn, the American University librarian, had also died in captivity.

Whatever the quality of the intelligence emerging from Tehran, the Americans had at last established contact with those in the Iranian regime who had influence over the fate of the remaining hostages, and a third deal was negotiated: the sale of eighty of the Hawk anti-aircraft missiles which the Iranians had always sought. On this occasion the arrangements were co-ordinated by Oliver North of the NSC, and they did not go entirely according to plan. To begin with, Hawk missiles were substantially larger than the TOWs, each weighing a ton and being some eighteen feet in length. Thus the physical challenge of collecting them from Israel and delivering them to Iran was considerable: North's solution was for an El Al 747 to fly them to Lisbon where they could be transferred to three other aircraft and then shipped in relays to Tabriz. A complicated schedule was negotiated, with the release of five American hostages (plus two Lebanese Jews) timed to coincide with the arrival of the Hawks in Iran. However the plan, set for execution on 22 November, went awry from the start. The Portuguese authorities[14] refused to sanction the El Al flight from Tel Aviv, even after the CIA Chief of Station in Lisbon had assured the government that the shipment consisted of innocuous oil-drilling equipment. The Portuguese wanted written certification of the cargo, and this could not be provided in the very limited time available. At the last possible moment, when the 747 was approaching French airspace, the plane was recalled to Israel, where it landed with practically no fuel left.

Undeterred, North pressed ahead with a second attempt, but had to ask for the CIA's help in obtaining suitable cargo aircraft now that the El Al jumbo was committed elsewhere. The CIA officer at Langley who took North's call, and embroiled the CIA in the entire affair for the very first time, was Duane (Dewey) Clarridge, Chief of the Western Europe Division in the Operations Directorate and the officer with Casey's counter-terrorism brief. Reluctantly, a CIA proprietary company, the Santa Lucia Corporation, registered in the Cayman Islands, provided a cargo-configured Boeing 707 to take the Hawks from Ben Gurion Airport to Iran, flying the same circuitous route through Turkey that had worked in September when the TOWs had been transferred. The aircraft was chartered in Frankfurt and flown by two German pilots to Tel Aviv on 23 November, ready for the first consignment of eighteen Hawks. On this occasion the flight did get to Tabriz, but it was not without incident. The original flightplan called for the aircraft to refuel in Turkey, but again North was unable to obtain permission for the plane to land without disclosing its cargo. Instead the 707 went to Nicosia, but the unprepared Cyprus authorities arrested the crew. This unfortunate development required the local CIA station chief to be roused from his bed so he could free the pilot and pay for the fuel needed for the onward leg of the journey to Iran, which was eventually completed, three days late, on 24 November. Upon landing the Hawks were inspected by an Iranian colonel who announced that the missiles were not the latest modified version, known as I-Hawk (I for improved), they had paid for. Worse, half of them bore a Star of David on the side, and other embarrassing Israeli markings that were supposed to have been deleted.

This disastrous episode not only soured the trust that the Iranians had manifested by paying for the Hawk missiles before they had been delivered, but directly entangled the CIA in the arms-for-hostages affair for the first time. Although Clarridge was later to deny knowing exactly what was aboard the aircraft, his involvement was to prove catastrophic for both himself and the Agency. In particular, it raised two questions which were to dog the remainder of the Reagan presidency: who authorised the CIA's involvement, and was the participation legal? Clarridge himself appears to have experienced some initial doubts, for he had contacted Edward Juchniewicz, then the acting

Deputy Director for Operations, for approval before sanctioning the transaction.

A subsequent attempt to fly into Mehrabad, Tehran's international airport, to remove the offending missiles and replace them with other hardware, collapsed when the CIA failed to obtain the necessary permission for its plane, then stuck in Portugal, to overfly certain countries *en route* to Iran. When the DDCI, John McMahon, learnt that the mission was to be undertaken in an aircraft chartered from a CIA proprietary company registered in the Cayman Islands, albeit on strictly commercial terms, he immediately banned the scheme on the grounds that the President's personal permission was required before the CIA could become directly involved in breaking the various trade embargoes. This legalistic nicety brought the whole matter to a standstill because of the conflicting views expressed in the White House about the wisdom of maintaining contact with the Iranians. Some believed that the release of the Reverend Weir was proof enough of Iranian goodwill. Others considered that supplying weapons to the kidnappers was nothing more than rewarding terrorism. The real problem, however, as revealed by the Tower Commission which later investigated the scandal, was that the CIA deeply distrusted Ghorbanifar, who had pocketed $40m from the Iranians in anticipation of a delivery of some three thousand TOW missiles. The CIA was also handicapped by a complete lack of any hard intelligence from inside Iran. Indeed, Terry Waite was described in one document presented in evidence by Oliver North as 'our only access to events in Lebanon'.[15] Waite and North had met at least twenty times, in New York, London, Switzerland and Germany, but the premature disclosure of their relationship was to prove disastrous for the archbishop's mediator. Without any independent sources of its own, the CIA was disadvantaged in the struggle within Reagan's White House, and the NSC staff continued to exploit the situation.

Although both the CIA and Mossad opposed any further

ransom initiatives to free the remaining hostages, the National Security Council persevered, and used Ghorbanifar as intermediary in another deal, his fourth. This time the arrangement was to be an exchange of sensitive intelligence data to restore goodwill, and then the delivery of five hundred TOWs from Eilat in Israel to Bandar Abbas. On the return journey the 707, belonging to yet another CIA proprietary, Southern Air Transport, was to fly into Tehran and collect the seventeen Hawks that had proved so unsatisfactory. The slight shortfall was accounted for by the eighteenth being fired, in a test, at an Iraqi aircraft flying over Kharg Island. In return the Iranians would be refunded the money they had paid for the Hawks, and would arrange to release the remaining five hostages in Beirut. The delivery was made on 18 February[16] but, again, no hostages were forthcoming. On 27 February a second delivery of five hundred TOWs was made by the same route but no hostages were released. Instead the Iranians suggested a high-level meeting in Tehran at which further negotiations could be conducted, and this proposal was accepted on the understanding that the hostages would be freed either before, or during, the talks. North and Ghorbanifar's discussions were assisted by a sweetener; a quantity of intelligence material relating to Soviet intentions towards Iran, provided by Robert Gates, the CIA's Deputy Director for Intelligence. Bud McFarlane was nominated to represent the American government, and the secret visit to Tehran took place on 25 May 1986. Among the delegation were George Cave, a retired CIA officer who spoke Farsi, and an Israeli, Amiram Nir, who went along as Shimon Peres's personal representative (in spite of the CIA's objections, which were overruled by the White House). The delegation spent two unproductive days in Tehran without meeting anyone they recognised as senior members of the Ayatollah's regime. Instead the Iranians removed a pallet of Hawk spare parts from the American aircraft and refused to let any hostages go.

The meeting was considered a disaster by the American participants, but at least they left Tehran with a greater understanding of how chaotically the Iranian regime managed its affairs. That view was reinforced on 26 July when Lawrence Jenco was handed over to the American Ambassador in Damascus, clutching a video cassette of David Jacobsen in which he was seen pleading for his release. Jenco was flown to Wiesbaden, where he was debriefed by Oliver North, and confirmed that the other hostages were in reasonable health. Jenco's release led to a further delivery of Hawk spare parts to Bandar Abbas on 4 August, again in an Israeli 707 with false markings, manned by an American crew. This was to be the last delivery, and marked the beginning of the end, with Ghorbanifar's complicated financial schemes starting to unravel.

The first overt sign that the arms-for-hostages contact had failed came on 9 September, when Frank Reed of the Lebanese International School was kidnapped in Beirut. Three days later Joseph Ciccipio, an accountant at the American University, was grabbed, and on 21 October a writer, Edward Tracey, was snatched. Perhaps worse, news of McFarlane's clandestine trip to Tehran appeared in some pamphlets distributed in Beirut, and then in a Hezbollah newspaper published in Baalbek.

The paradox of this apparent breakdown of relations is that North had opened negotiations with Tehran through a separate channel, that of Khomeini's son-in-law Sadegh Tabatabai, whom North and the CIA recognised as altogether more reliable and promising than the wheeler-dealer Ghorbanifar. A meeting was held in Frankfurt at which North and Cave made an offer, a schedule detailing the supply of weapons, in exchange for Buckley's body and the release of the remaining hostages together with John Pattis, an American businessman held in Iran on espionage charges. The Iranians made a counter-proposal, using the newly established alternative line of communication, and another five hundred TOWs were sent, on 30 October, to Tehran. Almost simultaneously an identical quantity of TOWs was delivered to Tel Aviv to cover the shortfall in the

Israeli inventory, taking a very traceable route from Kelly Air Force Base to Ramstein in Germany. Two days later David Jacobsen was released in Beirut but, to the disappointment of Oliver North, who flew to the Lebanon to supervise, no other hostages materialised. Instead the Speaker of the Iranian Majlis made public the American efforts to trade arms for Hezbollah hostages, thereby sparking a major political scandal in the US.

Although many of the details became known, there remained a continuing mystery about the huge sums paid by the Iranians for the TOWs and Hawks. On the first deal, for 508 TOWs, the Iranians paid $10,000 a missile, which netted the intermediaries a profit of roughly $3m. Equally large sums were involved in the subsequent sales, and it became evident that not all the money went to bank accounts in Central America to fund Oliver North's chosen cause, the Nicaraguan Contra rebels. According to the Tower Commission, cash totalling $2m went missing and was never recovered. This three-man commission, set up to determine the facts of the Iran-Contra affair, left many questions unanswered. Their enquiries were bound to be incomplete because the central figure in the whole affair, the DCI, was never cross-examined. Bill Casey had been taken to hospital suffering from brain cancer on 15 December 1986 and he resigned his office on 29 January the following year, six years and a day after his appointment, without ever having given his own version of what had occurred.

In retrospect it would seem that Casey's well-intentioned efforts to free Buckley were always bound to fail. Firstly there was an extraordinary gap in the CIA's understanding of events in the Middle East and, in particular, Tehran. This had been manifested in the past by the classic misreading of the political situation in Iran at the time of the Shah's downfall. It was alleged then that the CIA had possessed not a single Farsi speaker on its Iranian desk at Langley. The loss of so many clandestine service officers after Admiral Turner had taken control of the agency in 1977 had drastically reduced the expertise available to the Directorate of Operations, and the death of Robert Ames had exacerbated the situation further. Indeed, Michael Ledeen says that the chief of Near East operations, Dick Holm, had never worked in the region and had spent his entire career in Latin America. The DO's Iran desk was headed by a man identified only as 'Patrick' who spoke no Farsi and had no knowledge of the principal Iranian personalities in Khomeini's administration. Thus the CIA's approach throughout was characterised by an astonishing lack of professionalism.

Whether the situation at the CIA has improved in recent years is open to doubt. According to Tom Milligan, a recently retired senior CIA officer who conducted a survey for the Training Directorate before his departure from Langley, only 'about a third of all operations officers in the field had the foreign-language skill to do their job'.[17] An internal investigation into the Iran-Contra scandal conducted by the CIA's Inspector-General, Carroll Hauver, cleared the agency of misconduct; but a further inquiry, this time instituted by Judge Webster (who was appointed Casey's successor in 1987), led to the dismissal of two senior CIA officers from the Latin America Division, Joe Fernandez (the CIA station chief in San José, Costa Rica) and Jim Adkins (the CIA's liaison with the Contras),[18] and the resignations of two key figures in the arms-for-hostages deals: Dewey Clarridge, head of the Counter-Terrorist Unit, and Alan Fiers, the Central American Task Force chief. Curiously, three other careers have prospered: those of Tom Twetton the Near East operations head, his deputy, and 'Patrick', the head of the Iran desk. All have since received promotions, but there is reason to believe that the CIA's coverage of a crucial region has not improved. An example is the State Department's decision to allow the US Ambassador to Baghdad to take her annual vacation three days before Iraqi forces invaded Kuwait in August 1990.

The Irangate scandal undermined the last months of President Reagan's term of office and seriously eroded confidence in his administration. How much had he really known of the secret (and illegal) policy formulated and pursued by his subordinates? What had been the involvement of his vice-president? Was the NSC staff used in a deliberate attempt to circumvent the Congressional oversight committees that would certainly have vetoed the arms-for-hostages initiatives? The only person who could have answered these crucial questions was Casey, who took his knowledge to the grave on 6 May 1987, after surgery for a tumour. However, some of those who had been close to the DCI remain convinced that the single compulsion that drove Casey to mastermind the ill-fated scheme was the optimistic hope that William Buckley could be freed . . . alive. Paradoxically, Casey's single-minded commitment was to jeopardise even more lives, for as well as rewarding terrorism it prompted an all too public inquiry, the Tower Commission, that inadvertently disclosed the undercover role played by Terry Waite. No sooner was the commission's report released, revealing Waite's involvement with North and thereby compromising the special envoy, than he too became a victim of the kidnappers. Terry Waite was taken on 22 January 1987, having been escorted from the Riviera Hotel in Beirut by Druze militiamen. He had intended to meet Islamic Jihad representatives in the hope of getting news of four hostages: Terry Anderson, Thomas Sutherland, John McCarthy and Brian Keenan. Waite had been warned before his departure that leaks of testimony given to the Tower Commission had jeopardised his mission, and his safety had been further endangered by the arrest in Frankfurt of Muhammed Ali Hamadi, a key figure in the TWA hijacking in June 1985. Nevertheless Waite was adamant that he would not abandon the hostages and was to endure nearly five years of solitary confinement until he was released on 18 November 1991.[19]

CHAPTER IV

Anthony Blunt

In the middle of June 1940, soon after the evacuation of the British Expeditionary Forces from Dunkirk, a meeting took place in the second floor sitting room of Victor Rothschild's three-storey maisonette at 5 Bentinck Street, London. There were only three people present, one of them in uniform, and they exchanged pleasantries for about an hour; but it is no exaggeration to say that the repercussions of that single event were to have a profound impact on the West's intelligence community for the next forty years.

The host that evening was the third Baron Rothschild, a brilliant young scientist who had inherited his uncle's title after his death in 1937. His visitors were a civilian, Guy Liddell, then the recently appointed head of MI5's counter-espionage division, and Captain Anthony Blunt, on temporary leave from the Field Security Wing of the Intelligence Corps. The meeting had been arranged by Rothschild because he had recommended Blunt, who had taught him French at Cambridge, for a transfer to the Security Service and Liddell was in a position to authorise the move. However, to maintain good security, Liddell had not used his own name, and Rothschild had simply introduced him to Blunt as 'Captain Black of the War Office'.[1]

Blunt's military career was undistinguished. He had used his elder brother Christopher's influence to obtain a reserve commission the previous year and, after a spell at the Intelligence Corps training centre at Minley Manor, near the Corps's bleak Mytchett headquarters outside Aldershot, he had been posted to Boulogne on routine field-security duties such as censoring the mail. These the homosexual aesthete had found very disagreeable; hence the introduction to Liddell who, in Whitehall circles, was known to be a powerful figure in the Security Service. There was, of course, quite a paradox in one former Party member already in MI5, namely Rothschild, asking Liddell, who was a staunch anti-Bolshevik, to take on another Communist. Liddell, of course, had no idea of Blunt's political antecedents, but the fact that he was even contemplating taking on Blunt was a serious break with MI5's conventions. As well as being a former Communist, Blunt was a don and an active homosexual. If MI5's long-serving Director-General, Sir Vernon Kell, had not recently been dismissed by the Prime Minister,[2] Blunt could never have been considered for employment in an organisation that, at the outbreak of war, boasted a staff of just eighty-three officers, all personally approved by Kell. After working for Kell for many years, Liddell would not have dreamt of interviewing the effeminate Blunt with his university background. Not one of MI5's senior pre-war staff had received a university education.

Liddell, like his two brothers, had been decorated with the Military Cross for gallantry during the Great War, and thereafter he had joined the Special Branch of the Metropolitan Police, monitoring the rise of Communism. In October 1931 he and his small civilian staff had transferred to the Security Service and, following the dismissal on 10 June 1940 of Kell, then sixty-seven years old, and the simultaneous resignation of his deputy, Sir Eric Holt-Wilson, Liddell had been appointed Director of B Division (in succession to Brigadier O. A. Harker, who was made acting Director-General until a permanent replacement could be found). Liddell's long study of left-wing subversion in Britain had borne fruit in several important prosecutions which had exposed attempts at Soviet espionage in Britain. Three in particular had been significant: the conviction in 1928 of Wilfred Macartney, a Communist idealist who had been trapped after passing an RAF handbook to his Soviet contacts; the break-up of a spy-ring in the Woolwich Arsenal in 1938; and the discovery and secret trial of Captain John King, the source of a leak from within the Communications Department of the Foreign Office, in 1939. Of these three serious cases, two had been directly linked to the Communist Party of Great Britain, which Liddell had spent twenty years observing: Macartney had been a member of the Young Communist League, and Percy Glading, one of the three men convicted in the Woolwich case, had been the Party's National Organiser at the time of his arrest. Accordingly, the Security Service had good reason to maintain surveillance of the CPGB in the belief that Soviet espionage used the Party as a convenient vehicle for the recruitment of agents, and relied upon four principal methods of accumulating information about the Party: the interception of mail and telephone communications of both the Party and its key members; the acquisition of branch membership lists by informants; the recording of Party meetings, either by technical means or the attendance of Special Branch shorthand note takers; and the reports of well-placed informants.

The fact that the CPGB was vulnerable to all these techniques had become evident during the Woolwich trial, which disclosed the existence of a Security Service agent who had deliberately gained the confidence of the Party's hierarchy for the sole purpose of describing its activities to MI5. Unfortunately, the testimony of Olga Gray had been required during the Old Bailey trial, which had not only ended her career as a valuable informant but had also served to alert the Soviets to the kind of counter-measures deployed by their tenacious opponents.

It emerged during the Woolwich case that the Soviets relied heavily on the use of 'illegals', sources – not necessarily Soviet citizens – who travelled in and out of the country to service existing agents. One such individual, a German student named Georg Hansen, had been arrested with Wilfred Macartney but had resolutely insisted that he was merely a journalist seeking to improve his English. At the end of his ten-year prison sentence he had been deported to Germany and disappeared. Three similar people, known only as 'Mr Peters' and 'Mr and Mrs Stephens', evaded arrested in the Glading case ten years later, but the former was identified as an experienced Soviet agent of Austrian extraction called Theodore Maly. The latter pair are believed to have been Willy and Mary Brandes,[3] using a Canadian passport, who had been observed travelling to France in November 1937, two months before Glading was arrested.

The predictable Soviet response to MI5's surveillance was to develop an underground structure for certain CPGB members which would theoretically enable them to avoid the unwelcome attentions of the authorities. That Anthony Blunt abandoned his overt CPGB membership but continued to be an underground member is known because, in April 1964, he gave the Security Service a detailed account of his clandestine career. The evidence that Rothschild had taken a similar path is limited to the memory of another of his contemporaries at Cambridge, a distinguished paediatrician who was an overt CPGB member until he went down from university.[4] Liddell, of course, had no inkling in 1940 that the CPGB had created a two-tier mechanism; the assurances of those who had once had a youthful flirtation with the Party that they had severed their links were invariably taken at face value. It had been thus with Anthony Blunt, whose original application for a commission had been queried because of an adverse entry in his MI5 record. Blunt had been challenged about the two items listed: a visit to the Soviet Union in 1935, and a contribution to the Communist-orientated *Left Review*. No doubt relieved to discover that this represented the meagre sum of MI5's knowledge about his past, Blunt had been able to persuade his interviewer that he had long since forsaken his Soviet sympathies. His explanation had been accepted, and Blunt allowed to continue his training at Minley Manor. This kind of muddled approach was by no means unusual at that time. When Blunt had first written to the

War Office volunteering to join up, he had received two replies by the same post. The first turned him down; the second ordered him to report to Aldershot.

Victor Rothschild's entry into the Security Service had been via the civilian route, after submitting a paper on the German banking system. Thereafter he had been employed to study German strategic commodities and this had led to his entry into MI5 as a scientific adviser specialising in industrial sabotage. He had been in MI5 for less than six months when he wrote a memorandum to Liddell recommending Blunt for immediate recruitment. The invitation to drinks at Bentinck Street had followed, and thus Liddell's approval was gained for Blunt to join the Security Service as a military liaison officer in MI5's D Division, working for Brigadier Harry Allen and dealing with routine security matters. Recalling this episode forty-six years later, Rothschild remembered that half-way through their meeting Liddell had dropped his pseudonym, thus indicating to him and Blunt that the latter had been accepted.

At the time of Blunt's entry into the Security Service he was thirty-three years old. During the following five years he was to move from D Division, where he found the work uninteresting, to B Division, where the most sensitive counter-espionage operations were undertaken. It was here that Blunt inflicted the greatest damage on MI5. Whilst it could be argued that much of what he betrayed did not really harm long-term British interests, there were a few items that did immediate and lasting harm. In particular, he alerted his Soviet controllers, whom he met regularly in London throughout the war, to the existence of two important British agents. The first was an SIS source who for years had been supplying secrets from the Kremlin to Harold Gibson, a senior SIS officer. Although Blunt never knew this individual's exact identity, which was protected by a cryptonym in the documents he had read, he had given enough information to the Soviets for them to have arrested and executed Anastas Mikoyan's secretary. Another source, this time reporting to MI5 from within the CPGB, was Tom Driberg, whom Blunt was able to link to 'M8', an informant run by another B Division officer, Max Knight.[5] On the first occasion SIS had written off the loss of their star agent as an occupational hazard. Mikoyan's secretary was never heard of again but, much to Blunt's embarrassment, Driberg was merely expelled from the CPGB and complained to Max Knight that he had been accused by the CPGB's Secretary-General, Harry Pollitt, of leaking information under the sobriquet 'M8', which he resolutely denied because, of course, Knight had never told Driberg of the cryptonym by which he was known in MI5's internal documents. This incident proved to Knight that someone within the Security Service had compromised his agent, but the M8 reports received such wide circulation within MI5 that it was assumed the leak had occurred at low level, perhaps through the indiscretion of a clerk. In fact Blunt had read an M8 report which had been left on a colleague's desk at lunchtime, and one particular reference in the text, to something M8 had recently written for publication, had made him realise that 'M8' could only be Driberg. He had passed this nugget to his Soviet controller, never expecting that Pollitt's lack of finesse would place him in jeopardy. Driberg was indignant at his betrayal, and Knight pursued a relentless but futile molehunt among the MI5 officers who had been circulated with M8 reports to identify the culprit. Fortunately for Blunt, his glimpse at the document had been illicit, and his name had not appeared on the official M8 circulation list; therefore he never came under suspicion.

This episode, and the incident detailed below, persuaded Blunt to exercise great caution when passing information to the Soviets, and he tried to restrict this to details relating to his colleagues of the kind that could have come from almost anyone inside MI5, rather than specific items that might be traced back to him. An exception were decrypted enemy signals, code-named ISOS, which were highly prized by Blunt's Soviet contact. Initially Blunt had removed the documents from his office and lent them to the Soviets to be photographed, for the exact text of each was needed if they were to assist the Soviet efforts to decipher the German messages too. However on one occasion Blunt had been walking across a London park with one such document in his briefcase when he was stopped and searched by a policeman. Luckily the constable had no idea of the sensitivity of the paper in Blunt's case, and allowed Blunt to proceed unhindered. Later that same evening Blunt had told his contact, whom he knew only as 'George', that thenceforth he would memorise all ISOS decrypts, and would not risk physically taking any further classified material out of MI5's headquarters. Apparently he never did, which is perhaps one explanation of why he remained undetected throughout his entire service in MI5.

Blunt did not last long as Harry Allen's subordinate, and deliberately manoeuvred himself into being appointed Guy Liddell's personal assistant, thereafter staying in B Division until he moved to SHAEF in 1944 as part of MI5's liaison with the deception staff. Blunt's wholesale betrayal to the Soviets of all the information he could gather probably did not do any lasting harm to MI5's operations, although his review of the role of the watcher service, which at the outbreak of war had a full complement of eight, must have reassured the KGB that MI5 was not the ubiquitous organisation many believed it to be. In 1940, when Blunt undertook the efficiency survey for Liddell, the watcher teams were primarily deployed on following suspected Fascists around London, rather than on keeping Soviet diplomatic personnel under surveillance. Blunt also worked for a period in the section which diverted the diplomatic bags of some neutral diplomatic missions in London and photographed their contents. Whilst the information he obtained from this illicit source must have been of great interest to the KGB, there is no reason to believe it compromised any British operations. Blunt's final appointment, to SHAEF, must have helped reassure the Soviets that the Anglo-American invasion of Europe was indeed going to take place. Some might argue that Blunt's betrayal of the progress made by British cryptographers in their work on enemy ciphers might have been helpful to the Soviets but, as we shall see, whatever else it accomplished, it failed to persuade the KGB to tighten up its own coding procedures.

Blunt remained in MI5 until the end of hostilities, when, having turned down the chance of a permanent post in the Security Service, he returned to academic life. He only came under suspicion of having been a spy after the defections of Guy Burgess and Donald Maclean in 1951. Even then he resisted his interrogators, who had acquired some startling new evidence, of the most secret kind, that he had been a traitor.

The possibility that ideologically motivated spies might have deliberately inserted themselves into the British establishment so as to inflict the greatest possible damage was only really taken seriously following the mysterious disappearance of Burgess and Maclean, but prior to that extraordinary event there had been a continuing search for Soviet agents in Britain. The failure to recognise the concept of a mole was entirely understandable. No less than three wartime espionage cases had involved overt members of the CPGB who had made no attempt to disguise their political allegiance. George Armstrong had been hanged in July 1941 and in 1943 Douglas Springhall and Ormond Uren had been sentenced to ten years' imprisonment each. Another CPGB member, Cedric Belfrage, was to escape prosecution entirely as his espionage was only discovered at the end of the war, when he had taken up permanent residence in America.[6]

In the immediate post-war period Allan Nunn May was identified as a source of leaked atomic secrets, because clues to his identity had been contained in documents removed by a GRU defector, Igor S. Gouzenko, from the cipher-room of the Soviet Embassy in Ottawa. It had not been difficult to track Nunn May down, and his confession in 1946 was straightforward. In his work as a physicist he had come across data that he felt morally bound to share with the Soviets, and therefore he had volunteered it when the opportunity had arisen. There had never been any question of this Cambridge-educated scientist being a long-term mole who had manoeuvred himself into a position where he could gain access to secrets with the specific intention of betraying them. Accordingly, when Burgess and Maclean disappeared in 1951, the Security Service was obliged to rethink its strategy: evidently Soviet espionage was not merely the indulgence of foreigners, opportunists and overt members of the Communist Party.

MI5's pursuit of suspected Soviet agents rested on three principal sources: a huge archive of material recovered from Brussels at the end of the war relating to the Gestapo's investigations into the GRU's European networks; testimony in 1947 from another GRU defector, Allan Foote; and Soviet cryptographic data analysed by GCHQ. The first revealed the existence of a vast organisation of Soviet agents, broken up by the Germans, who had referred to it as Der Rote Kapelle (it was known sometimes also as the Red Orchestra).[7] Based primarily on commercial fronts, it boasted branches in practically every European country, and its tentacles even stretched to the United States. Information gleaned from a particular batch of these files, called the Robinson papers, had led MI5 to an agent in London code-named JEAN, actually a professional piano player calling himself 'Arnold Lock' who turned out to be Arnold B. Weiss from Breslau. Under interrogation, and without fear of prosecution in the post-war peace, Weiss had described his role in the British branch of the GRU's network which, for obvious reasons, the Gestapo had never been able to follow up. He had arrived in England in May 1932 and had acted as a courier for several Soviet agents until 1941, when he lost contact with the GRU. None of those named by Weiss were still active so no prosecutions were brought, but MI5's consequent analytical exercise, undertaken by Michael Serpell and Robert Hemblys-Scales, had been very helpful to the Security Service, and their report is now regarded as an essential key to understanding the methodology of Soviet espionage.

The second vital source of information on the GRU's European operations was Allan Foote, an experienced agent who decided to switch sides in August 1947 whilst *en route* to a new assignment in the West. He had been working as a GRU radio operator in Switzerland, servicing the Swiss branch of the Rote Kapelle. His evidence did much to enlarge MI5's knowledge of that organisation and fleshed out many of the personality dossiers recovered from the Gestapo headquarters in Brussels. In particular, Foote had enabled MI5 to trace another GRU agent, Ursula Kuczynski, then living in Oxfordshire, but when questioned in August 1947 she insisted that she had long since abandoned her wartime activities for the Soviets, and she denied any current involvement. In the absence of proof to the contrary she had been left alone by MI5 and was subsequently allowed to take her family to East Germany. It was only after a confession had been extracted from Klaus Fuchs in January 1950 that MI5 realised Ursula Kuczynski had lied. She had been active for the GRU after the war, helping to run Fuchs after his return from Los Alamos in June 1946.[8]

Finally, there was the most secret source of all, the intercepted Russian signal traffic known generically as VENONA. This consisted of a series of partial decrypts of wireless messages that had been accumulated since the last year of the war, and disclosed the existence of hundreds of Soviet agents around the globe. There were, in total, some two hundred thousand enciphered texts in the collection, containing references to about eight hundred cryptonyms of suspected Soviet agents. The scale of the Kremlin's espionage offensive was truly breathtaking, and the incriminating material was used to good effect to persuade Australia and Canada, which at that time possessed no effective counter-intelligence capability whatever, to take appropriate measures, including the creation of a specialist counter-espionage agency built on MI5's lines. VENONA's existence was properly regarded as the most sensitive secret, and potentially the most useful weapon, in the West's counter-intelligence armoury. In Britain only a handful of specialists were indoctrinated into VENONA and few of them ever spoke openly about it or used that particular term. Most either referred to 'V-traffic', or perhaps one of the VENONA code-worded sub-categories, such as VAROOCH (allocated to the KGB traffic dealing with KGB 'illegals'). Even after VENONA's existence had been publicly disclosed, those involved felt uncomfortable discussing the topic; none of the material has ever been declassified.

The fact that the VENONA material had been gathered, recorded and studied was disclosed to the Soviets in 1948 by William Weisband, a clerk in the US Armed Forces Security Agency (the National Security Agency's predecessor). Weisband was convicted of contempt, not espionage, that same year, and no details of his highly classified work were released.[9] This had prompted the KGB to change its cipher procedures, but there was nothing the Soviets could do about the wealth of material already in American hands, ticking away like an unexploded bomb, waiting to be detonated by a skilled cryptographer. Certainly Philby, when he was granted access to the treasure in 1949, took a tremendous interest in the progress made by the AFSA's code breakers on the various fragments of VENONA cables. Two years later, following the defections of Burgess and Maclean, his interest was given a different interpretation.

Even though it was realised that Weisband had betrayed the AFSA's ongoing decryption programme, known internally as Operation BRIDE, the American authorities went to great lengths to protect the degree of success they had achieved in reading the traffic. A cover story was disseminated, which still finds wide circulation, saying that breaks into the text had been accomplished through scraps of a partially burnt KGB code book recovered from the battlefield in Finland in 1941. In reality a complete code book had been photographed when the safe used by the KGB's *rezident* in New York, located in the Soviet

Consulate on East Sixty-first Street, had been burgled by the FBI. A similar attempt made in Washington, on Vassili Zubilin, the KGB's chief *rezident* in the US, had failed, but an illicit entry had been made on the consulate, where the Consul-General Pavel Mikhailov had himself been identified as the principal GRU officer in the States.[10] It had been the use of this code book that had facilitated much of the cryptographic activity that was to take place on both sides of the Atlantic. The tale of the Finnish code book neatly obscured the true, highly illegal source and persuaded the KGB not to dissolve their networks and start them over again. The fact that there was an alternative explanation is hinted at by Robert Lamphere,[11] one of the FBI Special Agents assigned to the Foreign Counter-Intelligence Section in New York, who referred obliquely in his memoirs to documents that 'had been photographed by the New York FBI agents in the course of an investigation into Soviet operations in New York in 1944'.[12]

Of particular interest to MI5 was the VENONA traffic that passed between Moscow and London during the week following the defection of Igor Gouzenko, the GRU cipher clerk in Ottawa. The Russians noticed his disappearance on 6 September 1945 and, once they realised the implications of his defection, together with a quantity of stolen papers, a world-wide alert was signalled by Moscow. Local *rezidents* were instructed to suspend operations temporarily and meetings with agents at risk were postponed while the panic lasted. The recipient in London of many of these signals had been Boris Krotov,[13] known to be a senior KGB officer, and study of the messages addressed to him revealed that he had then been in touch with no less than eight important spies in England, one of whom was a scientist with access to British defence secrets.

Putting names to eight cryptonyms revealed in Krotov's messages was to become a major preoccupation for the Security Service, which instantly understood the implications. Every reference was carefully indexed, and gradually the data on each increased. Occasionally there was a clue to an agent's movements which was logged in case it might one day fit the travel pattern of a suspect. In America an identical exercise was also under way and by the end of the decade the FBI was able to narrow down its espionage suspects and positively identify Alger Hiss and Julius and Ethel Rosenberg as Soviet agents. Hiss was the only person whose known peregrinations dovetailed with the reconstructed itinerary of the KGB source protected by the cryptonym ALES.[14] The FBI also matched Klaus Fuchs to another cryptonym and sent the evidence to London where MI5 used it skilfully to extract a confession from the physicist without having to compromise the source. In his statement Fuchs helpfully identified three key GRU personnel: Ursula Kuczynski, her brother Jurgen,[15] and Fuchs's very first contact, a Russian who appeared in MI5's photo album as Simon D. Kremer, the Soviet Military Attaché's secretary in London until 1941.[16]

Meanwhile MI5's research was concentrating on another American lead, a spy in the British Embassy in Washington during 1944–45 with the Soviet cryptonym HOMER,[17] who had passed the Russians copies of Churchill's private telegrams to President Truman. Included in the VENONA material were verbatim texts of the Prime Minister's most secret wartime correspondence, to which only a limited number of people could have had access. There were several possible suspects for HOMER but the fact that this particular VENONA series had emanated from New York suggested that either a KGB case officer had travelled to Washington to retrieve it – which seemed unlikely because there were so many other KGB personnel available to undertake such routine tasks in the capital – or that the spy had frequently visited New York. A check of the suspects showed that during the relevant period in 1944 a diplomat named Donald Maclean had sought, and received, permission to visit his wife in hospital in Manhattan each weekend. This breakthrough had prompted MI5 in May 1951 to obtain the Foreign Secretary's sanction to interrogate Maclean, but his subsequent escape was eloquent proof of his guilt. The fact that Guy Burgess, who had not yet come under suspicion, matched the cryptonym HICKS in Krotov's VENONA traffic was extremely convenient, but even though Kim Philby incriminated himself by assisting Maclean's defection he was not to be confirmed as the other cryptonym, STANLEY, until 1966.

MI5 soon realised that the key to unlocking the KGB's espionage in Britain lay in the VENONA decrypts, and in the years that followed a tremendous effort was made to put names to the remaining six spies who had been run by Krotov in London in September 1945. However, by 1956 MI5 believed it had exhausted all the VENONA leads, and the work was only restarted a decade later when more clues had been obtained. As more breaks were achieved, more spies emerged in the texts. Burgess was evidently the impulsive, temperamental HICKS, about whose erratic behaviour Krotov had been warned, and STANLEY must have been Philby who had been on a trip abroad at the time that Krotov received his warning to suspend operations in 1945. One message had noted that STANLEY was travelling overseas, but would be returning shortly: this neatly coincided with Philby's journey the same month to Egypt and Turkey.

Following the defections of Burgess and Maclean, Anthony Blunt had fallen under suspicion and been interviewed several times by those leading MI5's investigation. Blunt resolutely denied having spied, but his interrogators were convinced that he was the most likely candidate for another of Krotov's eight cryptonyms, JOHNSON. Thus there remained five more spies to be identified, and among them were a pair who were always linked together, DAVID and ROSA. In the aftermath of the Burgess and Maclean defections one further spy was positively identified, from his handwriting found on some Treasury documents left in Burgess's flat: John Cairncross, who at that stage admitted only to having been indiscreet about his work to Guy Burgess. Cairncross's career as a civil servant had included the pre-war Foreign Office, GCHQ at Bletchley Park, SIS's Yugoslav Section and finally the Treasury,[18] amounted to a remarkably useful *tour d'horizon* for the KGB. Thirteen years later, as we shall see, he was to make a much more candid and comprehensive confession. In the mean time MI5 made an exhaustive trawl through Burgess's coterie to find candidates for the missing cryptonyms. One strong suspect, who proved a useful informant and clearly knew more than he admitted, was the Welsh academic Goronwy Rees.

In recent years there has been much speculation about the identity of a master spy, the elusive 'fifth man'. That individual is any one of several different people, depending upon one's interpretation of events and perspective. Originally, as we have seen, MI5 sought the eight spies whose cryptonyms had shown up in the VENONA decrypts, and in 1951 there was a public outcry about the identity of the so-called 'third man' who had tipped off Burgess and Maclean just as the authorities were closing in on the latter. Although MI5 had fully satisfied itself of his complicity, there was no move made against Blunt, on the grounds that there was insufficient evidence to justify an arrest. Indeed when in 1954, three years after the defections, the KGB *rezident* in Canberra, Vladimir Petrov, confirmed that Burgess and Maclean had escaped to Moscow, and had both been long-term Soviet agents recruited whilst still at university, no public announcement had been made. However, in response to mounting public criticism the government had released a White Paper[19] on the defections and incidentally had absolved Philby of being the 'third man, if indeed there was one'. This effectively laid the matter to rest as far as the public was concerned, but in 1962 the situation changed again when a KGB defector, Anatoli M. Golitsyn, disclosed the existence of a 'Ring of Five': five agents in Britain whom the KGB believed were not only known to each other, *but who all knew each other's guilty secret*. They were known by the KGB as *pyat*, 'the five'. He also confirmed that Philby was probably STANLEY in Krotov's messages back in September 1945; there was some further circumstantial corroboration, for Golitsyn mentioned that STANLEY had recently been in the Middle East. In fact Philby, who had been sacked from SIS in November 1951, had subsequently moved to Beirut, where he was to remain until his hasty departure to Moscow in January 1963.

Considering that Burgess, Maclean and Philby had known each other, it seemed likely that they were members of Golitsyn's 'Ring of Five'. The idea that five spies all knew about each other's espionage breached all the usual tradecraft rules which required, for the sake of security, that agents should be compartmented so that the loss of one should not lead to others being compromised. Orthodoxy demanded isolation of sources so as to preserve their integrity yet here, according to Golitsyn, were five spies who broke all the conventions. The remaining question centred on the identity of the other two spies. Shortly before his own defection in January 1963 Philby tried to mislead the investigators by accepting an immunity from prosecution in return for his detailed confession; he left a statement in which he had named Tim Milne, formerly one of his closest SIS colleagues, as a Soviet spy, and simultaneously exonerated Anthony Blunt.[20]

At the time of Philby's false confession MI5 had already gleaned a certain amount of knowledge regarding Soviet intelligence methodology in England from three unexpected sources. The first was George Blake's confession and subsequent debriefing in 1961. He had provided MI5 with a comprehensive account of his dealings with the KGB stretching back over more than a decade and had identified Sergei Kondrashev as his Soviet case officer in London. The second source was John Vassall, a homosexual spy coerced into helping the KGB after being honeytrapped while serving in the British Embassy in Moscow. After his arrest in September 1962 Vassall had looked through MI5's album of Soviet diplomatic personnel and had pointed out Nikolai Karpekov as his KGB contact in London. The same person was also to be identified by Professor Giuseppe Martelli, the atomic physicist who was to be acquitted of espionage the following year. Golitsyn had helpfully confirmed that both Sergei Kondrashev and Nikolai Karpekov were senior specialists from the British department of the KGB's First Chief Directorate, case officers assigned to the embassy in London specifically to handle important spies.

Philby's mischievous 'confession' took some time to be disproved, and it was not until 1964 that MI5 finally recognised it for the fabrication it was, and decided to start its enquiries again, beginning with a review of all the old leads. This resulted in an inconclusive statement from Cairncross, then lecturing at Northwestern University, Ohio, who reluctantly named James Klugmann as his recruiter at Cambridge. Klugmann, then engaged in writing the CPGB's history,[21] was a veteran old-style Communist who had also played a murky role at Cambridge and, during the war, in the Cairo branch of Special Operations Executive. MI5 had little doubt that Klugmann had been a spy, but Cairncross's confirmation hardly carried matters much further, for there was no prospect whatever of MI5 talking directly to Klugmann. Apart from the fact that he would never have agreed to be interviewed, to have talked to him at all might have disclosed MI5's position to the KGB. However, further enlightenment was at hand, in the form of vital testimony from Michael Straight, an American who had recently given an account of his own activities to the FBI.[22] Petty inter-agency rivalry, exercised by J. Edgar Hoover, had prevented the FBI from sharing this crucial information with MI5. Straight had been one of Blunt's students at Trinity and had been approached, so he claimed, to drop out of the CPGB and undertake a secret mission for what Blunt had termed 'our friends in the International'. Straight, who had joined the US State Department after Cambridge, had subsequently held covert meetings with some mysterious foreigners, a pattern that was to be followed by a number of those close to Burgess and Blunt who were equally reluctant to recognise the reality of their situation. Understandably hesitant about his own role, Straight's damning statement was emphatic about his former mentor and proved to be the very first direct allegation of Blunt's involvement in espionage. It was this powerful weapon used by MI5, together with a formal offer of immunity from prosecution, which persuaded Blunt to switch sides. On 22 April 1964 Sir Anthony Blunt, after thirteen years of bland denials, and in the comfort of his flat in the Courtauld Institute, calmly admitted his duplicity. The Surveyor of the Queen's Pictures acknowledged that he had served the KGB since he had been invited to do so by Guy Burgess whilst still at Trinity College.

Blunt's decision to collaborate with MI5 was to remain a closely guarded secret within the Security Service. Only a handful of senior personnel knew that he had opted to co-operate, and MI5 certainly expected him to identify his fellow conspirators. Among the first were John Cairncross, who was already well known to MI5, and Leo Long, who had never previously been a suspect. Long had worked in military intelligence during the war, monitoring the enemy's order of battle, and afterwards had held a senior position in the Intelligence Division of the British Control Commission for Germany. Whilst on a visit to Long on 1945, Blunt had tried to engineer his transfer to the Security Service, but the attempt had failed and instead Long had taken up a job offer from a film company which effectively removed him from access to secrets.

Blunt appeared to be entirely co-operative, and spent hours poring over albums of photographs snatched of suspected Soviet intelligence personnel, occasionally identifying a picture as one of his contacts. In this way Anatoli Gromov[23] and Yuri Modin were confirmed as the Soviet intelligence officers who had taken over running at least some of the Cambridge spies from the KGB's original 'illegals'. This coincided with information volunteered by Anatoli Golitsyn a year earlier. However, it was noted that Blunt did not fulfil the objective MI5 had, perhaps over-optimistically, set him – the identification of *currently active*

Soviet spies. Certainly he had put MI5 on to Long, but he could have been regarded as something of a 'discard', whose loss could be borne by the KGB without any major inconvenience. Most of Blunt's other items were of only marginal contemporary importance and tended to concentrate on old cases, and definitely those that the Soviets had good reason to believe had already become known to the West's counter-intelligence authorities. This was true of Paddy Costello, the New Zealand academic who had already been compromised, by having used his consular position in Paris to authorise the New Zealand passports found in the possession of Lena and Morris Cohen back in 1961. The Cohens, previously implicated in the New York network headed by the Rosenbergs, had been arrested in a London suburb operating under illegal cover. After having fled from the States, the Cohens had settled temporarily in Vienna, long enough to make an application, supported by false birth and marriage certificates, for new passports. Costello's incriminating signature appeared on the resulting consular paperwork. Already a suspect, Costello's recruitment at Cambridge had been confirmed by Blunt. He had also named an army officer named Tom Wylie as one of Burgess's sources, but Wylie could not be interviewed because he had been dead for some years. This was equally true of the Canadian diplomat Herbert Norman, who had committed suicide on 4 April 1957 in Cairo, where he had been Ambassador.[24] For all his apparent willingness to co-operate enthusiastically with MI5, it certainly seemed that the KGB was not going to sustain any great damage inflicted by Blunt. Analysts were later to remark that Blunt's prodigious memory often failed him when his debriefers ventured close to someone who might still be operating in place for the KGB.

Blunt had described fondly how he had been recruited by Guy Burgess, and how Philby had often talked of his admiration for his recruiter, Theodore Maly. Blunt had never met him, but he had been introduced to 'Otto', another Soviet 'illegal' whose true name was believed to be Arnold Deutsch.[25] Blunt recalled that soon after he had started to pass names of potential recruits to Burgess. 'Otto' had disappeared and contact with the KGB had only been resumed after Philby returned from Vienna with Litzi Friedman as his wife. She had been Burgess's link to the Soviet Embassy in London through two further cut-outs, Robert Stewart and Edith Tudor Hart. Both the latter pair were senior figures in the CPGB, which again defied the usual well-established tenets of espionage demanding that agents be run in isolation from the potential contamination associated with political activism. Although the KGB's best agents had gone to elaborate lengths to sublimate their Party connections, much of the Cambridge ring had continued to rely on the CPGB to convey messages to the embassy. Both the couriers named by Blunt had maintained a very high profile and had continued their political exertions while engaged in their incompatible clandestine work. This seemed to be an unconscionable breach of security but, as Blunt pointed out, it had not proved in practice to be the weakest link. MI5's attempts to interview Stewart and Tudor Hart failed, so a further visit to Cairncross was made, using Blunt's information as a lever to obtain yet more co-operation. On this occasion, having demonstrated the depth of MI5's knowledge on the subject, Cairncross had been rather more forthcoming. He had already named James Klugmann as his recruiter, and this time he agreed to ask Klugmann to talk to MI5. His motive for doing so was the incentive offered by MI5 that he would not face prosecution if he returned to England and successfully 'turned' his recruiter. Klugmann, long a CPGB hardliner, rejected the request scornfully, leaving a wretched Cairncross to continue his exile abroad, and MI5 to wonder exactly what role he had fulfilled within the Soviet network in Britain. Apart from his wartime service in SOE, Klugmann had not had access to secrets, which ruled him out as having been an active spy at risk in September 1945, and therefore one of Krotov's eight cryptonyms. However, he had known that Burgess and Blunt were spies, which automatically made him eligible for membership of Golitsyn's Ring of Five.

The extraordinary feature of the Ring of Five, according to Golitsyn, was the fact that the KGB believed each of its members knew the others, and knew about their espionage. Into this category fitted Burgess, Maclean and Philby, but not necessarily Blunt. Although Blunt had been positively matched to JOHNSON in Krotov's messages, he had not known fully about Maclean's involvement until shortly before his defection. It seemed that the key figure in the network, at least according to Blunt, had been Burgess. Blunt had only a rough idea of whom Burgess had approached to spy. Some people Blunt had 'talent-spotted' for Burgess, passing the candidate's name on as suitable for further action; this had happened with John Cairncross, whom he had recommended for a recruitment subsequently dealt with by Klugmann. In fact Blunt claimed to have handled only a single agent himself, and that individual had been Leo Long. Blunt's main method of determining who had or had not been approached by Burgess rested on his belief that Burgess had probably made a pitch for everyone whom he admired. This left MI5 with the daunting prospect of researching all of Burgess's university connections and then interviewing each to see whether Burgess had made his move. Burgess had been an extraordinary predatory social animal, and the list of his acquaintances, drawn up with the help of some of his former friends, was a long one. Among those who assisted MI5 to rebuild Burgess's address book was the distinguished philosopher and former wartime intelligence officer Sir Isaiah Berlin, and the humorist Arthur Marshall, who possessed a fund of knowledge about the homosexual circles in Cambridge in which Blunt and Burgess had moved. Added to the list were names which had cropped up from other sources, such as those suggested by Goronwy Rees in 1951, and some others denounced by Flora Solomon who, in 1962, had belatedly supplied some incriminating testimony about Philby to MI5. Born in Russia,

Solomon had led a very colourful life,[26] having been the mistress of Alexander Kerensky. She had also been close to Edith Tudor Hart, and two of Philby's three wives, Litzi and Aileen. It was MI5's suspicion that Solomon had known a great deal about Soviet espionage during the late 1930s, but the researchers had been obliged to settle for simply adding the names she had volunteered to their growing list of suspected spies.

This distasteful exercise revealed a number of espionage candidates who had risen to high office in Whitehall, Sir Andrew Cohen, Sir Dennis Proctor and Sir Edward Playfair among them. Some were interviewed, some could only be seen after their retirement from the Civil Service, while others died before the investigators could get to them. Very gradually, and in conditions of great secrecy, the MI5 team reconstructed the university-based relationships that had been forged thirty years earlier. Each new name was put to Blunt, who offered an opinion on the likelihood of them having been approached or recruited. Occasionally, after some nudging, as happened in the case of Proctor, Blunt would recall some long-forgotten incident that tended to confirm an individual's involvement (he remembered that in a characteristically indiscreet slip before the war Burgess had mentioned getting papers straight from Stanley Baldwin's desk. At the relevant time Proctor had been Baldwin's private secretary.)

Blunt also identified (Sir) Stuart Hampshire, then Professor of Philosophy at Princeton, as having been recruited by Burgess. Five years later, when he was interviewed by MI5 at Princeton, Hampshire recalled a dinner party held in Paris in 1938 at which James Klugmann, Anthony Blunt, Guy Burgess and Blunt's boyfriend Ben Nicolson had been present. On that occasion Burgess had apparently approached Hampshire, but the latter had misunderstood what Burgess had meant by 'working for peace', a frequently used euphemism for spying. Despite Blunt's allegation, MI5's interrogators were satisfied that Hampshire had not been a spy; but they were equally certain that John

Lehrmann had. Lehrmann had been very active in the Communist underground in Austria before the war, and had been a close friend of Anthony Blunt's at Trinity, but he had never been entrusted with access to British secrets. Nevertheless, he was marked down as having operated as a courier for a KGB network, and he admitted as much when interviewed.

MI5's recognition of the need for secrecy prevented its research from becoming public knowledge until one of the investigators, Peter Wright, disclosed much of what had happened to Chapman Pincher, who then published *Their Trade is Treachery* in 1981. The official policy was to avoid any hint or accusation of pursuing a McCarthyite witch-hunt into the 1930s, and this had necessarily restricted the activities of the researchers, who frequently experienced frustration as a potentially promising avenue of enquiry was closed to them by a directive from on high. Despite the disappointment, strict discipline was maintained and very little freelancing took place. Only on one occasion did MI5's team leader resort to what might have been described as dirty tricks. As well as Bob Stewart and Edith Tudor Hart, Blunt had named Phoebe Pool as having worked as a courier for the Soviet network. There was no prospect of interrogating her, as she was in a long-term hospital, so a scheme was devised, using one of Blunt's colleagues at the Courtauld Institute, Anita Brookner, as an unwitting go-between.[27] Blunt asked Brookner to convey a message to Phoebe Pool when she next visited her. The gist of it was that Blunt needed to know whom to alert now that enquiries were being made into the events of the 1930s. Brookner reported back that Pool had mentioned Sir Andrew Cohen, Jenifer Fischer Williams and the Floud brothers as needing a warning.

Not all of these names were entirely unknown to MI5. Cohen had already been identified by Flora Solomon as a source recruited by Burgess at Oxford, and Jenifer Fischer Williams had married a former wartime MI5 officer, Herbert Hart.[28] The late Peter Floud had been the director of the Victoria & Albert

Museum, but his brother Bernard was then still a Labour Member of Parliament, tipped for a ministerial appointment. When interviewed, Jenifer Hart admitted having held clandestine meetings with a man who resembled 'Otto', and having dropped her overt CPGB affiliations at Bernard Floud's suggestion. Floud denied Mrs Hart's recollection, but committed suicide soon afterwards. Phoebe Pool also killed herself not long after these events but Blunt, who was deeply affected by her loss, comforted himself that at least Pool had never realised she had been tricked into betraying Cohen, Hart and the Flouds. Nor had she ever learnt that Blunt himself had thrown in his lot with MI5.

Further research on the Flouds revealed that both had been involved in intelligence during the war. Bernard had served in the Intelligence Corps until 1942 and his brother had worked in a senior post at the Ministry of Home Security until 1944. As for Jenifer Hart, she had worked in the Home Office department responsible for handling MI5's applications for telephone-intercept warrants. She also disclosed the existence of a Communist cell, known as the Leighton group, which operated in Whitehall, to which her sister Elais Judith belonged. Her husband, David Hubback, whom she married in 1939, was a civil service high-flyer who had been educated at Westminster and King's College, Cambridge. After being investigated by Peter Wright he was switched in 1968 from the Treasury to a less sensitive post in the Board of Trade. One of his contemporaries at King's, Peter Vinter, who also worked in the Treasury, moved to the Ministry of Technology at the same time. Cairncross had also been a member of the Leighton group, and some of them had been known to (Sir) Edward Playfair. Others connected to the group included a senior official of the Customs and Excise named Buckley and a civil servant in the Department of Trade named Chivers who had been at Cambridge with Cairncross.

The extent to which Blunt helped MI5 in the six years following his acceptance of the Attorney-General's immunity from prosecution can be gauged by his presence during the lengthy interrogation of Alister Watson, whose name had emerged as a good candidate for the scientist among Boris Krotov's eight spies. Watson had been named as a former CPGB member by Victor Rothschild, and been linked to Burgess by several different people, including Sir Isaiah Berlin. Watson performed badly while responding to MI5's questions and, although he never admitted having been a spy, all those present at the interviews were convinced of his guilt. He admitted having met 'Otto' and effectively incriminated himself when shown MI5's album of Soviet diplomats. He picked out Yuri Modin,[29] Sergei Kondrashev and Nikolai Karpekov, all confirmed KGB specialists, as men he had met secretly over the years. However, as the disastrous trial of Professor Martelli at the Old Bailey in 1963 had demonstrated, evidence of clandestine meetings with undercover Russian intelligence officers did not in itself amount to conclusive proof of espionage. However unconvincing his denials, Watson's refusal to confess saved him from prosecution. Even the offer of an immunity failed to budge him, partly because he was by then almost punch-drunk from the intensity of his interrogation, but mainly because, unlike Blunt, he was still a committed Marxist. Technical surveillance on Watson had also revealed other members of his family to be CPGB members, so there were compelling reasons for him not to go the extra distance for MI5.

The exposure of Alister Watson settled the outstanding problem of the elusive scientist whose cryptonym had appeared in the VENONA traffic. Although he could not be prosecuted for having betrayed secrets during an espionage career estimated to have lasted a quarter of a century, he was moved away from access to classified information at the Admiralty Research Station at Teddington to a more appropriate position in the National Institute of Oceanography. This was not an entirely unsatisfactory way to conclude the Watson case, considering that there had never been much prospect of turning him as Blunt had been turned.

The initial reluctance that Blunt had manifested when confronted with the names of Proctor and Watson suggested to some in MI5 that his co-operation had never been entirely whole-hearted, and might have been driven by sheer expediency. There were two issues that had yet to be resolved. The first was the thorny perennial of Soviet penetration of the Security Service itself. The fact that Blunt had been allowed to leave MI5 in 1945, although the KGB knew that he had been offered a permanent post, was a strong indication, if not absolute proof, that there must have been at least one other source, equally well-placed, in the organisation at that time. Blunt himself conceded this, stating that he had been surprised when Burgess relayed the welcome news that the Russians had given their consent to his return to academic life. He too had drawn the conclusion that there must have been someone else working in parallel with him, but he had been unable to suggest any candidates. The evidence of Soviet penetration had seemed overwhelming, right up to 1963, yet Blunt had offered no leads. MI5 had already embarked on a debilitating internal molehunt when Blunt had confessed, concentrating on the then Deputy Director-General, Graham Mitchell, which had proved inconclusive. Thereafter both Sir Roger Hollis and Sir Dick White had been the subject of secret investigations, but once again the molehunters had drawn a blank. Some of the circumstantial evidence regarding a spy inside MI5 dated back to the war and centred on a hitherto unidentified GRU source code-named ELLI. To date no credible explanation for ELLI, if there was such an individual, has materialised.[30]

The second area of disappointment over Blunt's performance was the identification of Boris Krotov's eight active spies. Burgess, Philby, Blunt, Cairncross and Watson were there, and it could be assumed that Long or Proctor could be the sixth, but what of the mysterious duo DAVID and ROSA? Golitsyn had

1. Dusko Popov, MI5's colourful double agent code-named TRICYCLE, pictured while in New York in 1941. The FBI's reluctance to assist a self-declared German spy led to a bitter dispute with MI5 and nearly cost Dusko his life.

2. Simone Simon, the French actress who was Popov's mistress while he was in America. Their behaviour so shocked FBI Director J. Edgar Hoover that he ordered Popov to leave the country or face arrest on espionage charges.

3. William Luke (*left*), Popov's first MI5 case officer, and T. A. Robertson, the architect of the double-cross system. They used TRICYCLE to build a network of agents that even included an Austrian beauty married to Ian Menzies, the brother of the SIS Chief.

4. Wulf Schmidt before the war, in the Danish Army uniform of his cavalry regiment. Born in Schleswig-Holstein, territory claimed by both Denmark and Germany, Schmidt had divided loyalties and became a key German spy . . . and a star MI5 double agent.

5. Code-named TATE by MI5, Wulf Schmidt adopted the identity given to him by the Abwehr: Harry Williamson, the name he uses to this day. Fifty years after his arrival by parachute in Cambridgeshire he is still under MI5's protection.

6. *top left, opposite* The State Department's officia portrait of William Buckley, the diplomat and undercover CIA officer. H served under diplomatic cover in Damascus, Cairo, Islamabad and Beirut as a counter-terrorism expert. His experience had been gained in Saigon where he had supervised Viet Cong defectors with the notoriou Provincial Reconnaissanc Units. His knowledge of th West's anti-terrorism techniques made him a prestige target for Hezbollah.

7. *below* Buckley, the CIA station chief in Beirut whose capture by Hezbollah in March 1984 led to his interrogation and torture. The CIA's top management was so anxious to obtain his release and prevent a haemorrhage of the CIA's secrets that clandestine negotiations were opened through Mossad and arms sold to Iran.

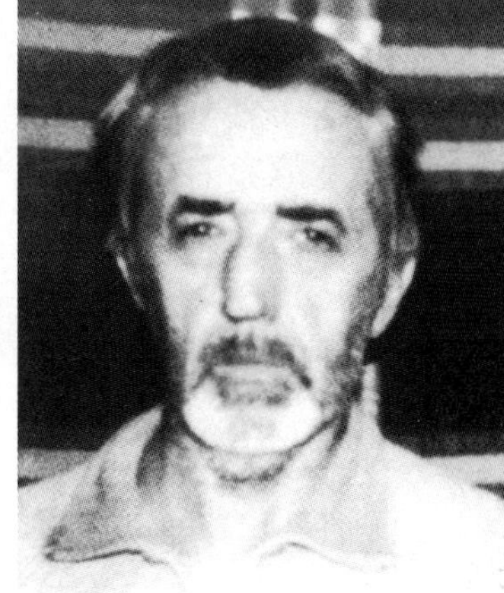

:. *below* Hezbollah released this photo of Buckley four months after he had died. Hezbollah promised to free him in exchange for cash and a consignment of weapons but instead released another hostage, Benjamin Weir, who turned out to be pro-fundamentalist.

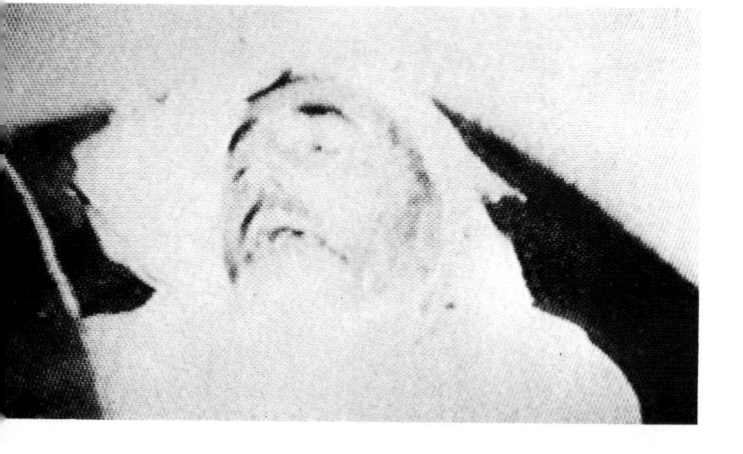

9. Terry Waite, surrounded by his Druze bodyguard. He communicated with Hezbollah in Beirut by walkie-talkie but ignored advice to stay away when his secret involvement with Oliver North had been disclosed inadvertently in Washington.

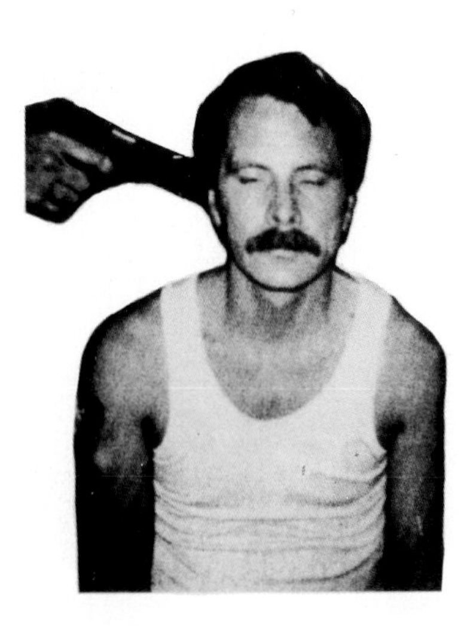

10. Arkadi Katkov, the popular KGB officer who was kidnapped with three other Soviet Embassy officials in September 1985. His captors removed the photograph's background to avoid giving any clue to their location. The KGB's ruthless response to his murder forced the kidnappers to release their remaining Soviet hostages.

11	
12	13
14	15

11. Anthony Blunt, a long-term Soviet asset who penetrated MI5 and then switched sides in return for an immunity from prosecution. His confession ruined the careers of a dozen top civil servants, but MI5 eventually concluded that he had duped his interrogators and had remained loyal to the KGB.

12. Leo Long, the order-of-battle specialist in MI14 who was one of Blunt's key agents recruited at Cambridge.

13. Victor Rothschild, the unpopular wartime MI5 officer and former underground member of the Communist Party who boasted an IQ of 184 but said he never realised several of his closest friends – including Burgess and Blunt, who were living in his house – were Soviet spies.

14. John Cairncross, a vital KGB source during the war, photographed at his home in the south of France where he now lives in self-imposed exile to avoid risking a British prosecution.

15. Yuri Modin, the legendary controller who ran the KGB's top spies in Britain while under diplomatic cover, photographed outside his old office in Dzerzinsky Square, Moscow, after being interviewed by the author. During his first assignment in London, which lasted six years, he had only three weeks' holiday.

16. George Blake in his Moscow flat, April 1991, the 'temporary' home where the KGB installed him on Christmas Eve 1966 after his unexpected escape from a record prison sentence in England and his rendezvous with his KGB controller, Vassili Dozhdalev, in East Berlin.

17. Now a member of the Canadian Senate, Philippe Gigantes adopted the name Philip Deane when he worked for the *Observer* during the Korean War. Imprisoned with George Blake, his nickname for one of their Soviet interrogators, 'Kuzma Kuzmich', led to the belief that such a KGB officer existed. The story was later embroidered to suggest that 'Kuzmich' had subsequently defected to the CIA.

18. Michael Randle and Pat Pottle, the peace campaigners who helped Blake escape, pictured outside the wall of Wormwood Scrubs prison that Blake scaled unnoticed in October 1966.

19. Francis Gary Powers, the U-2 pilot who appeared as a witness before the Senate Armed Services Committee and concealed how his plane had crashed. Following a secret CIA review, some senior offficers wanted him to face a court-martial on a charge of negligence but instead he was treated as a hero and given a pension.

20. Greville Wynne, SIS's disastrous courier, on his arrival at Northolt following his release in a spy swap in April 1964. After his arrest in Moscow Wynne had offered to switch sides and spy for the KGB.

21. *above right* Harold Shergold, the SIS officer who finally entrapped George Blake and subsequently ran Oleg Penkovsky as an agent in a joint operation with the CIA. When the Americans learnt of Wynne's erratic behaviour in Moscow they demanded he be dropped, but SIS continued to use him and thereby placed their star source in jeopardy.

22. Greville Wynne reunited with his wife and son outside their home in Upper Cheyne Row. After his release Wynne suffered a breakdown and abandoned his family. His Walter Mitty fantasies led him to collaborate with two ghost-writers and write two entirely spurious accounts of his espionage.

been convinced that this was a Jewish husband and wife team, and a reference to DAVID's scientific qualifications had suggested Victor and Tess Rothschild as possible candidates. Both had been active in the political Left while at university, and both had subsequently joined MI5. Even contemplating that Lord Rothschild might have been a Soviet spy sent shudders down MI5's institutional spine. As well as being a useful source for MI5, with whose top management he was on very friendly terms, he had become a respected figure in the British establishment and had been commissioned to write a government report on gambling. He had also been appointed by Prime Minister Edward Heath to run a high-powered policy-review think-tank for Downing Street. It seemed unthinkable that he might have been a spy, and yet he did behave strangely on occasions. The shock, a few days before his thirteenth birthday, of his father's suicide in their country home at Ashton, Northamptonshire, must have had a profound impact on the adolescent Rothschild. Nathaniel Rothschild, then aged forty-six, had cut his own throat 'while of unsound mind'.[31] At Trinity College Victor had been known as both a Leftist and a wild motorist.[32] His reputation in the Security Service had not been enhanced by his habit of referring to his IQ of 184 ('the highest ever recorded by the US Army, and equal to Hitler's favourite architect, Albert Speer'). Nor had his award of the George Cross, for defusing explosives concealed in a box of imported Spanish onions, been universally well received. Rothschild, as MI5's resident expert on enemy sabotage, had been called in by the army to deal with the device near Northampton on 10 February 1944. He had succeeded in rendering it harmless and had given a running commentary over a field-telephone line to his secretary, Tess Mayor, whom he subsequently married. Rothschild's gallantry had been undeniable but by convention MI5 officers were not supposed to be individually recommended for decorations. Indeed, there had been much speculation about how the GOC who had put Rothschild's name in for a medal had acquired a copy of the commentary transcript.[33] In short, Rothschild was a profoundly unpopular member of MI5, and in later life he actively sought to deny, rather unconvincingly, ever having met Philby. He most certainly played a part in unmasking Kim Philby in 1962, by introducing Flora Solomon to MI5, and he also denounced Alister Watson as a former Cambridge Marxist, and both these two actions had been counted in his favour whenever his credentials were doubted. Yet some cynics wondered why, if he truly was so intelligent, so many of his friends, including Burgess and Blunt, had turned out to be traitors.

This was not a subject that Blunt cared to speculate about. Nor was he able to contribute much in other areas of special interest to MI5, such as the KGB rings known to have been recruited in other universities in the 1930s – particularly at Oxford, where reportedly Burgess and Klugmann had also been active. According to Ann Orr-Ewing, who in 1971 wrote an exhaustive study of the leads he had provided to MI5, Blunt had probably never fully co-operated with the molehunters nor been entirely candid. Certainly he had been unable or unwilling to say anything about the GRU's networks, which were reckoned to be as extensive as the KGB's. Nor was he judged to have been wholly frank about his last contacts with the KGB. Blunt had never been shaken from his insistence that, apart from one task performed in 1954 to convey a message to Philby, he had remained out of touch with the KGB since he ignored its advice to flee the country immediately following the Burgess and Maclean defections. Not all the MI5 officers indoctrinated into the case were persuaded by this proposition. The unpalatable fact was that Blunt remained an enigma to the day he died and, as Ann Orr-Ewing concludes, never really changed his views. There are still, of course, numerous unanswered questions, and many lingering doubts about the veracity of replies he had previously given.

CHAPTER V

George Blake

Born George Behar in Holland, Blake is probably best known as the spy who received the longest prison sentence ever handed out by a British criminal court, a total of forty-two years. He is equally notorious for the fact that he served less than six years before making a dramatic escape to the Soviet Union in October 1966. But in the intelligence community he is regarded as someone who changed history because he was the very first SIS officer to be tried and convicted of having betrayed his country.

Blake's background was unusual. His father was a Jewish businessman born in Constantinople who had served in the French Foreign Legion during the Great War, and subsequently transferred to the British Army during the Mesopotamian campaign. Evidently he had fought with distinction, because he was decorated with the British Military Cross and the French Croix de Guerre. He also acquired British citizenship, and married a Dutch wife, Catherine, in London before settling in Rotterdam. Upon his death in April 1934, when young George was thirteen, the boy went to Egypt to live with his paternal aunt, and learnt for the first time of his Jewish origins. Those who know Blake say that his father's omission in not telling George of his Jewish heritage affected him profoundly. While in Cairo he also came to know his cousin, Henri Curiel, a left-wing activist eight years older than himself who was to be a founder member of the Egyptian Communist Party. Curiel was eventually to move to Paris, where he was murdered in 1978, in a political assassination linked to his enthusiastic support for the Palestine Liberation Organisation.

Blake's curiously cosmopolitan beginnings may have had some influence on his later development, but he denies that Henri Curiel did any more than awaken a religious awareness within him. Indeed, Blake was to consider taking holy orders at one stage. The suggestion that Blake was indoctrinated by Curiel came about through an analysis of Blake's case by H. Montgomery Hyde in *George Blake Superspy*, in which he incorrectly identified Curiel as Blake's uncle.[1] In 1939 Blake returned to Holland to complete his education, but the war intervened and he was interned by the Nazis because of his British citizenship. After a month of detention Blake was released and became active in the anti-Nazi resistance, working as a courier delivering messages and helping distribute underground newspapers. After the death of his grandmother in 1942 Blake decided to escape to England to join his mother and sisters who had already fled, and he made contact with the organisers of a route that guided *passeurs* from Paris to Lyons in the unoccupied zone, and then on to Spain. He crossed the frontier late in 1942 and, having been arrested by the Spanish police, was interned at the notorious Miranda del Ebro Camp. His release came two months later, in January 1943, after the intervention of the British Embassy in Madrid, and he then completed his journey to England via Gibraltar and a sea voyage aboard the *Empress of Australia*. He underwent the routine four-day screening process at the Royal Victoria Patriotic School at Wandsworth and, once cleared by the security authorities, joined his family, who had found a house in the London suburb of Northwood, and went to work for the Dutch government-in-exile. After five months of unremittingly dull clerical work in the Dutch Ministry of Economic Affairs, Blake, together with his mother and two sisters, Anglicised his name by deed poll; in October 1943 he joined the Royal Navy.

For the next year Blake underwent an officers' training course and had a spell at sea aboard the cruiser *Diomede*. It has been suggested, originally by Rebecca West in *The New Meaning of Treason*, that Blake 'had been abstracted by SOE to work in their Dutch Section',[2] but this is incorrect. Nevertheless other authors have perpetuated this particular myth, with Cookridge claiming that Blake 'was seconded by the Royal Navy to the Dutch Section of SOE'.[3] In fact Blake remained in the navy for a full year before he entered the intelligence community, and when he did so, it was to be SIS he joined, not Special Operations Executive.

Blake's naval career was short-lived. Assigned to submarine training, it was discovered that he had a medical condition which made him unsuitable for work underwater, and his name was passed to SIS as a potential recruit. A series of mysterious interviews in London followed, at the end of which Blake discovered in August 1944 that he had been enrolled as a member of the famed British Secret Service's Dutch Section, designated 'A2', and later 'P8'. Although surprised by this unexpected development, Blake apparently welcomed what he thought was an opportunity to return to Holland under cover, but he had not reckoned on the terms of an agreement between SIS and the Dutch intelligence service that precluded British subjects operating as agents anywhere in the Netherlands. Its purpose was to remove any fear that the British had long-term interests in Holland, and avoid the bitter accusation made so often of SOE and SIS in France of meddling in an occupied country's internal politics. Accordingly Blake was to spend the first part of his SIS career escorting agents as a conducting officer from one training school to another, and processing reports from SIS's networks in Holland. This was mainly office work in SIS's headquarters in Broadway Buildings, where he was in close proximity to some very attractive secretaries who, he recalled, 'were decidedly upper class and belonged to the higher strata of the establishment. There were among them daughters of Tory MPs and ministers, of bishops, of a Viceroy of India, of court dignitaries and some were even related to the Royal Family . . . They were mostly pretty, some very beautiful, but inclined to be vague and incompetent in varying degrees, though to this there could be exceptions. They were pleasant to work with and helped create a cheerful, friendly atmosphere in the office. I was a beneficiary of this as I spent most of my time there.'[4]

Three of those who worked very closely with Blake, in the same room in Broadway, truly characterised the blue-blooded women drafted into the wartime SIS by its equally well-born Chief, Colonel Sir Stewart Menzies DSO MC. Bearing in mind that Blake had already acquired some sensitivity about the British class system, it can be imagined what effect their proximity had upon him. The three were Diana Legh, Guinevere Grant and the Hon. Iris Peake. Diana's father was Colonel the Hon. Sir Piers Legh, then Master of the King's Household, while Guinevere's (now Dame Guinevere Tilney's) father was Sir Alfred Grant, the twelfth to succeed to a Scottish baronetcy that had been created in 1688. Iris was the daughter of the Rt Hon. Osbert Peake MP, a Tory minister later to be ennobled Viscount Ingleby. These young ex-débutantes had been brought up on weekend house-parties, country pursuits and the Four Hundred. In contrast Blake, who was rather younger, had spent the past three years hiding his Jewish ancestry in a Nazi tyranny. According to Charles Seymour, then head of SIS's Dutch Section, Blake became infatuated with Iris Peake, and was very embittered when her father told him one evening after dinner at their mansion in Yorkshire that there was no chance of him ever marrying his daughter. Whatever the truth of the story, or the degree of tact exercised on this delicate subject, Blake remains to this day acutely self-conscious of his Jewish background and his heavily accented English.

After the Liberation Blake stayed in SIS and was offered a permanent post. The alternatives were a job running pleasure cruises on the Rhine with an ex-SIS colleague with a wooden leg, or working as a buyer in a fashion house for a friend of his mother. Neither appealed, so he opted for a Russian-language course at Downing College, Cambridge, and a future with SIS. Having learnt Russian it must have been only natural, following the twisted logic so typical of the Foreign Office, that he should have been posted to Seoul in South Korea in October 1948. Scarcely eighteen months later he witnessed the capital being overrun by Communist troops, as the North Koreans unexpectedly invaded at the start of what was to become the Korean War. The remaining employees of the British Consulate-General, including Blake, were taken into custody, and for the next three years he was a prisoner of the North Koreans. It was during this period of captivity which he shared with several other internees, including the *Observer* war correspondent Philip Deane, that, according to Blake, he was to adopt the Marxist creed and volunteer to work for the Soviets.

The way Blake made his offer is of interest. In the autumn of 1951 he asked one of his guards to convey a message to the Soviet Embassy in Pyongyang, and in due course, some six weeks later, he was interviewed by 'a big burly man of about forty or forty-five with a pale complexion. What was remarkable about him was that he was completely bald, so that he looked very much like the film actor Erich von Stroheim.'[5] Blake made his pitch to 'von Stroheim' and recalls that 'he never told me his name, but many years later I learned that, at that time, he had been the head of the KGB in the Maritime Province'. This initial encounter was followed by many more over the coming months, and Blake noticed that 'while we were talking a young fair Russian with pleasant open features came in,' who was 'introduced as the man who would interview my companions'.[6] This second Soviet played no part in Blake's conversations with 'von Stroheim' but his appearance was later to have a special significance, particularly for some of Blake's biographers.

Thus Blake met two Soviets whilst in captivity in Korea, one older than the other, and Blake remembers that 'Philip Dean immediately thought up a name for him and called him Kuzma

Kuzmich, a character out of a Russian novel, and from then on we referred to him by that name.'[7] Blake insists that he 'was always seen by the KGB chief, the others by Kuzmich'.[8] In his memoirs, *Captive in Korea*, Deane writes:

> We had nicknamed him Kuzma Kuzmich after a character who appears regularly in every new Russian novel – the convert to Communism who still suffers from 'survivals of capitalism.' Our Kuzma Kuzmich, a White Russian from Harbin who had taken up the 'faith' in 1945, was not always successful in expressing the fanaticism expected of neophytes. He would speak longingly of 'business', and his eyes would light up so, when told of cabarets in Alexandria or of Beirut dives.

The point that Kuzmich was a nickname is significant because when Blake's story came to be told by his biographer E. H. Cookridge in *Shadow of a Spy* the author misunderstood the reference to Kuzmich by Philip Deane and drew two wholly incorrect conclusions: that 'Kuzmich' had been the true name of the younger Soviet interrogator, and that this had been the person responsible for recruiting Blake into the KGB. Neither assumption was valid. Another internee, Herbert Lord of the Salvation Army, who lived alongside Blake during their months of captivity, remembers the younger Russian as 'a tall man with aristocratic manners and he was obviously a university man. He spoke fluent English and he really set about trying to persuade us that the Communist system and way of life was the best. George Blake had numerous sessions with him. Afterwards Blake would return to his room and tell us he was treating these conversations as a huge joke.'[9] In fact, of course, Blake was not seeing 'Kuzmich', but the 'von Stroheim' character, but this he never revealed to his fellow prisoners and they never suspected that, ideologically, he had switched sides.

When Cookridge wrote of Blake's experiences he told of the

research he had undertaken to discover more about 'the most impressive of the persuaders . . . Although I have been unable to find out his real name, I found out that he was known as Gregory Kuzmitch or "Kuzma" for short. He was an official of the Political Education Department (*Prosveshtcheny Otdyel*) of the MGB, the Ministry of State Security, which controlled all espionage activities abroad. Kuzmitch was one of the cultivated and highly trained men, found serving outside the Soviet Union as cultural attachés, Press attachés, correspondents of TASS, the Soviet news agency or accompanying trade missions, theatrical and ballet companies on their foreign visits as security officers to prevent defections.'[10]

Whilst Cookridge at least admitted that 'Kuzmitch' was not the young officer's true name, he did not attribute the name to Philip Deane, who actually invented it, using a fictional character from a novel as a model. To compound this error Cookridge claimed that he had been able to

> trace Kuzmitch's diplomatic career prior to his employment as a 'brainwasher' in Korea. I discovered that he had served on the staff of Major General Georgi Nikolaievitch Zarubin, who had been Soviet ambassador in Canada until 1947, and afterwards in London, with his appointment at Washington in 1952. Kuzmitch had spent long spells both in Ottawa and London (though in London he had used the name Kuznetsov and the rank of an 'Attaché'). In 1950 or early in 1951, Kuzmitch was recalled to Moscow and eventually sent to Korea. His task was to turn around British and American prisoners. During his service in the West – he had spent also some months at the Soviet embassy in Sweden – he had acquired a thorough knowledge of the Western way of life; his command of English was almost faultless. From Moscow's point of view, his acquaintance with Western politics and philosophies proved disastrous. At the end of the war in Korea Gregory

> Kuzmitch defected to the Americans and was sent to Washington where he was employed for several years by Mr Allen Dulles's Central Intelligence Agency.[11]

This revelation, all the more astonishing because it concerns someone who never existed outside a Russian novel, unfortunately does not stand up to any detailed investigation. Virtually every aspect that can be checked from non-classified sources shows Cookridge's proposition to be deeply flawed. For example, there was no one on the staff of Ambassador Zaroubin in Ottawa in 1945 who subsequently transferred to London. It has always been the British government's policy not to accept the diplomatic credentials of anyone who has previously been implicated in espionage, and the defection of Igor Gouzenko, the Soviet Embassy's GRU coding clerk, in September 1945 meant that the British Security Service had received a very comprehensive picture of the intelligence personnel working under diplomatic cover. Any attempt to transfer someone to London would have been resisted. The subsequent movements of those compromised by Gouzenko were carefully monitored, as illustrated by another confirmed GRU officer, Sergei M. Kudriavtsev, who was later to work in Vienna, Paris and Cuba, but not London. According to another defector who gave the West Soviet intelligence 'order-of-battle' information and data on senior Russian personalities, Kudriavtsev's real name was Aleksandr Erdberg, and he had a long history of espionage even before his arrival in the Canadian capital.

Neither does Cookridge's identification of Kuzmitch's alias as 'Kuznetsov' bear close scrutiny. During the period of 1945–50 no one with the surname Kuznetsov was attached to the Soviet Embassy in London, yet the author is emphatic this was the name used, cautioning his readers 'not to be confused with Pavel S. Kuznetsov, second secretary at the Soviet embassy in London in 1952'.[12] This surname is very common in Russia and there were two Kuznetsovs working as attachés in London in 1951, named Piotr and Viktor respectively, but neither, of course, could have been in London and in Korea simultaneously. Pavel S. Kuznetsov himself did not arrive in London until 1952, so he might conceivably have been posted to Korea prior to his transfer to London but, of course, Cookridge had already ruled him out.

Perhaps more significantly, there is no record of any KGB defector fitting 'Kuzmitch's' description having sold out to the CIA in 1953 or 1954. In fact between 1948 and 1957 there were only seven KGB defectors received in the West and they are all accounted for; none of them ever served in Korea. *Perebezhchiki*, as defectors are known, from either of the Soviet intelligence services were in those days so rare, and therefore so highly valued, that their meal-ticket information was circulated widely among Western security agencies. Almost without exception each GRU and KGB defector has written a book about his experiences, but none of those published bear any relation to Kuzmitch. Nor is such a person mentioned in any of the standard works of reference on this arcane subject and, perhaps most convincing of all, his name does not appear on the KGB's own list of traitors. Such a document, identifying all defectors between 1945 and 1969, was acquired by the *émigré* NTS, the Ukrainian Nationalist organisation based in West Germany, and later published in their newspaper, *Possev*. Much analytical work on this extraordinary paper has been done by Professor Vladislav Krasnov,[13] who has been able to compile a very comprehensive study of the phenomenon of defection and has used the various different sentences passed on defectors *in absentia* by the Soviet Supreme Court as a guide to an individual's status in the regime. GRU and KGB defectors have invariably been given a death sentence by the military *collegium* of the court, yet Kuzmitch goes unmentioned: further evidence, albeit of the negative variety, that he never really existed.

Admittedly Ambassador Zaroubin did himself move to London and take up his appointment on 23 January 1947, but that is about the only detail in Cookridge's version that fits the facts and can be verified. Indeed, there is a further flaw in the idea that the KGB officer who converted Blake had switched sides – years before Blake himself was exposed as a Soviet agent. If so, why had Blake been left at liberty? Had Kuzmich not told the CIA, or had the CIA concealed the truth from its British allies?

In reality Cookridge misinterpreted Philip Deane's references to the young Soviet interrogator, and then must have invented his subsequent colourful career. However, because of this single slip the whole Kuzmich episode was to become part of intelligence folklore. Other commentators were to repeat Kuzmich's notional role in Blake's purported conversion, including H. Montgomery Hyde, who described him in familiar terms, mentioning 'the arrival of a Russian expert from the Political Education Department of the Ministry of State Security (MGB), forerunner of the present KGB. His name was Gregory Kuzmitch . . .'[14] Hyde says nothing about Kuzmitch's supposed defection, perhaps realising that there was a central implausibility about Kuzmitch defecting to the West and then failing to disclose Blake's crucial change in loyalties, which he purportedly had engineered. After all, if Kuzmich really had defected, why had he not denounced Blake? Such a nugget of information would have been a meal ticket for life and assured Kuzmich of a sizeable reward, not to mention the book contracts. But Blake, of course, remained at liberty, spying for the KGB until his eventual arrest years later, in 1961. This crucial obstacle to Kuzmich's authenticity did not however prevent another observer of the intelligence scene, James Rusbridger, repeating Kuzmich's role as the catalyst of Blake's conversion. In his account in *The Intelligence Game*, Rusbridger neatly avoids the problem of exactly when Kuzmich defected, by moving the date to *after* Blake's arrest in 1961: 'By a curious twist of fate Kuzmitch later defected to the CIA by which time Blake had been convicted of spying . . .'[15] Thus, according to Rusbridger, Kuzmich defected after Blake's arrest, thereby disposing of the chronological difficulties posed by Cookridge and H. Montgomery Hyde.

None of this would really have any great significance if it was not for the fact that Kuzmich's entirely fictional existence and his role as a defector were confirmed by another, genuine former KGB officer, Oleg Gordievsky. According to his credentials, as a former *rezident*-designate in London, and the historian entrusted with the First Chief Directorate's secret history of its British operations section, Gordievsky is ideally placed to shed some light on this puzzle. His escape to the West took place as recently as August 1985, and he claims to have had access to many of the KGB's most prized secrets. He could reasonably be expected to have studied Blake's dossier, and certainly to know about previous defectors from his own service. His *KGB: The Inside Story*, co-authored with the Cambridge academic Christopher Andrew, states that 'Blake's recruitment seems to have begun in the autumn of 1951, according to the first MGB officer to interrogate him, Grigori Kuzmich . . .'[16] The authors also assert that 'Kuzmich, the first MGB officer to interrogate Blake, later defected,'[17] and in the footnotes source the Kuzmich reference to H. Montgomery Hyde who, as we have seen, not only borrowed Cookridge's claim, but had also adopted his spelling of 'Kuzmitch'. Quite how Gordievsky and Andrew came to use the same spelling as Blake ('Kuzmich'), which does not coincide with Cookridge or Hyde's 'Kuzmitch', is unexplained. Suffice to say that the gentleman concerned only ever existed in Philip Deane's Russian literature, so it is rather odd to find him surfacing in so many places with the help of people who are supposedly well informed.

It may well be that Oleg Gordievsky never had an opportunity to take a good look at Blake's file, for he makes several elementary mistakes in his account of his case, not the least being his description of Blake's father as a 'Sephardic jew from Cairo'[18] when in reality Albert Behar MC had been born in Constantinople. Furthermore, Gordievsky asserts that Blake only joined

SIS 'after spending the academic year 1947–48 learning Russian at Downing College, Cambridge'[19] when in fact Blake had entered SIS formally *four years earlier*, in October 1944. Since Gordievsky had been commissioned to write the KGB's secret history, and Blake was arguably the most valuable KGB spy in SIS (if not in the whole of Britain) while he was still at liberty, one wonders about the standards of accuracy at Dzerzhinksy Square.

By Blake's own admission, he returned to London in March 1953, having been released by the North Koreans, determined to work for the KGB. His contact was Nikolai B. Korovin, the KGB *rezident* who had been operating under diplomatic cover in London with the rank of first secretary, and then counsellor, since 1949. Korovin was to stay in London until 1954, but returned from Moscow in 1956. In January 1961 he made a hasty departure following the arrests of the Portland spy-ring, no doubt fearing that he might be implicated by Gordon Lonsdale, a KGB 'illegal'. In fact he need not have worried, because Lonsdale maintained his silence until he was swapped in April 1964 for Greville Wynne.

Blake's initial meeting with Korovin was in the customs building at Otpor, the frontier crossing point on the Trans-Siberian railway between Peking and Moscow. 'He was a thick-set man of middle height aged about fifty,' says Blake. 'He spoke English well but with a marked Slav accent'.[20] They arranged to meet again in The Hague in July 1953 and thereafter they met early in October outside Belsize Park tube station at 7 p.m. 'every month or three weeks'.[21] Blake recalled, 'I cannot say that Korovin was the kind of man who naturally evoked very warm feelings in me. There was too much of the iron fist in the velvet glove about him for that, but I had a great admiration for his skill . . . even though he was known to MI5 to be the KGB resident in Great Britain and constantly followed by a highly experienced surveillance team, equipped with fast cars and modern radio communications, he always managed to get rid of his tail and meet me, punctually at the appointed time and appointed place. He once told me how it was done. In order to meet me at seven o'clock in the evening, he left his house at eight o'clock in the morning and was on the move all day. The operation involved several people and cars and a few safehouses. It was difficult and time-consuming, but it worked every time.'[22]

There must have been a moment of disbelief when Blake revealed to Korovin in October 1953 that he had resumed working for SIS the previous month, and had been moved to one of that organisation's most secret departments, known as Section Y. During the post-war era SIS had recognised the potential of using sophisticated listening devices to access Soviet military and diplomatic communications, and Section Y had been created specifically to exploit what were euphemistically termed 'technical' or 'special sources.' The very fact of Section Y's existence was itself a tightly guarded secret even within SIS because, as a source, it was immensely vulnerable. The slightest hint might alert the Soviets to the inadequacy of their security countermeasures, and discovery of a particular project might even lead them to turn it to their advantage in a classic deception operation of the kind they had proved so adept at mounting. In addition, the disclosures of the identities of those employed in Section Y would automatically compromise its intention to initiate a scheme in a third country. For example, eight months after he had joined Section Y Blake was sent to Geneva to bug the Eastern Bloc representatives at an international peace conference. Not surprisingly, as Blake recalls, 'the staff of the Communist delegations observed strict telephone security'.[23] No doubt there were other cases where his colleagues arrived in other cities with similar tasks, only to discover that the targets had recently improved their security procedures. Even the information that Section Y was accommodated at 2 Carlton Gardens, directly opposite the Foreign Secretary's official residence overlooking the Mall, would have assisted the KGB who, no doubt would have been pleased to put the elegant building under clandestine surveillance and photograph all those entering and leaving. If this happened, one of those betrayed would have been Blake's own wife, Gillian Allan, whom he married in October 1954, and who was then employed as a junior secretary in Section Y. One exceptionally profitable source that Blake alerted the Soviets to was at Schwechat in Vienna, and code-named LORD. For three years Section Y received a wealth of telephone recordings of the conversations relayed along the principal landline that ran from the Soviet military headquarters in the old Hotel Imperial to Moscow. An illicit tap had been placed on the main cable and then run along a specially dug tunnel to a small receiving station built in a neighbouring basement. Almost as soon as Blake had been indoctrinated into LORD the source dried up.

Early in January 1955 Blake was transferred from what was essentially an eavesdropping post to the Berlin Station. He admits that he 'had obtained all the operational intelligence which Section Y could provide',[24] but the KGB probably persuaded him that he should further his career by seeking a post abroad. Philby had observed that he 'could not reasonably resist a foreign posting without serious loss of standing in the service';[25] and the same was true for Blake. This move took him from processing the raw intelligence acquired from various clandestine microphone- and telephone-tapping operations around the world to just one of the many centres where the work was actually conducted, although in Berlin he was not assigned to the technical or scientific branches but to what was termed the Political Station, tasked to recruit Soviet personnel. Here the KGB assigned him a new case officer, a man he knew only as Dick. 'He was a thick-set man of about fifty with a pale complexion and a friendly twinkle in his eyes behind thick, horn-rimmed spectacles.'[26] For nearly the next five years Blake was to hold regular meetings with this man, handing over SIS's secrets on each occasion. Exactly what he betrayed during this period is known in part, for he later confirmed what he had provided to his British interrogators. He admitted, for example, that he had disclosed the full details of a technical operation code-named PRINCE which had intercepted Soviet telephone and teleprinter traffic in Berlin's Russian Zone. PRINCE was the most expensive single technical operation ever undertaken by SIS and the CIA, costing about $30m, and dated back to December 1953, when the original proposal had been discussed by the CIA with Section Y, at a meeting where the notes were taken by Blake.

A secret tunnel had been built at Rudow in the American sector extending under the boundary and into a cable conduit on the Soviet side. There British Post Office engineers helped construct what amounted to a combined telephone-switching centre and recording studio that stored on tape thousands of hours of Soviet communications. Blake had acted as the secretary to the joint CIA/SIS committee that had overseen the project and had ensured that the KGB had been alerted to it 'before even the first spade had been put in the ground'.[27] In technical terms the tunnel was an extraordinary achievement, stretching 1,776 feet, at a depth of twenty feet, to the Soviet cable conduit. That it was a genuinely practicable proposition was proved by a team of the Royal Engineers who built an identical shaft at Longmoor Camp near Kingshott in north Hampshire. Under SIS supervision the sappers established that a tunnel with a diameter of seventy-eight inches, suitably soundproofed and insulated, could be built undetected without any giveaway surface settlement. Work on the tunnel proper took seven months and elaborate steps were taken to ensure complete security. The CIA's own secret history of the project records that

> tunneling operations stopped each time the German guards walked over the tunnel on their regular patrols. Pumps were installed to take care of the excess water. Observation logs were maintained, and since the highway under obser-

> vation was the main road from East Berlin to the Schoenefeld Airport, considerable Order-of-Battle information was obtained.[28]

Air-conditioning equipment was installed to prevent the heat of all the electronic equipment from reaching the surface, thirteen and a half feet above, and perhaps melting the winter snow. The construction work was completed on 25 February 1955, six weeks after Blake's arrival in Berlin, and the first intercept was recorded successfully on 10 April. Altogether three telephone lines and one cable circuit were monitored, which together generated a vast quantity of raw materials, recorded on six banks of one hundred tape recorders located in the dummy radar station which covered the entrance to the tunnel. The volume of unprocessed tape was so great that two special centres were established, in Regents Park in London and in Washington Mall, Washington, DC to provide facilities for the dozens of *émigré* Russians employed to translate the product, which sometimes amounted to 1,200 hours a day.

Suddenly, without any warning, the tunnel was 'discovered' and closed down by Soviet troops on 22 April 1956, eighteen months after the operation had begun. At the time it was assumed that it was luck, not betrayal, that had brought the Soviets to the scene. As a contemporary CIA document states, 'Analysis of all available evidence – traffic passing on the target cables, conversations recorded from a microphone installed in the tap chamber, and vital observations from the site – indicates that the Soviet discovery of [PRINCE] was purely fortuitous.'[29] Apparently one of the telephone landlines, already in a poor condition at the start of the operation, had deteriorated after having been penetrated by moisture during a period of unusually heavy rainwater, and engineers had been sent to replace the cable. This seemed the most reasonable and logical explanation for PRINCE's demise. Despite the loss of the tunnel, the CIA and SIS continued to study the accumulated backlog of intercepts for the following twenty-nine months before the analytical end of the operation was wound down. One strange footnote to PRINCE is John Ranelagh's assertion in his respected history of the CIA, *The Agency*,[30] that the Soviets inadvertently came close to exposing Blake by transmitting compromising data on one of the tapped tunnel lines. Ranelagh says that Carl Nelson, a resourceful boffin from the CIA's Office of Communications, stumbled on to a method of decrypting Soviet enciphered text. Apparently the coding equipment used by the Soviets accidentally sent an echo-like electronic signal of a message's original clear text down the cable, which could be heard and recorded if intercepted close to the source. Thus, 'Through Carl Nelson's discovery the CIA learned that the Russians had a spy in the British Intelligence station in Berlin, although his identity [George Blake] was not discovered for several more years. Allen Dulles had the problem of alerting the British without giving Nelson's secret away.'[31] Whether Ranelagh's claim is correct is difficult to ascertain, but it is certainly true that no molehunt was initiated in SIS's Berlin Station in 1956. Indeed, had such an investigation been conducted, it would have led quite quickly to Blake, for PRINCE was only known to two people out of the 150 working in the Berlin Station: the Head of Station Peter Lunn, and Blake himself.

Blake's career was unaffected by the premature conclusion of PRINCE and he remained in Berlin, under the command of Lunn's successor Robert Dawson, until he was posted back to London in the summer of 1959. On this occasion he was assigned to a department known as Production Research, based in Artillery Mansions, Victoria Street, which had the task of recruiting contacts among British businessmen travelling abroad. Of special interest were those developing commercial links in the Eastern Bloc, and the Controller of Production Research, Blake's immediate superior, was Dickie Franks, who had been cultivating suitable agents for some years. He was an experienced intelligence officer, having previously served as

Head of Station in Tehran, after which he had returned to London as Controller Middle East. Franks, of course, was also Greville Wynne's case officer, and during the period of Blake's work in Production Research, between mid-1959 and September 1960, Wynne was reporting to Franks, but had yet to meet SIS's future star source, Colonel Oleg Penkovsky. Simultaneously, Blake had resumed contact with Nikolai Korovin, and another KGB officer whom he knew only as Vassili. He says that when Korovin 'was away . . . his place was taken by a younger man called Vassili, who differed from Korovin in that he had a much more cheerful disposition and looked typically English so that if he didn't open his mouth nobody would have dreamt of taking him for a foreigner'.[32]

In September 1960 Blake moved to the Lebanon, where he started to learn Arabic on a Foreign Office language course at Shemlan, in the hills outside Beirut; and it was from here that he received a summons back to London at the end of March 1961. The apparently innocuous request was relayed to Blake by Nicholas Elliott, then Head of Station in Beirut, but as soon as he reported to SIS's personnel department on Tuesday 4 April he was escorted across St James's Park to Carlton Gardens for interrogation. There he was confronted by a panel of four SIS officers who conducted a series of interviews which lasted until Thursday evening. The four were Harold Shergold, a colleague from Germany who had spent his career operating against the Soviets and the East Germans; John Quine, the former Head of Station in Tokyo and now head of SIS's counter-intelligence section, designated R5; Terence Lecky, another veteran of the German stations who had recently ended a two-year tour in Zurich; and an ex-policeman named Johnson. Together the four men took Blake through his career and confronted him with the mounting evidence that he had compromised virtually every operation to which he had been given access. In particular, he was challenged about the nature of his relationship with Horst Eitner, a German agent whom he had run in Berlin. Eitner had been arrested by the German police as a Soviet spy and once in custody he and his wife had denounced Blake as a KGB asset. There was other evidence, albeit of a circumstantial nature, that suggested SIS had harboured a traitor. A Polish intelligence officer, Michal Goleniewski, who had defected from Warsaw in December 1960, had proved that SIS documents had been leaking to the KGB for years. One particular paper, an annual review of SIS's performance in Poland, was positively identified by Goleniewski as having reached the Soviets, and a trace had shown that it had been distributed to Blake among others. With Eitner's damning testimony, and the failure of PRINCE and other technical surveillance operations, Blake had become a prime suspect.

There are two versions of what happened next. According to Blake he withstood the mounting pressure until Thursday afternoon, when he was accused of having sold out to the KGB for money and then been the victim of blackmail. Blake says he was outraged at this suggestion and momentarily lost control,[33] indignantly protesting that his collaboration with the Soviets had been ideologically motivated. That such a hardened professional should allow himself to be entrapped so easily sounds highly improbable, and it is not a recollection shared by those involved. The other version is that Blake successfully resisted the growing weight of evidence against him until Thursday lunchtime when, as usual, the participants broke for a midday meal. On the previous two days Blake had been allowed to wander unaccompanied through the West End and eat alone in a restaurant. On this occasion he lost his nerve and decided to seek advice from his Soviet contact. He had an emergency telephone number for Korovin and a code word to summon help, but at the very last moment, after he had approached and then circled a telephone kiosk, he decided against making the call. On his return to Carlton Gardens he was informed that his every move had been watched, and his interrogators demanded to know whom he had been thinking of telephoning. Not realising that he had been under surveillance, Blake panicked, and confessed he had thought of asking the Soviets to rescue him.

Whichever version is the truth, there is agreement about what happened next. He spent the weekend with his colleagues at a country cottage while a decision was reached about what action should be taken, and on Monday 10 April he was arrested by two Special Branch detectives, Louis Gale and Ferguson Smith. His trial lasted just one day, on 3 May 1961, because he pleaded guilty to the charges; he was sentenced to a total of forty-two years' imprisonment. It was only after Blake's appeal had been rejected that he was visited again by SIS. Curiously, Blake makes no mention of this important episode in his memoirs, but this was the first chance the Security Service had been given to question Blake and extract whatever relevant knowledge he still retained about his Soviet contacts. This was an entirely voluntary exercise, for Blake was under no obligation to receive Terence Lecky, representing his old service, and Tony Henley, MI5's principal interrogator (who habitually used the pseudonym Healey). He had passed into the criminal justice system and he had little to gain from helping his former colleagues. However, he co-operated to the full and together the two counter-intelligence experts made Blake reconstruct each meeting he had held with the KGB, and identified his three case officers, including Nikolai Korovin, and Vassili A. Dozhdalev, a first secretary. The third turned out to be Sergei A. Kondrashev, First Secretary at the Soviet Embassy since 1955, who was later to turn up attached to Soviet diplomatic missions in Austria and Bonn and, according to a KGB defector who confirmed his identity in 1962, was a key Soviet agent-handler. This unexpected source of knowledge about the KGB's First Chief Directorate was Anatoli Golitsyn, formerly attached to the Soviet Embassy in Helsinki, who revealed for the first time that 'Nikolai Korovin', the case officer who had met Blake on the Sino-Russian frontier, was actually General Nikolai Rodin.[34] Golitsyn possessed an encyclopaedic knowledge of the KGB's operations in northern Europe, and in 1962 travelled to London to help MI5. He explained that Rodin was a skilled case officer who had been appointed *Rezident* in 1949 in succession to Konstantin Kukin, an old-timer who had held the post since 1943. However, by the time Golitsyn made his revelation Rodin had already returned to Moscow.

During his long debriefing sessions held in Wormwood Scrubs Prison, which continued until the end of September 1962, Blake admitted that he had indiscriminately photographed everything that passed over his desk and given all of it to the Soviets. Considering that Philby had been fired from SIS in November 1951, the material supplied by Blake must have been of enormous value to the KGB, as Blake represented, as far as is now known, their sole source of information from within SIS. There is, none the less, some continuing doubt about exactly what intelligence disasters Blake could be held personally responsible for. He freely admitted his role in compromising PRINCE in Berlin, but he had so comprehensively betrayed SIS's secrets that he himself was not entirely sure of the details or of the scale of what he had done. An interesting case in point is that of Piotr S. Popov, a GRU officer run by the CIA since his recruitment in Vienna in 1953. According to one of his case officers, William Hood,[35] Major Popov had been transferred to Moscow in the autumn of 1955, where it had proved impossible for the CIA to communicate with him. Popov had been supplied with a list of dead-letter drops in Moscow, where he could leave messages for the CIA, but apparently he was unimpressed by the locations chosen and had dropped from sight. It subsequently emerged that the CIA station chief in Moscow at that time, Edward Ellis Smith,[36] had himself been compromised by the KGB and had been withdrawn more or less simultaneously with Popov's assignment to Germany. His reappearance in East Germany at the end of July 1956, without a method of re-establishing contact with the CIA, had forced him to take emergency action sometime the following year.

Popov had been instructed that, in the last resort, he could always reach the CIA by asking any American serviceman to relay a message. Perhaps unwisely, Popov attempted to do just that by slipping a six-page letter to two officers who were touring the Soviet Zone, as they were entitled to do under the quadripartite occupation treaty. However, the men he approached were not American but British and they in turn dutifully passed the message to the SIS station in Berlin . . . not direct to the CIA. SIS did eventually clear it for onward transmission to their American counterparts, but it is Hood's firm belief that Blake seized the opportunity to convey the contents of the letter to the KGB so that they could track down Popov. Blake emphatically denies his involvement, asserting that although he probably identified 'four hundred'[37] SIS agents to the KGB he had done so 'on the express understanding that they would not come to any harm'.[38] If he really received such an assurance, it is incredible that he should have believed it. Anyway, the question arises as to whether or not he was directly responsible for betraying Popov, who certainly did come to harm. In fact he was pitched live into a blazing furnace in front of an audience selected from among his GRU colleagues. Blake says in his defence that, firstly, he was not the proper conduit for liaison with the CIA in Berlin and therefore he would not have had access to Popov's note. He also suggests that the date of 1955, given by Montgomery Hyde as the year the supposed betrayal took place, does not tally with Popov's arrest, which did not occur until October 1959; and finally casts doubt on Popov's grisly fate, insisting that 'such a fact would have been kept a close secret in any country, let alone in a country as secretive as the Soviet Union'.[39]

All three issues can in fact be resolved. Since Blake admits he cannot be certain about what he photographed, his claim that he would not ordinarily have seen information destined for the local CIA station in Berlin does not deserve much credence. Following publication of his own book Blake gave a television interview in which he adjusted the figure of 'four hundred agents' to 'five hundred or six hundred',[40] so he clearly has not given much thought to the fate of those he delivered up to the KGB. According to William Hood, Popov's six-page letter, written in Russian, had been translated by the SIS officer with whom Blake shared an office. Thus the document was never alleged to have passed through Blake's hands, but it was a chance remark, about the CIA having acquired a GRU source, that alerted Blake. As for the delay in Popov's eventual arrest, it was not the four-year gap that Montgomery Hyde's version of events suggests, and which Blake sought to discredit. He mistakenly implied that the note-passing incident had occurred in Germany in 1955 or soon afterwards, when William Hood is quite specific that the episode happened rather later, in the spring of 1957. It may well be that the contents of the note were insufficiently compromising for the KGB to track down Popov immediately. In any event, although Popov was not arrested until October 1959, it is known for certain that prior to that date he had come under KGB control and an attempt was made to run him as a double agent. Whilst no exact date can be put on the moment Popov was identified as the CIA's source, many commentators have held that General Mikhail A. Shalin's sudden resignation as head of the GRU in December 1958, and his replacement by the dreaded Ivan Serov of the KGB, is probably the best indication. Clearly, whatever the catalyst for Shalin's removal, it must have been extraordinarily serious, and the transfer of Serov from the KGB suggests strongly that the incident had been a major failure in the GRU's security. On that basis the KGB's molehunt had been completed within eighteen months, which is not unreasonable.

Finally, as for the dreadful circumstances of Popov's gruesome execution, a GRU officer who defected to the West in June 1978, Vladimir Rezun, has given a graphic account in his autobiography *Aquarium*[41] (written under the pseudonym Viktor Suvorov) of an initiation ceremony undergone by recruits into the Soviet military intelligence organisation. He describes having had the distasteful experience of being made to watch an old black-and-white home movie of a traitor's execution:

> Once again I can see before me the colonel's face at the very last moment when his feet are already in the fire, but his head is still living, blood is still circulating and his eyes reflect the powerful intellect, the fear of death, the cruel torture and an unconquerable desire to live.[42]

Although Rezun does not name the wretched GRU officer, and gives his rank as colonel, while Popov was a major (but is mentioned occasionally as a lieutenant-colonel), his testimony does serve to support the claim that the GRU was not averse to the ruthless despatch of traitors. Whether Blake was truly responsible for this horrific incident cannot be verified, but he has shown no remorse for what he did and at his trial he even instructed his defence counsel, Jeremy Hutchinson QC, not to tell the judge during his plea for mitigation that he harboured any regrets. As a professional who had willingly betrayed his country, and had made a determined effort over a period of seven years to inflict maximum damage to SIS, Blake richly deserved his punishment. However, the severity of the sentence persuaded several other prisoners in Wormwood Scrubs that the Lord Chief Justice had been too harsh, and three in particular plotted his escape. Sean Bourke, Pat Pottle and Michael Randle offered Blake their services, and following their own release helped Blake to disappear on 22 October 1966.

Bourke was an Irish criminal who had served a seven-year sentence for mailing a letter bomb to a detective in Sussex against whom he had a personal grudge. Strangely, Oleg Gordievsky says that Bourke was a member of the IRA, but there was nothing political about Bourke's crime and he had never previously been accused of terrorism. Randle and Pottle were political activists who had been imprisoned with a group of others for eighteen months for their part in an anti-nuclear demonstration at RAF Wethersfield in Essex in December 1961. Together the three men had agreed to find and finance a safe house for Blake, with whom they communicated by two-way radio, if he managed to scale one of the perimeter walls. Through a series of security lapses Blake was able to approach the wall under cover of darkness one wet Saturday evening and climb a home-made rope ladder thrown over the top by Bourke. According to *The Blake Escape*[43] – the account subsequently published unapologetically by Randle and Pottle, which coincides in almost every respect with the versions given by Sean Bourke in his *The Springing of George Blake*[44] – the spy hid for the next two months in London, nursing the fractured wrist he had sustained in his fall to freedom from the prison wall. Then he was driven by Randle and his wife in a concealed compartment of a camper van to Berlin, where he was welcomed to the Eastern Bloc by one of his KGB contacts, Vassili Dozhdalev, who happened by coincidence to be in the Soviet Zone at the time, and therefore available to confirm Blake's identity. Having dropped Blake off in Berlin, Randle and his wife (and two young children, brought along as additional cover) motored back to London via Ostend and resumed their life.

Blake's audacious escape prompted a major review of prison security, conducted by Earl Mountbatten with a panel of three assessors and given expert advice in secret by a veteran intelligence officer, Tony Brooks. He was especially well qualified to help Mountbatten, having parachuted twice into France to work for the wartime resistance, for which he was decorated with the Distinguished Service Order and the Military Cross. Aged only twenty, he had been the youngest agent sent by SOE into the field, and he had worked continuously in the underground between July 1942 and the Liberation, apart from a period of ten weeks spent in England for briefing, and three days spent in prison. Since the war he had operated for SIS in Sofia, Belgrade and Cyprus, and more recently had transferred to MI5, where he was to score some impressive achievements, including the recruitment of a KGB defector at the Soviet Embassy in London. Brooks's contribution to the Mountbatten review[45] was to go deliberately unacknowledged in the report which was drawn up by the inquiry's secretary, (Sir) Philip Woodfield, so as to protect his identity. Woodfield, of course, was an ideal choice because, until the previous year when he had moved to the Home Office, he had been private secretary to three successive prime ministers and therefore considered the very soul of discretion. His report, published in December 1966, just as Blake was settling into his new life in Moscow, cast no fresh light on exactly how Blake had managed to elude the police but it did highlight several flaws in prison security which, too late, were tightened up.

Blake's incredible escape baffled both the police and the Security Service, and their inability to solve the mystery led to several rumours about his possible role as a double or triple agent. One theory, subsequently reproduced uncritically by Bernard Porter in *Plots and Paranoia*, suggested that Blake 'when he was first discovered to be spying for the Russians was asked to carry on, as a double agent for Britain'.[46] A similar theme was adopted by James Rusbridger, who concluded that 'Blake's escape was the result of a deal between MI6 and the KGB. MI6 was very shocked at the severity of Blake's 42-year sentence. They saw it as a betrayal of their promise that by making a full confession Blake would be more leniently treated and felt that such a heavy sentence would deter any future traitors from confessing.'[47] Certainly those SIS officers privy to the case were dismayed that a decision had been taken on the very highest level to prosecute Blake, but no offers or inducements made to him to extract a confession. His statement to Detective Superintendent Ferguson Smith, made under caution, was to be the basis of the charges preferred against him. It may well be that those who would have opted to keep this embarrassing case out of the courts did not fully appreciate the political implications of suppressing such a matter, following as it did only a month after Gordon Lonsdale and the other members of the Portland spy-ring had each received substantial sentences in a well-publicised prosecution. Indeed, in that case Lonsdale, a KGB professional, had been given a sentence of twenty-five years by the same judge, Lord Parker, so Blake must have known what the current rate was likely to be. Therefore there can be little to substantiate the idea that SIS conspired with the KGB to free Blake from a sentence perceived to be savage. One unforeseen consequence of this interesting but misguided speculation was the caution with which Blake was eventually welcomed to Moscow. Apparently even the KGB found it hard to believe that their man could have engineered his own escape with just £700 and the help of two naïve peace campaigners and a hard-drinking Irishman. Nevertheless, a month after his arrival he was decorated with the Order of Lenin.

SIS may have calculated that with most of the evidence against Blake being heard in camera, and the imposition of a D-notice to prevent press speculation, his embarrassment value to the government would be kept to a minimum. No expulsion of Soviet diplomats was necessary, Nikolai Korovin having already slipped out of the country, and Blake's wife, who had herself served in SIS as a secretary, could be relied upon to maintain a discreet silence about the nature of her husband's work, even if the Prime Minister had a little disingenuously distanced the Foreign Office from Blake by assuring the Commons that he 'had never been an established member of the Foreign Service'.[48] However, Blake's true function quickly leaked to Fleet Street and word spread that Blake had received a year of his sentence for every British agent he had betrayed. The government must have been further irritated when it was alleged in 1964 that Blake had not been segregated from Gordon Lonsdale in C Hall, one of five prison wings in the Scrubs. The Home Secretary, Henry Brooke, denied the allegation in response to a Parliamentary Question, but Blake (and some other ex-prisoners) are adamant that he and Lonsdale met regularly each afternoon while taking their daily half-hour exercise in the yard.[49]

The reality was that both MI6 and the Security Service were keen to find out how Blake had left the country and who had been involved. Their initial list of suspects included Sean Bourke – who had been discharged from the Scrubs just three months before the escape – Michael Randle and Pat Pottle, as all three had been friendly to Blake in prison, and Randle had sent Blake a Christmas card after his release. When MI5 obtained a pre-publication copy of Bourke's book, *The Springing of George Blake*, the conclusion was reached that the two central conspirators referred to as 'Pat Porter' and 'Michael Reynolds'[50] were Pat Pottle and Michael Randle. Both men exactly matched Bourke's descriptions. They both had an Irish mother and English father,[51] and Reynolds had a wife called Anne and two small children, and lived in Camden in a 'modest house' with a 'modest income'.[52] Pottle was indeed 'a couple of years younger than Michael', lived in a flat and had 'recently started a little business' with some friends[53] (in fact it was an antiques business). Although MI5 and Special Branch recognised the implications of Bourke's story, no attempt was made by the police to interview either of his fellow conspirators. A warrant had been issued for Bourke's arrest, but he had successfully fought an extradition hearing in Dublin in February 1969, and died in 1982, refusing to the last to name his helpers even though he had long since fallen out with Blake. There the matter rested until 1987, when H. Montgomery Hyde published his biography of George Blake and disclosed that Pat Porter and Michael Reynolds 'had belonged to the Committee of 100, the nuclear disarmament group formed by Bertrand Russell'.[54] He stated that the pair had been imprisoned from 1961 to 1963 because they had 'helped to organise the civil disobedience at Wethersfield RAF base in December 1961',[55] and thereby effectively identified their real names, because only six people had been tried for the incident at Wethersfield. They were Helen Allegranza,

Terry Chandler, Ian Dixon, Trevor Hatton, Patrick Pottle and Michael Randle. There could be little doubt who 'Pat Porter' and 'Michael Reynolds' were meant to be. As a former lawyer, Member of Parliament, wartime SIS officer and distinguished author, Hyde's confident assertion carried great weight. Confronted by newspaper journalists, the pair admitted their involvement. Pottle was still in the antiques trade in north London while Randle had moved to Bradford where he had been appointed a lecturer in peace studies. Responding to the sudden media interest in what they had done nearly a quarter of a century earlier, they wrote their own account, forcing the authorities to prosecute them. Clearly, declining to sue newspapers and authors who had named them was one thing, but openly boasting of what they had accomplished was quite another. The first trial, held in 1990, was delayed by a legal wrangle over the lengthy delay in bringing proceedings, with the defence arguing that a decision had been taken more than twenty years earlier not to pursue Randle and Pottle even though their complicity had become known to Special Branch and the Security Service. Retired officers of both organisations gave evidence, and during the course of the hearings it was disclosed, but not explained, by ex-Commander Rollo Watts of Scotland Yard that no further enquiries had been made of Randle and Pottle even though they were believed to have been responsible for aiding Blake's escape. Nor, for that matter, has anyone suggested why Bourke chose to incriminate his two friends in his book. Blake was among those who was appalled when he read Bourke's story and realised how easy it would be for the British authorities to identify Randle and Pottle.

Blake's original autobiography, entitled *No Abiding City*, was written at much the same time as Bourke's book, but no Western publisher who examined it was prepared to buy the manuscript. Robin Denniston of the Oxford University Press recalls accompanying an American colleague named Hal Schalatt to Moscow in 1968 to read it, but they found it dull fare. Instead

Denniston wrote a brief report on its contents for SIS upon his return and was entertained to lunch by MI5's long-serving Legal Adviser, Bernard Sheldon, in a private room at St Ermin's Hotel with a party of interested SIS officers. Their intention, obviously, was to determine whether Blake had the capacity to inflict further damage on SIS from behind the Iron Curtain. Their conclusion was that he had probably done enough mischief and although publication of Blake's book might well offend the public it would be unlikely to have any operational relevance to the Service. Since that very subjective assessment, a law has been passed to prevent former security and intelligence officers from capitalising in print on their experiences, but no attempt was made either to prevent the release in 1990 of an updated version of *No Abiding City*, entitled *No Other Choice*. Perhaps this may have surprised or even disappointed the English publisher, who went to elaborate lengths to conceal his intentions. Either way a substantial advance was paid for the manuscript and it is understood that various Sunday newspapers also competed to acquire the serial rights. As far as is known the Crown has not bothered formally to sequester these royalties.

Blake's career as a spy lasted for seven years, from the moment of his first interrogation in Korea in 1951 to his arrest nearly ten years later. However, his value to the Soviets extended well beyond that period, for he certainly had useful information to impart after he escaped to Moscow, filling in the inevitable blanks in the messages he had conveyed earlier, and helping the KGB to spot previously unidentified SIS personnel overseas in 1966. From the Soviet standpoint Blake must have been able to supply a wealth of information to which Philby had never gained access. Blake says that while he was in SIS he never met, and had never even heard of, Philby. 'This is not so strange if one bears in mind . . . we had worked in quite different fields; he in counter-espionage and I in espionage.'[56] His offer to work for the KGB came at a time when Philby had been excluded from SIS, so the Soviets could double-check his material against what Philby had already provided, and give the continuity in the flow of data which is the ambition of every case officer.

There is good reason to believe that Blake played a part (albeit unconscious) in betraying at least two GRU officers who volunteered to help the West. Piotr Popov was probably traced as a result of Blake's tip in 1957, having learnt from his office colleague that the CIA had acquired a good Soviet intelligence source. He may also have been instrumental in Colonel Oleg Penkovsky's arrest in October 1962, even though that event took place while he was in Wormwood Scrubs. The SIS Head of Station in Moscow who had run Penkovsky in 1961, and whose wife had relayed messages from him, was Ruari Chisholm. When the Chisholms were posted to the Soviet Union in May 1960, SIS believed that he had survived his tour of duty in Berlin without having been identified as an SIS officer. Blake's interrogators realised too late that for four years he had worked alongside Blake, who confirmed that he had told the KGB of his role. Thus the Chisholm family had been under intensive surveillance from the moment they had arrived in Moscow, which in turn had made it very unlikely that Penkovsky could escape detection.

Whether Blake's life in the Soviet Union has proved rewarding is doubtful. Jews have been discriminated against by the Communist regime in recent years as mercilessly as ever, and he has been cut off from his elderly mother who, now very frail, lives in Holland and cannot travel. The irony is that for all of the severity of his term of imprisonment in England, he would today be free, perhaps still living with his first wife and his two adored sons, if he had stayed to serve out his sentence.

CHAPTER VI

Francis Gary Powers

The meeting, held in a CIA safe house, a villa at 3 Litzensee-strasse in the American Sector of West Berlin, was tense. The two participants were Piotr S. Popov, a major in the Soviet military intelligence service, the GRU, and George Kisevalter, a case officer from the Soviet Russia Division of the CIA's Directorate of Operations. This particular rendezvous was just one of dozens that had been held since Popov first unexpectedly volunteered to spy for the Americans in Vienna back in November 1952. His technique for making contact with his CIA case officer had not changed since he had been transferred from Austria to East Berlin. He would habitually travel into the Western sector on the elevated S-bahn to the See Ufer Bahnhof, as he was authorised to do, and then jump into a car driven by his CIA contact at an agreed place and time, usually the Muellerstrasse. Then Popov would be taken to a safe house and debriefed over a leisurely meal, with plenty of vodka supplied. At the conclusion of the meeting Popov would be dropped back close to a crossing point for his journey home to the suburb of Schwerin.

What made this meeting, held sometime late in 1958, so special was a single item of information conveyed by Popov. He mentioned that he had recently heard a drunken Soviet officer bragging in the officers' club in Karlshorst about how the KGB had acquired 'full technical details on a special high-altitude aircraft the CIA had been flying over the Soviet Union'.[1] Although this snippet of intelligence meant little to Kisevalter, who had not been privy to the secret of the U-2 overflights which had commenced three years earlier, or to anyone else in the CIA's Berlin base, it rang alarm bells in Washington, DC, where the Deputy Director for Plans, Dick Helms, immediately informed the project manager, Richard Bissell, that his operation, code-named ACQUATONE, appeared to have sprung a leak.

Bissell had supervised the development of the U-2 aircraft since the concept of an ultra-high-altitude reconnaissance plane was dreamt up in 1954. No project was considered more secret, and while ACQUATONE was active it was administered in separate accommodation, a comfortable town house on the north side of H Street, well away from the CIA's offices around the Reflecting Pool by the Lincoln Memorial. The idea had been to build a single-seater, jet-powered glider that could operate at heights comfortably above the maximum ceiling of Soviet missiles and interceptors for many hours at a time. The latest Soviet anti-aircraft missile, the SAM-2 *Guideline*, was reckoned to be accurate up to sixty thousand feet, and only capable of reaching seventy thousand feet in an unguided state. The CIA calculated that if its twin criteria of height and duration could be met, the entire Soviet Union could be overflown at will, and every sensitive location in the Eastern Bloc mapped. Sophisticated photographic equipment that covered an area a hundred miles wide had already been designed and tested, but until the advent of the U-2 no suitable platform for this equipment existed.

In strategic terms the U-2 project would give the West an unprecedented advantage in the Cold War. The key, of course, was to ensure complete security over the entire undertaking, for although the Soviets were bound to spot and even track the unusual aircraft on its defence radar, they would be powerless to interdict the flights unless they somehow acquired detailed knowledge of the plane and its operating procedures. Critical to Soviet counter-measures would be data relating to the plane's height and speed, so the news conveyed by Kisevalter from

Berlin, that the KGB had acquired just such intelligence, caused considerable anxiety back at headquarters. 'It brought me right out of my seat. Bissell and I wondered where they could be getting their information from,' recalled Helms.

The U-2 was a unique plane and the CIA had taken elaborate precautions to conceal its development of a prototype and the deployment of twenty aircraft. It had been designed and constructed by hand in conditions of great secrecy by Lockheed at the 'skunk works' in Burbank, and although the very existence of the U-2 could not remain classified, its purposes and capabilities most certainly were. A comprehensive cover plan was prepared, in which the U-2 was assigned ostensibly harmless tasks, such as climate research, for civilian agencies like the Air Weather Service and NASA's predecessor, the National Advisory Committee on Aeronautics. However, in parallel a clandestine US Air Force unit, designated Detachment 10-10, started to fly missions from Wiesbaden along the Iron Curtain. Its maiden flight, deep into Soviet territory, the first of a total of twenty, took place on Wednesday 4 July 1956, when a U-2 flew from Germany over Moscow and Leningrad before returning safely to base. More flights followed over the weekend, but on 10 July the Soviet Ambassador in Washington delivered a formal protest to the State Department, which in response denied all knowledge of the offending flights. In reality only a handful of senior members of the administration knew anything at all about ACQUATONE. Thereafter each incursion was authorised individually by President Eisenhower, with an additional sanction from Prime Minister Harold Macmillan for those flights originating from the U-2's other European home, RAF Lakenheath in England.

According to the 1959 edition of *Jane's*, the U-2 could attain an altitude of sixty-five thousand feet for a period of up to four hours, whereas in reality the plane could cruise comfortably for nearly nine hours at around eighty thousand feet. This was exactly the kind of performance data that the CIA was so anxious to keep from its Soviet counterparts. The Agency was also keen to protect the secrets of GRANGER, an ingenious electronic counter-measures device fitted into the tail of every plane, which emitted signals to confuse the SAM-2's guidance radar.

That the KGB had long expressed an interest in the U-2 had been recognised since 1958, when cars with Soviet diplomats would park at the end of the runway in Wiesbaden and watch the unusual aircraft soar into the sky. As a precaution the CIA had shifted to a more discreet and remote location, Giebelstadt, but that too eventually came under observation by the KGB. The Soviets undoubtedly knew that the U-2 had a reconnaissance role, and had probably monitored flights from its various different operating bases. The U-2 deployment to Lakenheath had been given some unfortunate publicity on 1 June 1956 when *Flight* magazine reported the appearance of the strange craft over Suffolk. Other bases included Incirlik in Turkey, Atsugi in Japan, Lahore and Peshawar in Pakistan, and Bödo in Norway. Indeed, the Red Air Force newspaper *Soviet Aviation* published an article about the U-2, describing it as 'the black lady of espionage'. There was also interest in the U-2 in the West. In March 1958 *Model Airplane News* reported that 'an unconfirmed rumour says that U-2s are flying across the Iron Curtain taking aerial photographs'. Occasionally the distinctive matt-black plane made the news in other ways. In September 1959 a U-2 made an embarrassingly public emergency landing at a glider club's field ten miles short of Atsugi, having experienced fuel starvation, and the incident received much publicity, despite the efforts of armed US military policemen, who arrived on the scene by helicopter minutes later.

The Soviets also learnt more about the U-2 from an American defector, a US Marine radar operator who had been posted to Atsugi while U-2s were conducting routine operations there. The defector received his discharge from the Marines in September 1959, after three years' service, and travelled to London and Helsinki before arriving in Moscow by train on 15 October.

He remained in the Soviet Union continuously for the next thirty months until June 1963, and although it is the CIA's belief that this individual, Lee Harvey Oswald,[2] who was later to acquire world-wide notoriety in another role, was a source for the KGB's detailed information about the U-2, Piotr Popov must have been referring to another when he spoke to Kisevalter. That conversation had taken place in Berlin in November 1958, eleven months before Oswald reached the Soviet capital. By an odd coincidence, one of Popov's CIA contacts, Russell Langelle, was arrested by the KGB while passing a note to him on the very day Oswald arrived in Moscow.[3]

It is, therefore, quite likely that Popov's warning to the CIA had been a reference to an entirely different source, and there is some evidence to show that the KGB had concentrated its not inconsiderable resources on learning more about the U-2. One example is Selmer Nilsen, a Norwegian convicted for spying for the Soviets, who alleged that he had been under instructions to keep the Bödo airfield under observation and report the movements of U-2 aircraft.

Despite its fragile airframe and its complete lack of any armament, the U-2 was one of the most revolutionary achievements in intelligence-gathering. For the first time an adversary could penetrate an opponent's airspace at will and take photographs of astonishing clarity from an altitude of three miles or more. Nor were the American flights made exclusively over Soviet territory. The U-2s roamed across Eastern Europe and the Middle East, charted French missile experiments in the Sahara and operated from Formosa to monitor the development of a Chinese atomic bomb. The U-2 was of special significance to the Western Alliance because, for the first time, a truly reliable source of information had been achieved about what was happening behind the Iron Curtain. It is only by putting the then current state of play into context that the U-2 can be fully understood.[4]

Only rarely during the decade following the end of the Second

World War did the West obtain even the most fleeting glimpse into what was taking place inside the Soviet Union. The intelligence environment was considered so hostile that even the CIA opted not to establish a station in the US Embassy in Moscow until 1954, and when it did so the first Chief of Station, Edward Ellis Smith, was soon compromised by the KGB in a classic honeytrap. A thirty-four-year-old divorcee, Smith started an affair with his attractive Russian maid, and in July 1956 was hastily withdrawn from Moscow after rumours circulated that they had been photographed in bed together. There were no high-level sources of information in the Kremlin, the last being a British agent who had been arrested and executed in 1941. Whilst the West received a steady trickle of low-echelon line-crossers in Berlin and Vienna, few had enjoyed access to really useful data, and certainly nothing with any strategic value. The West's experience behind the Iron Curtain had been consistently unsuccessful. Even the GIDEON case, which had promised to be the exception to the rule, had come unstuck. GIDEON was a KGB 'illegal' who either was, or called himself, David Soboloff, the son of Russian immigrants who had moved to Canada in the 1920s, and had worked for Amtorg, the Comintern front trading organisation in New York.[5] Soboloff had been born in Canada and therefore was perfectly entitled to settle there after his parents returned to the Soviet Union. However, having travelled back to Montreal in 1952, and acquired a Canadian mistress, Soboloff had approached the RCMP Security Service in November 1953 and revealed his clandestine mission for the KGB. The RCMP had responded by enrolling Soboloff as a double agent, dubbing him GIDEON. For the next two years GIDEON helped the Canadians identify other Soviet intelligence personnel, and when he was recalled to Moscow for what were described by the KGB as 'routine consultations', the RCMP reluctantly agreed that he should go. In Moscow arrangements were made with SIS to maintain contact because the Canadians had no suitable facilities in the Russian capital.

GIDEON arrived safely, and continued to leave signals for SIS for only a short period before he simply disappeared. The British and Canadians concluded that GIDEON must have inadvertently incriminated himself, and suffered the consequences at the hands of the KGB. The whole episode served to highlight the immense difficulties involved in running an agent in Moscow's xenophobic atmosphere, and resulted in the loss of someone who, in the opinion of Terry Guernsey, then head of the RCMP's counter-espionage branch, was 'the most valuable double agent the West had had since the Second World War'.

It was the same dismal picture right across the international counter-intelligence front, with only a handful of Soviet defectors switching sides. Apart from Vladimir and Evdokia Petrov, the KGB *rezident* in Canberra and his wife, who opted to stay in Australia when they were recalled to Moscow at the end of their tour of duty in April 1954, the West received very few field operatives, and no one who could offer an authentic insight into Soviet intentions. Although the Petrovs exposed the existence of a massive spy network in Australia, they had little to offer when it came to interpreting the political nuances of the post-Stalin era. In short, the West was powerless to know what was happening inside the Politburo. Whilst the Soviets could rely on legions of illicit sources, agents of influence and fellow travellers to keep it informed on the very latest technical achievements in the West, neither the CIA nor SIS could boast the same. In consequence, the West's strategic assessments were in general hopelessly inadequate, as is demonstrated by the way in which the West was caught out in Korea. Without any warning whatever the Communist regime in the north had launched its invasion in 1950, taking the United States completely unawares. Of greatest concern was the lack of knowledge about the latest Soviet advances in atomic weaponry. That the Soviets had successfully detonated an atomic device in August 1949, and had been testing continuously thereafter at Novaya Zemlya and Semipalatinsk, was public knowledge. Seismic apparatus sited in neighbouring countries and high-altitude air-sampling had kept the Pentagon planners informed on the pace of Soviet research, as had the routine debriefing of emigrating technicians and the blanket interrogation of repatriated German scientists captured during the war and transported eastwards. Western travellers in Russia were also encouraged to keep their eyes open, particularly when flying internally, and the CIA employed a domestic-contacts division to debrief selected returning visitors, the so-called 'directed tourists'. The CIA also scrutinised all Soviet technical publications for clues to scientific progress, and heavy reliance was placed on the interception of signals from Soviet missile ranges; radar stations located in Iran and Turkey obtained telemetry data that enabled analysts to deduce the level of progress made in developing a strategic delivery system. The unanswered question, however, was the degree of accuracy of the official strategic assessments circulated at the highest level in NATO. Who could say whether they were wide of the mark or spot-on?

That the Soviets already boasted sufficient numbers of medium-range bombers to pose a credible threat was widely accepted in the West. In April 1954 an American air attaché reported spotting 'between twelve and twenty' of the new long-range bomber designated *Bison*. The proof had been demonstrated to observers at an airshow which opened on Aviation Day, 3 July 1955, at the Tushino military airfield outside Moscow. Three new bombers were given their début, the MYA-4 and two Tupolevs, the TU-16 and the TU-95, and the air attachés present had counted dozens of each aircraft, not realising that in fact only a single squadron was being flown continuously over the airfield, circling out of sight only to appear again in yet another impressive fly-past. Estimates of Soviet bomber strengths based on this single episode, working on the rough and ready principle that double the number observed must have been built, led to some extraordinarily exaggerated assessments of Soviet bomber production, and consequently to the so-called 'bomber gap', the narrowing difference between American and

Soviet inventories. Using this deeply flawed formula, the USAF decided that the Red Air Force would overtake Strategic Air Command in bomber strength by 1959. Having successfully deceived the West over bomber strengths, the Soviets proceeded to create further alarm over the relative success it had achieved in the development of a viable intercontinental missile.

The first Soviet rockets were almost exclusively based on German wartime designs and – until tests conducted at Kapustin Yar in 1957, watched on radar from the West – they were limited to relatively small systems. Most were variations of the *Guideline*, the most modern surface-to-air missile, which posed no strategic threat whatever. However, by late 1956 nearly fifty separate tests had been monitored which were on a rather larger scale. Then on 26 August 1957 TASS confirmed that a multi-stage ballistic missile had been launched successfully. Two months later *Sputnik 1* was put into an earth orbit on a huge booster, an eloquent demonstration of Soviet achievement in the space race. Indeed, Khrushchev announced that he had control of twenty other similar rockets, all with an ICBM capability, a claim that was accepted generally at face value and caused consternation in Washington and London. Although some experts may have been inclined to challenge Khrushchev's statement that warheads and satellites were interchangeable on the Soviet booster, only the CIA possessed the means of checking.

Located seventy-five miles east of Stalingrad, the 'cosmodrome' at Kapustin Yar was out of range of the reconnaissance aircraft that routinely patrolled the skies close to the Soviet border. The U-2 allowed the entire area to be photographed in detail on special filmstrips twelve thousand feet long that were duplicated after exposure and then flown to Westover Air Force Base for onward delivery to HT/AUTOMAT, the code name of Arthur Lundahl's legendary photo-interpretation laboratory located on the corner of Fifth and K Streets in Washington, DC. Simultaneously, a magnetic tape of radar emissions and other intercepted radio signals was couriered for analysis to the National Security Agency at Fort Meade, near Baltimore. From Lundahl's unremarkable office in an unfashionable part of downtown Washington, DC, his skilled analysts watched every Soviet development, and in August 1957 actually caught on celluloid an ICBM on the launchpad at Kapustin Yar. There were two immediate consequences of this new, more reliable source of information: a revision downwards of the previous US estimates of *Bison* heavy bombers, and the conclusion that the Kremlin had decided to concentrate its resources not on expanding its bomber force, but on an accelerated ICBM programme. The Soviet ICBM project had begun in earnest in the spring of 1957 with half a dozen tests, followed in August by two launches which achieved a range of 3,500 miles.

The Russian breakthrough resulted in a comprehensive review of Soviet capabilities, conducted by a joint civilian and military committee, and culminated in what was to become known as the Gaither Report, which was circulated under a top-secret classification on 7 November 1957. The report noted that the Americans had so far failed to launch their own ICBM, the Atlas, and anticipated a deployment of up to ten operational Soviet ICBMs by early 1959. Although the successful insertion of *Sputnik 1* into orbit had been a tremendous accomplishment, it was evident from the continuing tests that the Soviets still had some way to go before they were likely to perfect all the techniques required to guide a ballistic missile to a target three thousand miles away.

No sooner had the CIA released its predictions to Congress than the Soviets inexplicably suspended their ICBM test programme; it was not resumed until March 1959, when it suddenly restarted at an unprecedented rate of four tests a month. In an equally sinister development, the Soviets began nuclear testing again in September 1958 after a lull of six months. The CIA revised its estimates accordingly in the following November to show a smaller number of operational Soviet ICBMs, now designated SS-6. It was a huge, unwieldy booster, a full ninety-five feet long, that required a tracked permanent way to transport it into its final launch position. There was considerable mystery surrounding this particular missile, for although it was spotted by the U-2 at Kapustin Yar and at the other Soviet test site at Tyuratam, east of the Aral Sea, its characteristic railway lines could not be found anywhere else, leading some analysts to conclude that, contrary to Khrushchev's public pronouncements, it was not really intended for operational deployment.

Although the U-2 had proved itself invaluable in correcting the Pentagon's gross over-estimates of Soviet power, there were still persistent doubts about Soviet intentions. Subject to good visibility and presidential approval, the U-2 could determine the physical location of Soviet hardware (but there were limitations: it could not discern what obstacles had been encountered by Soviet technicians, nor determine what plans had been formulated for eventual deployment). Indeed, the two restrictions of weather and political sanction were occasionally insurmountable. Cloud cover in the winter and heavy bands of fog in the summer handicapped even the U-2's sophisticated cameras, and President Eisenhower had twice banned overflights, at the end of June 1956 when the Vice-Chief of the US Air Force, General Nathan Twining, visited Moscow, and from 15 to 28 September 1959 while Khrushchev had been touring the United States. Although greatly dependent upon the U-2, Eisenhower had no wish to be provocative at moments of diplomatic sensitivity.

By the spring of 1960 there was considerable pressure on the CIA to resolve the remaining mysteries regarding the SS-6. How many had been constructed, and had any been deployed anywhere apart from the two sites already recorded? One possibility was Plesetsk in the far north, six hundred miles from Moscow, where – according to radio intercepts and other information, possibly from human sources – an ICBM base was under construction. There was also a wide variation in the number of missiles believed to have come off the production line. In 1959 the CIA suggested a Soviet inventory of one hundred ICBMs by 1960. However, the US Air Force gave a figure five times greater and predicted 1,100 by mid-1961. Was the true number somewhere between the two estimates, or was it entirely different? In the absence of any well-placed mole, only the U-2 was judged to hold the key to the puzzle. The CIA's best agent in the Soviet Union, Piotr Popov, was known to have been in the KGB's hands at least since his rendezvous with Russell Langelle on a Moscow bus on 16 October 1959, and in all probability had been detected as a spy in December 1958. Subsequently he had been executed, convicted of supplying the CIA with the GRU's secrets since 1952. Included in the material he compromised was, according to Bill Hood, who was one of his CIA handlers, 'data on missiles and guidance systems'.[6] Whether any of this data was relevant to NATO's search for the SS-6 missiles is unknown, but Eisenhower had consistently declined to authorise any U-2 overflights after he had entertained Nikita Khrushchev for the weekend at the presidential retreat at Camp David at the end of his tour the previous September. This hiatus, which lasted six months, was to have profound implications for the balance of power because the CIA had no alternative source of information on which to fall back.

The fact that the Pentagon had been receiving sharply differing advice was known to the Kremlin through a Soviet agent, Colonel William H. Whalen, who worked for the Joint Chiefs of Staff and had access to the National Intelligence Estimates for 1959 and 1960. He subsequently confessed to having been in touch with two GRU officers in Washington, Mikhail M. Shumaev and Colonel Sergei A. Edenski, from December 1959 onwards. Whalen was not arrested until July 1966, and in March the following year he was to be sentenced to fifteen years' imprisonment. Thus the Soviets were fully aware of the American dilemma and may even have been in a position to exploit it. However, whether or not the Soviets knew of the importance attached to the overflight scheduled for the beginning of April

1960, much was to hang on its success, as it was the U-2's first opportunity to look at the suspected ICBM base at Plesetsk. Examination of the developed filmstrip was likely to solve the missile-gap conundrum once and for all, and this may have been the key argument in persuading President Eisenhower to give his consent to the CIA for a further U-2 overflight. When the CIA submitted its request it also highlighted the restricted amount of time in which it was obliged to operate. It pointed out that the weather conditions prevalent in Plesetsk's latitude would only allow aerial photography between April and July, when the angle of the sun would cast shadows from vertical structures that would ease the task of the analysts. If the President delayed, he was warned, it might not be possible to mount another mission until the following year, by which time a hundred more ICBMs might have been built, deployed and camouflaged. But there were also serious diplomatic considerations to be taken into account. The President was due to meet Khrushchev again at the Paris summit conference in less than a month, and there were three further strong reasons for suspending the flights, perhaps permanently: the aircraft themselves were getting old, and their plastic and balsa-wood airframes had certainly already lasted much longer than their expected life of two years each; the missions had been flown intermittently for more than four years and there was every reason to believe that the U–2's covert role had been compromised, if not its bases; the main base in the Middle East, at Incirlik, was close to Adana, Turkey's fourth-largest city, and had been home for Detachment 10-10 since 1956. Locally, it was no secret that clandestine missions were flown from the USAF compound. On 2 September 1958 an EC-130 Hercules flown from the base had been brought down by MiG fighters near Yerevan in Soviet Armenia while researching 'radio wave propagation', according to the official bulletin, and all seventeen of the crew had been killed. Finally, it had to be recognised that one of the U-2's principal objectives, the acquisition of targets for Strategic Air Command strikes, had been accomplished. The SAC's list of economic centres and defence installations had been extended to several thousand because of the reconnaissance flights, and there was no longer a need in this regard.

Eisenhower weighed up all the conflicting arguments and decided to authorise the flight. Because the U-2 was to fly from Pakistan, a Commonwealth country, this news was conveyed as a courtesy to London where the Chairman of the Joint Intelligence Committee, Sir Patrick Dean, prepared to travel to Chequers to brief Macmillan.

The preparations for the flight itself were entirely routine. Two experienced U-2 pilots, a lead and his back-up, were selected from Detachment 10-10 at Incirlik and flown to Peshawar via Bahrein in a C-130 military transport. Accompanying them were the eighteen support personnel: the ground crew, navigator, briefing officer, doctor, electronic specialists and photographic technicians needed to service the U-2 when it was delivered by a ferry pilot to its staging base the night before the mission. In addition there was a self-contained signals section, which would receive the final 'go' signal relayed from the liaison staff at the White House. On 9 April the plane, flown by the lead pilot, took off on a flight lasting nine hours, terminating 3,800 miles later at the NATO airfield in Bödo, Norway.[7] His back-up, present only as a contingency in case the lead experienced a health problem at the last minute, duly returned to Turkey. The mission went without a hitch, but when the filmstrip was developed in Washington the photo-analysts discovered that vital frames had been obscured by cloud cover. Cheated of answers to the crucial missile-gap questions, the CIA asked the President for another overflight for Thursday 28 April.

Powers had first overflown Soviet territory from Incirlik in November 1958 and since then had notched a number of overflights equal to the then record-holding U-2 pilot. He had been flying since joining the Air Force in 1950, but in January 1956, while assigned to F-84 interceptors at Turner Air Force Base in

Georgia, had been recruited into the U-2 pilot-training programme. Having passed through the seven-month course, conducted at an isolated camp known as Watertown Strip on the Groom Dry Lake in the Nevada desert, Powers was required to be sheep-dipped, i.e. to resign his Air Force commission and be re-employed as a civilian – all part of the CIA's policy to give the illicit overflights 'plausible deniability' in the event of anything going wrong.

Powers and his back-up flew into Peshawar on Wednesday 27 April, expecting to fly early the following morning, but bad weather forced a postponement. There was no improvement the following day, and the further delay forced the aircraft to be replaced. For the sake of security, and to avoid the U-2 staying in Pakistan a moment longer than absolutely necessary, the plane had been ferried to and from Turkey twice, and was now due for its periodic maintenance. A substitute aircraft arrived at Peshawar late on Saturday evening, and a new departure time was fixed for 6 a.m. on Sunday morning.

Powers experienced a further half-hour delay after he had been strapped into the cockpit, but he was eventually given permission to start his mission. The U-2 soared into the sky over the Hindu Kush and then headed north to overfly the Tyuratam cosmodrome. This part of the flight went without a hitch, but as the aircraft approached its mid-point the autopilot failed. Powers was later to claim that the particular aircraft he had been assigned, serial number 360, had frequently experienced mechanical breakdown, and he had not been surprised when he was obliged to take manual control. Soon afterwards there was a sudden flash and the plane started to break up. Powers clambered out of the cockpit and parachuted safely to the ground; the airframe disintegrated on impact.

The loss of the U-2 was recorded by the National Security Agency, which had been routinely intercepting Soviet ground-defence communications, and as soon as Powers was overdue at Bödo, Washington was notified. However, when the CIA broke the news of the incident to the President it was assumed that the pilot had perished in the crash. The CIA's pilots had been trained to engage a self-destruct mechanism before abandoning their aircraft, and had been issued with a curare-tipped needle so as to avoid capture and interrogation. Accordingly, President Eisenhower had good reason to believe that he would not be contradicted when he confirmed the official cover story that Powers was a civilian pilot, engaged on innocent weather research when he had accidentally strayed into Soviet airspace. He had no way of knowing that Powers had been captured alive outside Sverdlovsk and, contrary to orders, had been carrying incriminating personal identification papers which showed him to be an employee of the US Department of Defence. In short, Powers became an embarrassing political liability the moment he was taken into custody by three bemused Soviet onlookers, and was to hand Khrushchev the propaganda victory of the era by proving that Eisenhower had lied in protesting the U-2's innocence. Damning testimony from Powers, combined with incontrovertible physical evidence recovered from the plane wreckage, proved that the U-2 had been engaged on an officially sponsored act of espionage when it was downed over Soviet territory.[8] Khrushchev's surprise announcement that Powers was alive and undergoing interrogation spelt the end of the Paris summit and humiliated Eisenhower. Perhaps more significantly, it brought the overflights to a swift conclusion.

The loss of the U-2 as a means of obtaining aerial pictures of the Soviet Union was only temporary, and heralded a further generation of aerial-reconnaissance platforms, the orbiting satellites. The first US photo-satellite, *Discoverer 13*, was launched on 10 August 1960, three months after Powers had been taken into custody. The exposed film from this experimental spacecraft was jettisoned to earth in a canister intended to be recovered in mid-air by a specially adapted plane. Although theoretically possible, the latter part of the project proved quite impractical and only a tiny proportion of canisters was ever successfully intercepted and brought to Washington for analysis. Nevertheless, despite this unpromising start, satellite surveillance was to prove the most reliable and enduring method of obtaining information from within the Soviet Union, and the *Discoverer* series was to be superseded by other overhead platforms.

In August 1960 the President acknowledged the permanent nature of this new dimension to clandestine intelligence-gathering by authorising the creation of the National Reconnaissance Office, a new co-ordinating unit to supervise the development and exploitation of satellite surveillance systems.

These developments, of course, remained unknown to Powers, who had committed the two cardinal errors of failing to ensure his aircraft disintegrated by engaging the self-destruct mechanism before he bailed out, and of surviving the experience. Although the practice was not advocated officially, the CIA presumed that its pilot would have committed suicide to avoid capture, and had no contingency plans to cater for Powers's arrest and confession. Once the airman had admitted his status and role he was transformed from the Agency's priceless asset into a liability of horrendous proportions. His testimony, backed by the equipment recovered from the U-2's wreckage, proved that Eisenhower had lied, and that the US had engaged in a deliberately calculated long-term programme of aerial incursions. Fortunately Powers's confession amounted to such a damning indictment of Soviet air defences that only a small proportion of it was used in evidence during his show trial, which opened in Moscow on 17 August 1960. Indeed, the quality of the photographs printed from the negatives removed from the U-2 cameras was of such an unprecedented high standard that some rather grainy, relatively low-resolution pictures were substituted for them before being released publicly.

Powers underwent a period of intensive interrogation in Moscow's notorious Lubyanka Prison, but was always well treated. Upon conviction he was sentenced to ten years' imprisonment, leaving the CIA with two mysteries to be solved: how had the plane been brought down, and to what extent had its future been compromised by Powers's disclosures? According to the Soviet prosecution's account, the U-2 had been hit by an anti-aircraft battery near Sverdlovsk, presumably equipped with SA-2 *Guidelines*. But this version hardly made sense if the plane had been at its correct altitude. This therefore suggested to those conducting the CIA's post-mortem that the plane had either fallen victim to the freak chance of a *Guideline* reaching the U-2, or that the aircraft had lost height and accidentally come into the missile's range. The latter seemed the most plausible explanation, prompted either by a 'flame-out' (when a jet occasionally loses power in the rarified atmosphere at eighty thousand feet, forcing the pilot to fly lower to reignite the engine), or by some other malfunction perhaps due to pilot error. Flying the U-2 was no easy task, even with the assistance of the autopilot, and a combination of air turbulence and a phenomenon known as 'mach buffet' made the fragile airframe very vulnerable even in the very best conditions. By the time Powers had been downed, no less than five experienced CIA pilots had lost their planes.[9] One possibility, reckoned by some to be the most likely explanation for the incident, was pilot error. If a pilot fell asleep, or even lost concentration momentarily, the U-2 had a tendency to go into an uncontrollable dive.

The CIA was torn between its desire to know exactly how the U-2 had been shot down and its embarrassment at having to acknowledge its connection with the pilot. It was particularly keen to learn what Powers had compromised while under hostile interrogation, and some in the Agency thought he ought to be charged with negligence or dereliction of duty for having humiliated his country. There was also some anxiety that Powers might himself defect, and choose to stay in the Soviet Union. This particular worry was eliminated when a woman purporting to be the wife of Colonel Abel, the convicted Soviet spy, approached James B. Donovan, a lawyer who had worked in the wartime Office of Strategic Services, and asked him to lobby for her husband's release, in exchange for Powers.[10]

The idea of an exchange was not entirely new. On 27 October 1960, two months after Powers's imprisonment, a forty-seven-year-old KGB officer named Igor Y. Melekh had been arrested in New York where he was operating under United Nations cover as head of the Russian Section of the UN Secretariat's Languages and Meetings Service. The charge had been espionage, based on three years of intensive surveillance by the FBI which revealed that Melekh had been illicitly purchasing aerial photographs of the Chicago area from an illustrator of medical journals named John Gilmore. The FBI discovered that 'Gilmore' was in fact a German immigrant, Willie Hirsch, who had come to America as a boy. The FBI had first taken an interest in him back in 1958 when a man he had approached in Chicago about obtaining maps and photographs had reported the incident. The lengthy investigation that followed revealed Melekh as one of Hirsch's contacts. Another was Kirill S. Doronkin, a member of the Soviet Mission to the UN, a highly professional KGB officer who realised he was under surveillance and was expelled on 11 March 1959. The FBI had hoped optimistically that Melekh would resume contact with Hirsch, but he never did. Instead, nineteen months later, both men had been taken into custody. Melekh was soon released on $50,000 bail offered by his wife, Irina, and by agreement with the Justice Department returned to Moscow on 8 April 1961. Charges against Hirsch were also dropped, but in July he was deported to Czechoslovakia. No explanation was ever given for Melekh's release, but the suspicion remains that it was an attempt to interest the KGB in the idea of a swap for an agent considered a much larger fish.

The man who called himself Colonel Rudolf I. Abel is now a central figure in modern espionage mythology. He was arrested by the FBI in June 1957 in New York masquerading as Mark Collins, a talented commercial artist. In reality he was a KGB 'illegal' who had crossed the Canadian border late in 1948, having arrived in Quebec in November as a German refugee called Andrew Kayotis. For the previous two years he had lived in a series of displaced persons' camps in Europe. Abel had made his way to New York, subsequently adopting the identity of Emil R. Goldfus, and under interrogation he had displayed a cool professionalism, declining to reveal how he acquired his rather distinctive English accent. Further research later established that Abel was probably an Englishman, William Fisher, who had been born to a Russian mother in Newcastle upon Tyne and who had spent the first eighteen years of his life in northern England before emigrating to the Soviet Union in 1921 with his parents. According to the man who denounced Abel and helped the FBI run him to earth in a Manhatten hotel, an alcoholic KGB defector named Reino Hayhanen, Abel was the KGB illegal *rezident* in the US, and therefore an impressive prize. However, despite Abel's evident stature, the FBI could find no evidence that he had ever been called into action to run any spies in North America. No classified documents were found in his possession and Hayhanen, his former assistant, could shed little light on what Abel had been up to. A search of his possessions had provided plenty of incriminating paraphernalia, including wireless equipment and cipher material, and a link to the ill-fated Rosenberg spy-ring in the form of two photographs of Lena and Morris Cohen, both espionage suspects who had fled abroad after the Rosenbergs had been caught back in 1950.[11] The Cohens were not to re-emerge until January 1961, when they were arrested in London, living as dealers in rare books under the alias Peter and Helen Kroger, and servicing a spy-ring in the Royal Navy's underwater-weapons research establishment at Portland.[12] Abel had been convicted by a federal court and sentenced to thirty years' imprisonment in October 1957. Thus by the time Powers received his sentence Abel had already served three years in a penitentiary in Georgia.

Donovan's intervention received the approval of the US

government and a swap was arranged: Gary Powers for Colonel Abel. The exchange took place at the Glienicke Bridge in Berlin on 8 February 1962; Powers was swiftly flown to Andrews Air Force Base outside Washington, where he was disappointed to discover there were no official dignitaries to welcome him home. When the crew of an RB-47 reconnaissance aircraft, downed by the Soviets on 1 July 1960 in international airspace over the Barents Sea, had been freed, they had been met at Andrews by the President.[13] But instead of the expected celebrations Powers was whisked off to Ashford Farm, a remote property on the Choptank River in Talbot County, Maryland, for an intensive debriefing. The conclusions reached during the hours of interviews that followed are still classified, but rumour quickly spread through the CIA's new headquarters building at Langley, Virginia, that Powers had attempted to mislead his interrogators, and had probably lied when he insisted that his aircraft had been lost because of mechanical malfunction, not pilot error. Allen Dulles's successor as DCI, the businessman John McCone, enpanelled a formal board of enquiry to sift the evidence. Led by a federal judge, E. Barrett Prettyman, the board included John Bross from the Operations Directorate and General Harold Bull of the CIA's Office of National Estimates. For twelve days they heard testimony from other U-2 pilots and support staff, a National Security Agency signals expert and a member of the CIA's Counterintelligence Staff. They also watched news-reel footage of Powers's trial in Moscow, and studied the results of a polygraph test he had volunteered to take. Then the board submitted a twelve-page document to McCone, who showed it to the President. According to the version publicly released, the report concluded that Powers had 'acted in accordance with the terms of his employment and his instructions and briefings',[14] but those reading between the lines noted that Powers was described as only having made a 'reasonable' effort to have destroyed his aircraft. Powers himself was incensed at the faint praise but was delighted by the recommendation that he should receive his back pay in full for the period he had been in captivity. On the thorny issue of exactly what height the U-2 had been flying at when the pilot lost control, there was no general consensus. The NSA, which had radar recordings to show that the U-2 had glided gently down to thirty or forty thousand feet, suggested that the Soviet claim to have scored a hit with a SAM at sixty-five thousand feet was nonsense. The aircraft's designer, Kelly Johnson, believed there had been no direct hit but that the U-2's right stabiliser had been blown off by a missile detonating near by. He had not been able to examine what was left of the U-2, of course, but he had studied a film of the debris which had been put on display in Moscow's Gorky Park at the time of the trial. The board's deliberations on this topic were bogged down by the speculative nature of the opinions on offer from the experts, and the board's implied reluctance to accept Powers's own recollection:

> Some information from confidential sources was available. Some of it corroborated Powers and some of it was inconsistent in parts with Powers's story, but that which was inconsistent was in part contradictory with itself and subject to various interpretations.[15]

Publicly John McCone endorsed the conclusion that the plane had experienced a near miss at sixty-eight thousand feet and then glided down to a lower altitude, where Powers clambered out of the cockpit. Privately he was sure that Powers was a liar who had probably fallen asleep at the controls.

Once the sanitised version of the verdict on Powers had been released he acquired celebrity status, and on 6 March 1962 appeared before the Senate Armed Services Committee where he was received as a hero. There was no longer any talk of pilot error, or even pilot defection, as Powers described how he had wrestled with the controls as his plane plunged towards the ground. Officially absolved from any charges of misconduct,

Powers subsequently found it hard to adjust to the fact that rumours still abounded at Langley, where he was given a desk job. In January 1963 he divorced his hard-drinking wife, Barbara, and six months later married a CIA colleague, Sue Downey. In that same year he left the CIA and moved to California, where Lockheed employed him as a test pilot on U-2s at Van Nuys Airport. It was only five years later, when Powers accepted an offer to write an account of his experiences, subsequently published as *Operation Overflight*,[16] that he discovered that the CIA had been reimbursing Lockheed for his salary. When the Agency read his draft manuscript that arrangement came to an abrupt end, and Lockheed fired him. Powers was by now more embittered than ever. He was convinced that the Agency had deliberately withheld one crucial item of information from the public, namely the operating height of the U-2. He insisted that suicide to avoid capture had never been included in his instructions, and that he had kept silent under KGB interrogation about the most sensitive aspects of his flight. His critics maintained that he had disclosed far too much, and should never have made a humiliating public apology in Moscow for his mission.

Eventually KGIL, a local radio station in Los Angeles, hired Powers to fly their Cessna and broadcast weather and traffic reports, and in November 1976 he moved to KNBC, the television affiliate for whom he flew a Bell Jet Ranger helicopter. His last flight, on 1 August 1977, ended when his craft ran out of fuel and fell from the sky, killing him and his television crew. Some believed that he had been the victim of sabotage but, once again, the evidence pointed towards a much more straightforward explanation: simple pilot error.

After his death Powers received an unexpected honour: burial in the Arlington National Cemetery, with the full approval of the CIA and President Jimmy Carter. Finally, the man who changed the history of the Cold War by surviving what was probably the most diplomatically catastrophic aircrash ever was laid to rest, his achievement having been to prove what many had suspected: that Presidents of the United States occasionally tell lies. In the neighbouring plot rests another authentic American hero, Tucker Gougelmann, the veteran CIA officer accidentally left behind in Saigon after that city fell to the Viet Cong in April 1975.

CHAPTER VII

Greville Wynne

On a bleak, windswept morning, 22 April 1964, a slightly bewildered prisoner was escorted by a group of KGB guards to the Heerstrasse checkpoint in the Berlin Wall, where he was released to the West. Simultaneously, a Soviet agent named Konon Molody walked in the opposite direction, having been freed from a twenty-five-year prison sentence in England. Using the alias 'Gordon Lonsdale' and posing as a Canadian, he had been convicted three years earlier of breaches of the Official Secrets Act. The British businessman for whom his swap had been negotiated was Greville M. Wynne, a forty-three-year-old engineer and foreign-trade negotiator arrested in Budapest in November 1962 and tried in Moscow in May the following year, together with his fellow conspirator, Colonel Oleg V. Penkovsky. After their convictions Wynne had been sentenced to eight years' imprisonment, five of which were to be spent in a labour camp, and Penkovsky had been executed by a firing squad.

Their relationship began when Penkovsky approached Wynne and asked him to pass secrets to London, his previous attempts having been rebuffed by the Americans and Canadians the previous year. It is at this early stage that a difference of opinion emerges between various different versions of even this single event. At their trial Penkovsky and Wynne confirmed that Penkovsky's approach had occurred in a Moscow restaurant on 12 April 1961. However, Wynne was later to say that he had been deliberately but unsuccessfully 'dangled' in front of Penkovsky during two earilier trips to Moscow, in November and

December 1960. The link forged in April 1961 was then to remain firm until both men were arrested eighteen months later.

The story that brought Wynne, the dyslexic son of a foreman in an engineering works from a poor mining village in south Wales, to the East-West frontier was truly remarkable. He and his three sisters had been brought up in a small Victorian terrace house in Tredomen Villas, Ystrad Mynach, and he had left school at the height of the depression in 1933, aged fourteen, to work as a labourer for an electrical contractor in Caerphilly. Later he was apprenticed to a telephone company in Nottingham and, according to Wynne, this was to lead him into the world of espionage.

The pretence that Wynne had been an innocent traveller deliberately entrapped by the KGB came to an end in 1965, when Wynne learnt that Penkovsky's story was to be published.[1] Up until that moment the official British line was that Wynne had been an ordinary businessman and the victim of a tit-for-tat retaliation by the KGB. In fact Wynne's trading company in London, in which he and his wife were sole directors, had a sleeping partner: Dickie Franks of SIS. The company's main asset, at the time the longest articulated truck ever built in England, had been paid for in full by SIS so as to provide Wynne with suitable cover: a mobile trade fair demonstrating British goods in Eastern Europe. However, all the elaborate deception came to an abrupt end when the CIA authorised a Soviet defector, Piotr Derabian, and a *Time* journalist, Frank Gibney, to reconstruct *The Penkovsky Papers*. These purported, somewhat improbably, to be the daily observations of Colonel Penkovsky of the GRU, having been written before his arrest and smuggled out of his Moscow apartment before the KGB could act. Outraged that he had not been mentioned anywhere in the text, Wynne insisted on writing a short foreword which, though brief, disclosed his true role as a conscious agent for the very first time. Wynne's own book, ghosted by his brother-in-law John Gilbert, was released two years later as *The Man*

From Moscow.[2] Far from being innocent of the charges he was convicted of Wynne revealed that he had been specifically recruited by the Secret Intelligence Service to contact Penkovsky and act as his courier, carrying microfilms of GRU secrets to London.

Wynne is probably best known in his role as the vital link between Penkovsky and his British and American controllers based in London. Yet his full story is really much more remarkable than the eighteen months he spent as an agent that earned him world-wide fame. Indeed, so much new information has come into the public domain recently about Wynne and Penkovsky that many of the histories of the Cold War will have to be rewritten.

Wynne himself died on 27 February 1990 and during his lifetime had exercised what amounted to proprietorial rights over almost anything to do with Penkovsky. In some respects this was quite understandable. His prison ordeal in the Soviet Union was devastating, and upon his return to England he had undergone a complete nervous breakdown. He had divorced his wife Sheila, virtually disowned his only son Andrew, and developed an acute alcohol problem which sometimes made him violent. The episode for which he became so well known dominated him entirely, and none of his subsequent business ventures ever amounted to the successes he claimed them to be. His second marriage, to a Dutch girl named Hermione Van Buren in 1980, ended 'because of his drunken rages' caused by his abuse of alcohol which, she claimed in a newspaper interview, had 'changed his personality'.[3] He moved from the Canaries to Malta, Marbella and finally Majorca, and became a well-known figure in the bars frequented by the expatriate community in Palma. 'Wynne's drink problem started in Lanzarote where whisky was cheaper than a glass of mineral water,' recalled Hermione.[4] Wynne had been employed to sell villas at a development in the grounds of the San Antonio Hotel, but his efforts ended in failure. Perhaps because of his inability to sustain relationships, Wynne became increasingly litigious and brought numerous legal actions against almost anybody who wrote about him. He variously sued or threatened to sue the BBC, the *Sunday Telegraph*, Sir Fitzroy Maclean[5] and this author, but none of his cases ever met with success in court. He usually abandoned them before they came to trial, with one notable exception which will be described later.

Getting to the truth about Wynne is no easy task, mainly because of the measures he took to obscure the truth. In addition to *The Man From Moscow* and the sequel that was published in 1981, *The Man From Odessa*,[6] written with Bob Latona, he gave numerous newspaper interviews and was an eager commentator on events relating to the cold war. According to his own account, Wynne first came into contact with British intelligence in 1938 just prior to the Second World War, when he accidentally discovered a German spy using a clandestine transmitter in the Nottingham factory where they were both working. Having denounced the Nazi agent Wynne was selected for an undercover security role as an *agent provocateur*, identifying potentially disloyal Fascist sympathisers. Although posing as an ordinary soldier, Wynne allegedly ended the war with the rank of major and then went into business on his own, first as a property developer and club owner, and then as a representative abroad of several leading British engineering companies.

Wynne's first book included intriguing references to Odessa, and a visit he had made there 'about five years ago',[7] which would have placed him there in 1957. Further details were to follow in *The Man From Odessa*, in which Wynne revealed that before his involvement with Penkovsky he had undertaken an earlier mission for his SIS contact, whom he referred to only as James. This dangerous operation, he alleged, occurred in 1959 and had enabled a Soviet GRU officer, known to Wynne as Sergei Kuznov, to defect to the West with vital information. Indeed, Wynne's second book also made new disclosures about the celebrated Penkovsky case. Apparently Wynne had accompanied Penkovsky on a secret visit to Washington where they had been received by President Kennedy.

Wynne's remarkable claims which formed the basis of a BBC drama documentary in 1983 were only challenged in 1988 when they became the subject of libel proceedings following some very critical observations published in *The Friends*,[8] which for the first time challenged Wynne's veracity. What emerged during the lengthy litigation was to cast doubt on practically every aspect of Wynne's bizarre life and expose his memoirs as sheer fiction.

The first contradiction in Wynne's life concerns the day in which he says he was first recruited into British intelligence. His account describes how in November 1938 he accidentally discovered a German spy operating an illicit wireless from within the factory at Beeston, Nottingham, where they both worked. At the time Wynne was an engineering apprentice at the Ericsson Telephone Company and had returned to a storehouse after hours to recover some tools he had forgotten, when he stumbled upon the Nazi agent. This episode is important because it is the foundation of Wynne's clandestine career as an undercover agent. According to his story, the spy was in an underground cellar, and Wynne heard 'a series of staccato-like phrases in German'.[9] When he looked more closely, he could see a transmitter and an aerial, and this is what he reported to the military authorities and subsequently led to his recruitment.

There are two immediate difficulties with Wynne's story. Firstly, there is no record of any espionage case even remotely resembling that described by Wynne. In 1938 there was a single example of a German spy for the Abwehr being caught in Britain, but none of the details concerning Mrs Jessie Jordan, who was arrested in Dundee, coincide with Wynne's. Furthermore, it was learnt after the war that even Mrs Jordan's case had been unusual because the Nazi government had placed a ban on Abwehr activity in England in order to avoid provoking the British authorities. The second problem relates to the technical feasibility of a small portable transmitter, operating underground, being able to transmit a voice channel over the distance to Germany. Indeed, even with an antenna above ground level, no equipment then available would have had such a range.

Although Wynne's military record makes no mention of any service other than as a member of an anti-aircraft battery, with the rank of private, he invented for himself an alternative undercover career as an *agent provocateur*, testing the loyalty of suspect Communists and Fascists. On the issue of rank, Wynne always insisted that he 'finished up at the end of World War II a major'.[10] This is not borne out by the *Army List*, which catalogues comprehensively the progress of all those holding a commission. Wynne's name appears nowhere in it. That Wynne manifested some distinctly Leftist politics while still in the army is demonstrated by his authorship of an undated four-page pamphlet calling for a post-war socialist administration. Entitled *After the War – What then, Soldier?*,[11] it denounced capitalism and the government in strident terms and demanded a new order to replace the system that had been responsible for the slump after the Great War.

> In those days, like at the present time, there were among our Government and leading statesmen many false prophets, men who planned large profits for themselves rather than for the need of ordinary people. The great landlords and directors of industrial combines through their false prophets and vested interests gained a majority in the House of Commons, and they governed our country. Through their Tory policy and money invested interests we saw in our country between the Great Wars millions of unemployed, millions of money held from circulation, factory and industrial areas in a criminal state of depression, mines standing idle, fields uncultivated, raw materials unused. Yet all this time millions of our people were in want of the bare necessities of life, and the great

> industrial combines still continued to manufacture luxury at a profit for the rich . . . The past twenty-five years is sufficient proof that the old system has failed; there is something wrong about any system which allows millions of its people to exist permanently upon the verge of starvation amidst plenty.

That Wynne should have put his name to a leaflet espousing doctrinaire Marxism is remarkable, but the document's aims were clear:

> The majority of poor people between the Wars were without sufficient of the bare necessities of life. Many were unemployed, many were underpaid, yet industries were not producing sufficient commodities to supply the needs of ordinary people. Our country was still wealthy yet raw material lay unused. Mines were idle, fields lay uncultivated. All this takes place when the resources of the country are owned by a few rich people. They own the goods produced in the country, and they use their rights, as owners, to make themselves rich. The ordinary people who have no share in owning the land and its industries, but only work for wages, have no control over what happens to the things they produce. This system is known as capitalism and it is the system which we have been living under for twenty-five years. Under capitalism the interest and profits of a few people are considered far more important than the interests and living conditions of the majority of people. The fact that this system leads to waste and inefficiency has already been proved; for instance, it is necessary under capitalism to have unemployed in order to hold a reserve of labour and thus keep the wages of the worker at a low level for with cheap labour higher profits can be gained.

Wynne concluded his pamphlet with a direct appeal to soldiers which appears to border on incitement:

> You, Soldier, are you content to let your country fall back and be run on the old system, back to 1939 Capitalism, or will you take up the fight now and do all you can to build a real land fit for heroes to live in? Is it right that our soldiers are underpaid and their dependants suffering in poverty? The magnificent achievements brought about by Socialism in Soviet Russia should be all the proof that is needed to the thinking mind as to – WILL IT WORK.

Whether this was truly inspired by the security authorities with whom he claimed to be in touch is difficult to ascertain, but, signed 'yours fraternally in Socialism, Greville M. Wynne, Ystrad Mynach, Cardiff', there could be no doubt about the identity of its author. The text refers to the forthcoming general election, which suggests that it was distributed before the 1945 polls, but it also asks

> Is it right that the present Government, after nearly five years of war, does not tell our Soldiers what sort of country is being planned for them? Is it right that our soldiers are denied political freedom in their own country for which they are fighting?

This passage implies that it was written before September 1944 when, according to Wynne's account in *The Man From Odessa*, he was stationed in northern Europe in a vehicle repair unit, having reached France 'ten days after D-Day'[12] and made it in September 1944 'as far as the outskirts of Brussels.'[13] Like so many of Wynne's assertions, this contradiction is unexplained. Certainly many of his other claims do not appear credible.

For example, Wynne recalls a tragic love affair he conducted with a beautiful girl named Vicki, 'the first and only time'[14] he had ever been in love. He recalled 'her high cheekbones, lustrous ash-brown hair and an ineffable air of chic, so charmingly French . . . and exotic'.[15] They saw each other regularly over a period of months, and Wynne learnt that Vicki was a wireless instructor and an army lieutenant, working as a liaison officer with the Free French. Their relationship came to a sudden end when Vicki disappeared; Wynne subsequently discovered that she had been captured by the Nazis in France. Apparently she had been dropped in and pulled out of occupied territory 'several times',[16] and had been teaching the French Maquis when she had been caught.

Although Wynne gave few details about Vicki, apart from the fact that she wore an army uniform, 'had spent a good part of her childhood in France' and worked at an office in Whitehall, there is good reason to doubt she ever existed. The principal organisation that employed women agents in France was Special Operations Executive, and the personnel files of all fifty of those who were parachuted on missions into France have been carefully preserved. What makes Wynne's story so odd is that if Vicki had been French, and he mentions that her mother had been French and the time she had spent in France,[17] she would probably have been in a branch known as RF Section – yet none of its women agents bear even the slightest resemblance to 'Vicki'. A study of SOE's archives reveals that none of the British women agents sent to France held army ranks. Twenty-four were nominally members of the First Aid Nursing Yeomanry and fourteen held commissions in the Women's Auxiliary Air Force. Nor were any women wireless instructors sent into enemy territory. For security reasons, all training was conducted in England.

SOE agents deployed in France worked for one of two separate sections. F Section did recruit British nationals, but of the three women sent on more than one mission to France, and captured, Lise de Baissac and Virginia Hall survived. Only Violette Szabo was executed, and she was emphatically not

Wynne's 'Vicki'. She had been a FANY, and a courier, not a wireless operator. Furthermore, she had never been employed, as 'Vicki' had been, as a liaison officer with the Free French. SOE's F Section had been created specifically to operate in isolation from the Free French. As for RF Section, which did liaise closely with de Gaulle's forces, it only employed Frenchwomen, and none of its eleven female agents was ever captured. Thus it would certainly seem as though Vicki was nothing more than Wynne's invention. One possible explanation is that he had fantasised a relationship with 'Vicki' after seeing *Carve Her Name With Pride*, a movie based on Violette Szabo's experiences in the field. This may be the reason why Wynne omits any date regarding his affair with Vicki and says vaguely that it lasted months, when he was 'in London between postings'.[18]

Attempts to verify Wynne's claims concerning his relationship with the Security Service, under whose instructions he alleged he had operated during the war, meet with failure because of the erroneous information Wynne has propagated about 'Captain James', his case officer. This is the individual who supposedly recruited Wynne in 1940 and supervised him while he undertook three different types of enquiry for the Security Service. As well as undercover surveillance of Fascist sympathisers, he also monitored Communist subversives in the army and investigated the activities of suspect Czech and Polish exiles. Perhaps surprisingly, his admission of being 'hopeless' at languages apparently did not undermine his effectiveness in the latter task. As for 'James', Wynne vouchsafed the following about him: he was 'a good ten years older than I', a 'Sandhurst man', he had been 'educated at Trinity College, Cambridge',[19] had been 'parachuted into Yugoslavia to make contact with Tito's partisans'[20] and finally, at the time of writing, 'now approaching eighty is retired and farming in Sussex'.[21]

In reality Wynne was run by Dickie Franks, whose career coincided with none of the claims made for him. Franks was never in the Security Service, never jumped into Yugoslavia, and in 1981 (when *The Man From Odessa* was published), aged sixty, was still the Chief of SIS. He had been educated at Queen's College, Oxford, had not gone to Sandhurst, and his home was in Aldeburgh, Suffolk.

Wynne says that James made contact with him again in 1959 in anticipation of a secret mission to Odessa where he was to assist in the exfiltration of an officer who 'held a high position in the GRU'.[22] Since this is the central issue in Wynne's second book it is worth examining in some detail what he says took place. According to his version he acquired a visa to visit Odessa from a senior commercial attaché at the Soviet Trade Delegation in Highgate named Pavlov.[23] Once at the port he was introduced to the man he was to know as Major Sergei Kuznov. Having made successful contact, Wynne received an important package from him which he hid on the *Uzbekistan*, a Russian liner on which he was scheduled to travel to Varna. However, the original plan for Kuznov's escape had called for Wynne to act as a decoy and distract certain guards away from the area in the port where Kuznov was to be. In the event Wynne fell off the *Uzbekistan* at the vital moment and broke his leg. Nevertheless, Kuznov had managed to escape, and his package had later been retrieved from the *Uzbekistan*. Once in the West, Kuznov had supplied a wealth of information and eventually retired under a new identity to the United States, where he was rewarded with a consultancy post in the Pentagon.

There are, characteristically, more than a few problems with Wynne's account, bearing in mind that *The Man From Odessa* was set in 1959. Starting at the beginning, there was no Pavlov at the Soviet Trade Delegation in 1959. The record shows that Anatoli G. Pavlov did not arrive in London until 1961. Nor was the *Uzbekistan*, which Wynne described as 'a fairly new ship',[24] launched until 1962 – *two years after* these adventures. Further research casts doubt on other aspects of Wynne's story.

The key figure in the book is Sergei Kuznov, and there are three fundamental problems concerning him. First there is the question of whether he ever existed, for there is no record of any GRU officer defecting to the West in 1959. In fact, as we shall see, there were no defections at all from that organisation between 1948 and 1971. Secondly, the way in which Wynne says he made contact with Kuznov is, upon analysis, impossible. Thirdly, there is the information Kuznov is alleged to have conveyed to the West, which entirely contradicts what the history books tell us.

Over the years there has been much research undertaken into the phenomenon of political defection and, as might be expected, the world's counter-intelligence agencies have devoted much of their resources to this most valued method of acquiring data on their opponents. There are no less than three basic sources of non-classified information regarding Soviet intelligence defectors: the arrest list of suspects previously referred to (see p. 130) covering the period May 1945 to April 1969 maintained by the KGB but released by *Possev*,[25] a Russian *émigré* newspaper; a comprehensive list of GRU and KGB post-war defectors accurate until April 1988 published in *Games of Intelligence*;[26] and the memoirs of the defectors themselves. Of the fifty Soviet intelligence officers who defected during the post-war era, no less than twenty-six have either released their own autobiographies or co-operated with writers who have published accounts of their lives while in the Soviet service. That so many should have done so is hardly surprising: there are relatively few opportunities for a Soviet intelligence defector to make a living in the West, and a book collaboration is an easy and safe way to capitalise on his experiences. There are also numerous references in the burgeoning open literature to the minority of individual cases which did not go into print. Uniquely, there is absolutely no reference to Sergei Kuznov, or any GRU officer resembling him, *in any of the literature*. Indeed, only two Soviet intelligence officers defected to the West in 1959. One was operating under diplomatic cover in Rangoon, the other was an 'illegal' in the United States, and both were KGB officers, not

GRU. If Kuznov was truly a GRU officer who had successfully defected one would certainly have expected his name to appear on the KGB's arrest list, which has been the subject of intensive analysis by Professor Vladimir Krasnov, or at least to be mentioned by subsequent GRU or KGB defectors. Significantly, none have. In fact, of the hundreds of books published on Soviet and American clandestine operations since 1959, not one has referred even obliquely to Sergei Kuznov. Vladimir B. Rezun, who defected from the GRU in 1978 and subsequently wrote (under the pseudonym Viktor Suvorov) the standard textbook on his former service, *The Aquarium*,[27] has confirmed that he has never heard of Kuznov. Until Rezun sought political asylum at the British Embassy in Geneva, only seven GRU had defected to the West, and the cases of each were well known.

As previously mentioned, obtaining employment for defectors is a specialist field, and Wynne mentions that Kuznov was rewarded with a consultancy post 'at the Soviet desk in the Pentagon'. Curiously, none of the CIA counter-intelligence experts who were serving at this time have any recollection of such an individual. Nor does the Jamestown Foundation, an organisation specifically dedicated to the task of placing Soviet defectors in suitable employment.

According to Wynne, his initial contact with Kuznov was set up in January 1959, when he was first shown his photograph in preparation for their meeting in Odessa, which took place shortly before Easter of that year. Now Wynne insisted at the outset that 'Major Sergei Kuznov' was not the true name of the man from Odessa. It was merely the name by which he was referred to by SIS in Wynne's presence. He explains that he was never told Kuznov's real name in case he 'was arrested and interrogated'[28] by the Soviet authorities. All of this makes perfect sense, yet in *The Man From Odessa* Wynne describes how he was first introduced to Kuznov by two fellow Britons in the Savoy Hotel in Odessa:

> We . . . had a round of introductions and warm handshakes. When I was presented to Kuznov, he hesitated a moment when I told him my name.[29]

The issue of Kuznov's name is important because the agreed recognition signal to be made when the two men met was to be what would appear to the bystander as a slight confusion over Greville Wynne's own first name. Kuznov was to mistake it for Gabriel, and Wynne was to correct him. 'This was the recognition signal that had been decided on back in London,'[30] Wynne says. But if this introduction took place in the way Wynne later described, *he must have learned Kuznov's real name.*

There must be some scepticism attached to Wynne's insistence that it was security considerations that prevented him from learning Kuznov's real name. Certainly before the exfiltration had been accomplished security had been a low priority, for even if he had not been informed of the GRU officer's name, he knew plenty about him, more than enough for the Soviet authorities to identify Kuznov if they extracted the information from him. Wynne confirms that he had been issued with photographs of him, which he had been allowed to keep, and had been informed that Kuznov 'had been a member of the Soviet Commission in Vienna after the war, which is where he had first made contact with MI6'.[31] Furthermore, Wynne was supposedly told that Kuznov's parents lived in Odessa. Worse still, Wynne was in possession of all this vital data weeks before the operation was undertaken, and during a period when he made two visits to the Soviet Union and several trips to Romania, Hungary, Poland and Czechoslovakia! If this were all true, one wonders how SIS ever expected to pull off the exfiltration successfully.

Credibility is stretched even further when Wynne explains that one of the reasons that Kuznov was to be brought to the West was that he had fallen under suspicion. His security clearance had been withdrawn, yet SIS had somehow managed to pass him photographs of Wynne so he might recognise his contact.

Once Wynne had made contact with Kuznov, and handed over a gold ingot 'to pay off'[32] his helpers, the scheme devised by Kuznov called for Wynne to operate as a decoy. The plan itself seems unnecessarily complex and risky, considering Kuznov was supposedly already under suspicion. It required 'a lifelong friend'[33] of Kuznov's to drug a colleague, take control of a pilot vessel in Odessa harbour, collect Kuznov from 'a deserted loading facility'[34] and then put him aboard a foreign cargo vessel scheduled to leave the port shortly before midnight. Wynne's role as decoy was to fall off the *Uzbekistan* at exactly that moment, thereby creating a diversion that would allow Kuznov to escape.

What is not explained about this elaborate plan is quite why Wynne should have been needed at all. SIS apparently had the means to deliver a set of photographs to the enterprising Kuznov, so why not a gold ingot too? Was it really necessary to have Wynne travel out from England to fall off a ship when, according to his own account, SIS already had people in the area? Wynne says (twice) that SIS had made arrangements to place some sand on the dockside to break his fall.

One of the most interesting aspects of the Kuznov story is the question of his value to the West as a source of information. Undoubtedly, if he really had been haemorrhaging secrets since the Soviet occupation of Vienna, he must have been responsible for a very great deal of valuable data, and he would have been by far the West's most successful Soviet source. In contrast, Oleg Penkovsky survived just eighteen months as an agent, and the only other GRU officer known to have spied for the West during that period was Major Piotr S. Popov, who had been recruited in 1953 and was arrested and executed in 1959. Thus if Kuznov had really existed, he would have attained something approaching celebrity status within the intelligence community and, until Major Dmitri F. Polyakov of the GRU was revealed to have been a long-term CIA source dating back to 1961, would have been the most successful spy ever run by the West in the Soviet Union.

Considering that in 1959 the CIA would have had at least ten years to test Kuznov's bona fides as a reliable source of information, it is surprising that Wynne asserts that SIS anticipated difficulty in 'convincing the Americans that the stories Kuznov's been telling us are on the level'.[35] And despite his unequalled record as an agent in place, Wynne was only able to identify four specific items of intelligence Kuznov had vouchsafed to his SIS controllers. This itself is unusual, for a defector's meal ticket is his guarantee of continued support from his host country. The more secret his information, the greater the welcome he can expect to receive. But in Kuznov's case two items are ridiculous, and the other two fail to stand up to examination. The first was details of 'the first factory in the Soviet Union to manufacture Wellington boots',[36] where all the initial production had apparently been allocated to the KGB, so British agents 'were out on the streets clicking away with hidden cameras at anyone wearing the tell-tale gum boots'. The second was almost as preposterous: details of the production of defective trilby hats which had been delivered to 'Party officials and government functionaries'. This information was especially valued, claimed Wynne, because it 'enabled MI6 to extend their list of known or suspected Soviet agents'.[37]

Whilst it would be hard to take the above seriously, and scarcely justifies a decade of investment in Kuznov, two further items would appear to be more plausible: 'a list giving hundreds of names of Soviet agents from both the KGB and the GRU currently undergoing special training' and a 'photostat' of a plan 'with Khrushchev's signature on it' to build a wall across Berlin.[38]

As to the first, it is quite true that a list of GRU personnel deployed under diplomatic cover in the West was circulated to intelligence and security agencies in the early 1960s, but the information it contained is usually attributed to another, better documented GRU source, Oleg Penkovsky. The material was code-named RUPEE, but was not received by counter-intelligence staffs until 1961 at the earliest, which implies that if its true provenance was Kuznov, as alleged by Wynne, then SIS must have suppressed it for two years before distributing it. This seems very strange behaviour, given the data's limited shelf-life. Turning to the claim relating to the Berlin Wall, which really amounts to saying that the West had more than twenty-eight months' warning of Khrushchev's intention to build the Wall, this is indeed a grave charge, but it is entirely unsubstantiated. All contemporary accounts of this episode concur on one central point: that the Soviet and East German authorities took elaborate measures to conceal their intentions, and the construction work initiated in August 1961 took the American, French and British intelligence agencies completely by surprise.

Although he does not mention this in the context of Kuznov's meal ticket, Wynne states that the GRU man had 'given advance warning of the Russian plan to station their short and medium-range missiles on the Caribbean island where Castro had come to power just three months earlier'.[39] This, upon examination, seems quite unlikely. Of course, in April 1959 Castro had not yet declared himself a Marxist or committed his country to the Eastern Bloc, and we now know that Khrushchev's decision to deploy MRBMs and IRBMs (but never SRBMs) was not taken until very late in 1961. But even if Khrushchev had exercised breathtaking foresight and drawn up a plan as early as 1959, one wonders how a GRU major whose security clearance had been withdrawn could have acquired it.

Some of this documentary material was, so Wynne tells us, entrusted to him in the form of a package. This 'most vital information' had to be delivered to SIS 'with all possible speed' because it contained the 'evidence to convince the politicians'[40] that the Eastern and Western zones of Berlin were to be divided by a wall. Wynne took the package and apparently followed Kuznov's meticulous instructions about exactly where on the *Uzbekistan* it should be concealed. However, because of the injuries he sustained in the fall from the ship, Wynne says that he was unable to recover the bundle from its hiding place until August 1959 when the *Uzbekistan* called in to a Bulgarian port. Wynne then travelled to Vienna via Sofia and Budapest with Kuznov's documents still in his 'breast pocket'.[41]

Quite apart from the most obvious problem in Wynne's account, namely that the *Uzbekistan* was still under construction in a Leningrad shipyard while these events were supposed to have taken place, there is no explanation as to why Kuznov could not have carried them to the West himself. Nor, indeed, is there any obvious reason why SIS should have waited four months before recovering the package from the ship.

Given the many absurdities in Wynne's tale about Kuznov one is bound to conclude that this individual never existed outside Wynne's imagination. In fact a slip by Wynne supports such a conclusion. While discussing the obstacles to making a recruitment pitch to Oleg Penkovsky after he had allegedly first been spotted in Ankara in 1955, Wynne inadvertently remarked that 'no regular British agent existed in the Soviet Union who was in the sort of position that might cross or have any connection with Penkovsky's career as an army officer'.[42] Now this is an astonishing statement to have made (in 1967 in *The Man From Moscow*) if he knew about 'Kuznov'. Based on what Wynne has said about Kuznov, describing his age ('in his late forties'[43]) and his 'high position' in the GRU,[44] he would have been the ideal person to service Penkovsky, as they were both of roughly the same age and rank in the same organisation. The reality of course, is that Kuznov was an invention, dreamt up long after *The Man From Moscow* was published. One is therefore left wondering about the validity of some of his other more extraordinary claims. Two in particular seem rather unlikely, and the first concerns Oleg Penkovsky himself.

Although he made no mention of it in *The Man From Moscow*, Wynne claimed in his later book that he had accompanied Oleg Penkovsky on a secret visit to the White House during the latter's second visit to London, during the summer of 1961. Wynne's sensational disclosure revealed that both men had been flown to Washington, DC, where they had been received by the President, who had taken the opportunity to thank them for their vital undercover work. This was an extraordinary breach of the protocol which keeps heads of government (and heads of state) aloof from the sordid business of espionage, and was a key incident in Wynne's book. Indeed, the episode was accepted as true by the BBC researchers, who never questioned it and faithfully reconstructed it when the BBC filmed its television series *Wynne and Penkovsky*. In fact, the truth is that Wynne duped his readers and the BBC, for no such visit ever took place.

Although Wynne was always characteristically vague about exactly when the visit occurred, he inadvertently left just enough information in the text to pin it down. He mentioned that the journey to America had taken place 'in eighteen hours'[45] when Penkovsky had been smuggled out of his London hotel, SIS having taken care to avoid alerting the other members of the Soviet delegation. The exact day can be identified because Wynne states elsewhere that the secret trip immediately followed the weekend that Penkovsky had seen the Queen at a polo match at Windsor. From this single slender clue it has been possible to narrow down the exact date upon which Penkovsky is alleged to have been received by President Kennedy.

Penkovsky's second visit to London took place between Tuesday 18 July and Thursday 10 August, a total of twenty-four days which spanned three separate weekends. According to Buckingham Palace, which keeps a record of all the Queen's movements, she was at Cowes on 29–30 July 1961, Scotland on 5–6 August, and at Windsor on 22–23 July. On Sunday 23 July 1961 she had watched Prince Philip umpire the Captains and

Subalterns final at the Guards Polo Club, and this was the only time Penkovsky could have seen her in the flesh, as Wynne described. Accordingly, 'twenty-four hours later'[46] would have had the secret flight to America occurring on the evening of Monday 24 July 1961.

Wynne asserts that the entire journey, from London to Washington and back, was accomplished in eighteen hours and recalls that they were flown in a 'military jet liner'.[47] Having landed at an unnamed Air Force base, they were whisked to the White House for a short reception, and then flown in time for Penkovsky to be restored to his hotel without his Soviet colleagues having noticed his absence.

When it was pointed out to Wynne during litigation in 1989 that it would be a physical impossibility to have undertaken such a journey in 1961 in the time claimed, Wynne conceded having made a slight error and provided further details of the trip which, he suggested, proved the authenticity of his claims. His revised itinerary included a car journey to Manchester, a further ride to an RAF airfield, and then a transatlantic flight.[48] Significantly, he failed to alter the other details, such as the military jet liner. In fact, in 1961 the United States Air Force possessed only one such plane, and that was President Kennedy's personal Boeing 707, which was actually deployed elsewhere. The additional details supplied by Wynne lengthened the journey's duration and made it more improbable than ever.

Research in Washington and the Kennedy Archive in Boston confirmed that neither Wynne nor Penkovsky ever visited the President. The recently declassified visitors' log for the period Wynne said he had been in Washington shows that Kennedy had been constantly in the company of others, and that his time was fully accounted for on a minute-by-minute basis. This was further confirmed by his personal secretary, Mrs Lincoln, who swore an affidavit insisting that Wynne was mistaken. Indeed, she was supported in this view by the then Deputy Director for Plans, Dick Helms; Penkovsky's CIA case officer, George

Kisevalter; and the CIA's distinguished counsel, Walter Pforzheimer, who had briefed Congress on the case. All swore that Penkovsky never came to America in July 1961 – nor at any other time. Their recollection was supported by nine other CIA officers who had a knowledge of the case.

That Wynne could have expected to get away with such a blatant invention says much about the man, and further research into his claims in regard to Penkovsky show that not only did he exaggerate his own role in the case, but he made numerous claims on behalf of the GRU colonel that are themselves completely unsustainable. Some, indeed, have a marked resemblance to previous claims made on behalf of the imaginary Kuznov. For example, Wynne says that Penkovsky, whom he called Alex, 'named the day – 12th August'[49] that the Berlin Wall was to be erected. Wynne states elsewhere that work on the Wall had begun 'just days after Alex returned with his delegation to Moscow'.[50] Wynne tried to turn this incident into a matter of political controversy by charging that the United States administration had 'wanted the Berlin Wall' to be constructed, for its own obscure motives, and had 'cynically overruled'[51] British demands to prevent the wall from being completed. There is no evidence to suggest that any such inter-Allied dispute ever took place.

Study of Wynne's claims in the light of his tendency to invention reveals that much of what he wrote about Penkovsky is completely untrue. He did not supply him with a 'long range transmitter'[52] and there are several instances of Wynne exaggerating Penkovsky's access to Soviet secrets. It seems improbable that Penkovsky told the West of the 'location of hidden rocket sites'[53] in the Soviet Union. If he did, it was not because the indiscreet Marshal Varentsov was Penkovsky's father-in-law.[54] Nor is it likely that Penkovsky obtained 'official minutes of the Central Committee meetings at which the Soviet Premier admitted his country's vulnerability'.[55] Not even Penkovsky ever claimed to have enjoyed access to sensitive political intelligence. Nor, apparently, was this kind of material ever made available to President Kennedy, judging by his private correspondence with Khrushchev, subsequently published by Robert Kennedy in *Thirteen Days*.[56]

The inventions are not all restricted to *The Man From Odessa*. Wynne's first book has its own share of dubious material, and one incident in particular is worth highlighting. Wynne recalled an episode in which Penkovsky, while in London, had been reunited with an army colleague whom he believed dead. In fact the friend had defected, and the Soviet authorities had faked his funeral to conceal his escape to the West. Indeed, a week after this emotional meeting, another was arranged at which Penkovsky was reunited with no less than 'twenty men, all Russians, whom he had known long ago',[57] old friends he had believed to be dead also. Whilst such a grotesque breach of security, exposing an agent currently in place to twenty-one defectors, would have been unthinkable, the incident was pursued further by Wynne in *The Man From Odessa*, in which he added further, even more ludicrous details. In the second account, Penkovsky's first Russian friend, formerly referred to as 'a Russian officer who had served with him, [and] had been his friend,'[58] is promoted to 'a general in Alex's service'.[59] In fact no GRU officer over the rank of major has ever defected to the West.

Wynne makes a trifling error in timing over the meeting with the twenty old friends, 'all former top Soviet officials',[60] saying in his first account that it took place 'less than a week'[61] after Penkovsky was reunited with his friend. In *The Man From Odessa* the meeting happened instantly, when his friend 'took Alex by the arm like a little child and led him into the next room. There were twenty others like him . . .'[62] The BBC swallowed the latter version whole and apparently failed to notice another interesting discrepancy: while elaborating on the drama of the second account, Wynne included Sergei Kuznov as one of the twenty old friends of Penkovsky who had defected. Thus

Wynne alleged, albeit indirectly, that Kuznov and Penkovsky knew each other.

There can be little doubt that Wynne was a shrewd opportunist who sought to capitalise on his brief but harrowing experience as Penkovsky's courier. It will be recalled that when Wynne's second book was published in 1981, one of the topical issues of the day was Soviet penetration of the British Security Service. Wynne latched on to this subject by suggesting that Penkovsky had warned SIS in 'April 1961' that 'the KGB have placed one of their agents at the very highest level of MI5'.[63] This proposition is scarcely credible, since it is now known that the first allegations of a Soviet mole inside MI5 were not made until 1963, a good two years later. By straying into this uncharted territory Wynne quickly found himself in difficulties. Having fabricated Penkovsky's warning about a Soviet spy in MI5, it was logical for Wynne to claim that Penkovsky had insisted that MI5 should be excluded from any involvement in his case. Wynne gave 'a personal guarantee that MI5 would not be brought in' and that Penkovsky was being handled by SIS . . .[64] but omitted to mention that (if his own tales were true) he and 'James' had both previously worked for MI5 during the war. In fact, as is confirmed by Peter Wright, MI5 had been indoctrinated into the case at an early stage and had played a key role in taking counter-surveillance measures throughout Penkovsky's two visits to London.[64] Wynne's clumsy attempt to draw on the controversy then surrounding the loyalty of the late Sir Roger Hollis goes awry when he makes a series of fundamental errors, mistakenly referring to him as an 'MI6 mole'[65] when Hollis had never worked for SIS, and suggesting that in 1961 Hollis had been 'the acting director' of that organisation. In reality Hollis was Director-General of the Security Service in 1961, a post he had held since 1956.

Apart from Wynne's two accounts of his dealings with Penkovsky, there are two other published sources which give some insight into their case. One is the transcript of their four-day trial in Moscow in May 1963, and the other is a little-known English-language booklet entitled *Penkovsky: Facts and Fancy*,[66] published by Novosti. Much of the latter is devoted to denigrating Penkovsky and ridiculing the idea that he might have been an ideologically motivated spy, but by far the most interesting material concerns Wynne, and in particular the transcript of his interrogation by Nikolai Chistiakov and Aleksandr Zagvozdin of the KGB on 22 November 1962:

> Wynne: Good morning!
> Official: Good morning! How do you feel?
> Wynne: Oh, quite well, thank you.
> Official: I invited you in order to come back to that conversation, which you have repeatedly started, when you were here during the interrogations on your spy connections with Penkovsky. We rejected everything regarding your proposals of using you in intelligence activities against England and other Western powers.
>
> Yesterday, you asked the investigator to return to this question again, and I am ready to hear you on this matter.
>
> Wynne: Well, I would like to make it clear that I have no quarrel with the Soviet Union. And meeting you, I have realized more how bad previously I've done it, not intentionally. Therefore I ask you to give me an opportunity for putting this matter right.
>
> And I have no serious loyalty to my country now, because they put me into this affair. They have forced me.
>
> The serious situation I find myself in has been caused because I have been forced into it. Therefore I have no loyalty. I have a clear conscience to help you.
>
> And the way that I can see it . . . is several ways. The first one, as you know and your people know here, I am well connected with a vast amount of industries of all kinds. I have access through long established associations with most main industries in England and a great many in West-

ern Europe too. I have made friends in industry, and up to the present day I have access into these factories. So let us take the example first on the industrial side, on how I can help you, and then I will go on to the other means, which I have been thinking to use.

There are many factories. We take the example of Thompson, who has a 'John Thompson' factory, who has an armament, the development of armament factory which your delegation did not see and go near. I know and I go. That is just one example.

This is another example – the firm 'West Tools' are manufacturing ultrasonic equipment which is on the embargo list not allowed for Eastern Europe. I have pictures of the thing. Every large industry is doing some work for the Government, every large industry. Every large industry is doing something. I can find for you what they are doing. I can take some of your people there who'd normally not be allowed to go. I can introduce people to one another, who are perhaps sympathetic towards the Soviet cause. There are some people in England who speak to me, because they know I come to Eastern Europe and they speak well about the prospects. This sort of people I do a lot of entertaining in my house. I have a big house, I can get people to meet together if necessary. Apart from this field I have in Western Europe many contacts because we have many agents for the companies, not only the 8 companies on paper, sometimes I work for private companies on commission basis. I've also met members of many associations: Institute of Directors, Institute of Engineers, Institute of Supervising Electrical Engineers. I can attend many meetings and make many contacts if you need them.

I am able to make many contacts in industry and find out quite a lot of information upon research and development that is going on. This is quite not difficult for me. Sometimes I might need some money to buy samples but

I don't need you to pay me, I think maybe I would need from you some money to buy samples or to pay for something but not so much.

Now this is one side of my commercial business which I can do. Now the other side of my commercial business is the 'Mobile Exhibitions' units. Now I have arranged with the Hungarians and the Rumanians to come to England with their own people to sell Hungarian and Rumanian goods in England, to make propaganda for them all around the country. This I could do quite easily for the Soviet Union – its offerings. But not only in England. The Hungarians are thinking in terms of going into France and into Switzerland hiring my 'Mobile' unit. This could work to your advantage: where, as any place you want to go, I can arrange a programme in that place, and I can make contacts for you and introductions for you, and what you think you want on this side. This could work to your advantage because you could have your own people on the vehicles to make your contacts and I would help you in going to any area of the country that you want to go. This could apply to Western Europe too.

If you could invite the machines to come to the Soviet Union with British equipment it seems, from King's idea, that he has some idea of making trouble in April or May, because he has already mentioned that. You could work this to your advantage. I would play along with King. I would not make trouble for you and I would do as King told me to keep you informed on what is happening. He says he has other contacts or there are other people, he told me. King told me there are other people. So that it means that they have some plan for April or May. I don't know who it is. I would be prepared to work for you and to make . . . You see, I would like to explain to the General, that it's necessary. I cannot play false with you, I cannot be a fool twice, I've learned my lesson. So I have to be correct with you. And if you give an invitation . . . your enterprise here or your . . . somebody gives me an invitation to come with my machines to the Soviet Union, well, King, I am sure, would be very interested if I was coming. And I would work with you. I could not play false with you because I am sure you have your means to control me.

I am under obligation to you. It seems to me that it could work to your advantage. I will cooperate in any plan you have. I've tried to show my willingness to cooperate with you by not demanding some of the British Embassy here. It seems to me, I was thinking you have more experience of these matters, so forgive me I am thinking in my own way. I will work for you. How many bad times have I done, one and a half years? I will work for two years for you but give me my freedom after that. I don't want to have it on my head . . . but give me my freedom after this. I don't want to be mixed up in anything after this.

Supposing you have an Englishman, a high man in industry or scientist, that you were thinking maybe he would be good for you. I could in my social way, I am well connected. I have a good house, good presentation, I could become friends with this man within a month, two months and I would make my business to find out what organization he belongs to and what clubs he goes to. Oh, it's my business to make contacts with this man. I could make contacts, and I make good friend, I invite him to my house, speak with him about my experiences in Eastern European countries and I can report to you exactly as an Englishman, as I find another Englishman. These things I can do for you.

I have now a big house to myself. I have built an office at the back – used some money. And I have a big lounge with a bar. And I do some pretty high entertaining for contacts, if you want contacts, if you have high people that you think are sympathetic to your cause. This is a thing I could do very correctly and very quietly.

Official: Are you not afraid of the consequences if those people manage to find out about you being here, if suppose they learn at a later date that you have not told them the whole truth? And let's take the worst possibility, that you are caught working for us. Aren't you afraid of the risk?

Wynne: This is the way I see it. This is the way I see it. If I'm caught I'll take a risk for you. With your guidance, you have to help me and professionally. I'll take a risk, any risks for you for two years. I promise you. If they catch me, I shall say: 'Yes, I have done it for the Soviet Union. Why? Because the Soviet Union had treated me correctly. Your people did not treat me correctly.'

It seems to me that they . . . it would be difficult to do something against me because, if they put me in prison, it has to be a court case. I would speak about the bad things that they got me into. And the worst that can happen is that they make my business bad, stop me from going abroad or again take my passport away, and do this thing privately. That is the worst that can happen to me. So my risk for working for you is not so great, I don't think.

This, you see, I have money in the bank. So I could live in a small way without trouble, if my business was finished, just a small way. But it seems to me that if I worked for you and did well for you, I'm sure that you would help me, if I was in trouble, financially.

But I want some understanding with you if you agree with my proposals for two years on the maximum, because I couldn't stand this strain any longer. I would agree on two years of cooperation.

Official: We have understood your proposal. I am unable to promise you anything now.

(Speaking to the interpreter) I decided to listen to Mr.

Wynne's suggestions only because he repeatedly raised this question. Tell him that it is necessary to consider all this carefully and to think about it.

Wynne: I would work for you. I don't believe the Soviets want war. You have too much to do in your own country and I would help you in this. I would do anything you ask. Either I would concentrate on the industrial relations for you or I would concentrate on working with King and Ackroyd to help you to know the organizations, or on both, which you think is better for you.

Official: Do you think that you have told during the investigation everything about your espionage activities against the Soviet Union?

Wynne: Yes. Yes, really and truly. I have nothing to hide from you.

Wynne's offer to work for the KGB for a period of two years after his release may have been a convenient ploy to facilitate an escape from his predicament, or it might have been more serious, one cannot tell; but the reference to 'King' in the transcript is intriguing, for this was the name of one of the SIS officers who had handled Wynne.

SIS had run Penkovsky at four levels. The then Chief, Sir Dick White, was introduced to Penkovsky during the latter's second visit to London. During his trial Penkovsky disclosed that White had been referred to simply as 'RAJ'. The operation itself had been supervised by Oliver St John, a veteran SIS officer who had once run a network of agents in Cairo, leaving two case officers to deal with Penkovsky and Wynne separately. They were Harold Shergold, who never met Wynne, and Dickie Franks, who was transferred to Bonn from SIS headquarters as soon as Wynne was arrested. In addition, there were two other senior officers indoctrinated into the case: Harry Stokes, then the Deputy Head of Station in Washington to (Sir) Maurice Oldfield, who liaised closely with the CIA; and Herbert J. Collins, Shergold's controller. The latter's London flat, at 52 Coleherne Court, had been used to entertain Penkovsky in town, and had been the venue for Dick White's meeting with him. While giving evidence at his trial Wynne could say very little about the involvement of the CIA, as precautions had been taken to prevent him from learning the identities of Penkovsky's two American case officers, George Kisevalter and Joe Bulik. However, Wynne had identified various SIS personnel, including Ruari Chisholm, who had run SIS's station in Moscow until July 1962, and his wife Janet, who had held regular meetings with Penkovsky in December 1961 and January 1962. The clandestine role of this pair, of course, had already been disclosed to the KGB by Chisholm's former colleague in Berlin, George Blake. Indeed, Blake admitted to SIS in April 1961 that he had compromised Chisholm, which makes one wonder about the wisdom of the decision to allow the couple to maintain contact with Penkovsky eight months later. Wynne also named three people as having pressured him into what he had presented as his reluctant collaboration with SIS: a security officer named Hartley, a Foreign Office official named Ackroyd,[67] and his subordinate, Mr King.[68] What makes Wynne's statement so intriguing is that when Wynne and John Gilbert came to write *The Man From Moscow*, they changed King's name to 'Robbins'.[69] The name Robbins appears nowhere in the trial transcript, and King is repeatedly identified as one of Wynne's SIS handlers. Yet in *The Man From Moscow* the authors have substituted 'Robbins' for King. The most reasonable explanation is that although 'Ackroyd' was a pseudonym, 'King' was an authentic name. In fact the SIS officer who had assisted Franks was Roger Andrew Ivan King who, according to recently declassified CIA files, had once come under suspicion for having illicit contacts with the GRU in 1940.[70] This mystery has never been resolved.

Another area of speculation regarding the Wynne and Penkovsky case revolves around the exact date that Penkovsky was arrested. The official documents refer to Penkovsky having been taken into custody in Gorky Street at 1.55 on the afternoon of Monday 22 October 1962.[71] Curiously, on this date Wynne was still in the West, for he only crossed over from Vienna to Hungary on 31 October (only to be arrested there, in Budapest, at 7 p.m.[72] on Friday 2 November). Thus, by the time Wynne was arrested in Budapest, still oblivious to the fate of his friend, *Penkovsky had been in the hands of the KGB for at least ten days.*

On the day that Wynne was arrested, the KGB had conducted an experiment in Moscow to test the information extracted from Penkovsky during his lengthy interrogation. Penkovsky had revealed his instructions on how to make contact with the CIA, and described the elaborate procedure they had adopted. It was tradecraft of the most classic variety. First, a signal had to be sent to two American diplomats at their homes. Shortly before nine in the morning they had telephoned 43-26-94, which had been answered by Alexis Davison, an assistant air attaché. Without speaking the KGB had hung up and repeated the exercise with 42-36-87, which had been answered by Hugh Montgomery, who also lived in an apartment at 18 Kutuzovsky Prospekt. In addition, a black mark had been placed on lamppost Number 35 on Kutuzovsky Prospekt. The American reaction had been for Davison to drive along Kutuzovsky Prospekt and, at the appropriate lamppost, get out of his car to examine it. He then was seen to drive to the US Embassy. At 3.15 later the same day another American diplomat, Richard C. Jacob, was seized by the KGB while attempting to recover a small canister concealed behind a central-heating radiator in the hallway of 5/6 Pushkin Street. Thus, having demonstrated that Penkovsky's confession was certainly true in as much as it referred to his means of communicating with the CIA via dead-letter drops, the KGB arranged for Wynne's arrest.

It would certainly appear from the CIA's reaction that the

first its Moscow Station knew that its star agent had been compromised came on 2 November, when Richard Jacob was trapped while attempting to retrieve Penkovsky's dead drop in Pushkin Street. Under these circumstances it would be understandable that there was insufficient time to warn Wynne in Budapest of the danger he was in. However, there is another bizarre side to the story, for it would seem that shortly before his arrest Penkovsky had sent a coded 'Doomsday message' to his new SIS case officer, Gervase Cowell, indicating that a Soviet nuclear strike on the West was imminent. At the time Penkovsky's behaviour had caused consternation among those indoctrinated into the case, but in retrospect it may have been his way of alerting SIS to the fact that he had either come under direct KGB control, or had merely detected hostile surveillance.

Penkovsky's last contact with the CIA had been in September when he had noticed his principal contact, Rodney Carlson, at a reception given by the US Ambassador for a group of visiting executives from the American electrical industry. On 6 September he had attended a film show of *A Taste of Honey* at the British Embassy where he had been spotted by Gervase Cowell, his new British case officer, who had taken over from Ruari Chisholm after the latter's return to London on 14 July 1962.

There are still many question marks hanging over the Wynne and Penkovsky case, not a few of them placed there by Wynne himself. Some of those who worked with him on his overseas trips considered his consumption of alcohol to be a hazard to his regular business, quite apart from any espionage on the side, and he was a familiar figure to *habitués* of the British Club at the embassy who frequently saw him the worse for wear.

The KGB's opinion of Wynne was also pretty low. Viktor Kutuzov, speaking on behalf of the organisation, remarked:

> Wynne hated the British secret service agents who had ruined him, used him and discarded him like so much

> refuse. He wept and sobbed in front of the Interrogating Judge and in court, castigated himself, his rashness, his trust in those ruthless sharks from the Intelligence Service. Apparently this was why Wynne made to Soviet authorities some important revelation about certain high ranking person in the British secret service, which with time may be made public. Wynne did not stop there. He cynically offered the Soviet authorities to perform espionage assignments against the West.

Certainly Wynne's experience in the Soviet Union changed his life. Thereafter he was regarded as a pest by SIS and, to a lesser extent, by the CIA, which twice tried to accommodate him on visits to America. On neither occasion did Wynne take any interest in the business leads he was offered, but instead concentrated on drinking. He led a nomadic existence, working initially in Malta selling holiday apartments, a project that was abandoned in 1972, and then moving to the Canary Islands where a friend employed him to promote a villa development on Lanzarote. Finally he bought an apartment in Palma de Majorca, where he became a well-known member of the hard-drinking British expatriate community led by Lady Docker. It was here that he went into a rose-growing partnership, and later contracted cancer of the throat. His continued alcohol-induced abuse of his second wife led to their estrangement, and she went to live in a windowless basement sauna at a property he had once owned in Lexham Gardens, south-west London. In 1985, in an interview with Philippa Kennedy of the *Daily Express*, Hermione complained that she had been deserted by Wynne and said that he 'missed the secrecy and tension of his other life'.[73]

Shortly before his death Wynne brought libel proceedings against the author and publisher of *The Friends*, which had mentioned in passing that many of Wynne's claims relating to 'Sergei Kuznov' and Oleg Penkovsky were simply untrue. Short of money, Wynne sought financial backing from a business contact and launched an action for defamation. His case against the author faltered when it emerged that a copy of Wynne's military record had been acquired from the army, showing that Wynne had never received the commission he claimed. Indeed, it also transpired that Wynne had a history of using a bogus military rank, and even elevated himself to the rank of lieutenant-colonel when applying for membership of the Naval Club in London.

The issue of Wynne's exact rank, combined with overwhelming evidence that he had fabricated every detail of the visit he and Penkovsky had supposedly made to Washington, DC, in 1961, forced Wynne to abandon his action just two days before it was due to be tried in the High Court in London. This last-moment withdrawal, without payment of the damages demanded, his costs or even a face-saving apology, was eloquent proof that Wynne had no intention of being exposed publicly as a Walter Mitty character.

The sad reality is that Wynne suffered from what might be termed a 'post-usefulness syndrome', a craving for attention from the media. This is a fairly familiar phenomenon, particularly among ex-intelligence agents who have been unable to replace the excitement and adrenalin of their operational experience. He probably never really fully recovered from the physical and nervous breakdown he endured after his return to London from Moscow in 1964. As we have seen, *The Man From Odessa* was full of bizarre claims that could not be substantiated, and some must have been deliberately included to make the book controversial. He even suggested that the destruction of the Tupolov 144 supersonic jet which crashed so spectacularly at the Paris airshow in June 1973 had been a consequence of a scheme to plant deliberately falsified Concorde data on the Tupolev's Soviet designers.[74] In a television interview to promote *The Man From Odessa* he even implied that he and Penkovsky had been granted a secret audience by the Queen. However, in a far more revealing radio programme, in which Wynne was analysed by the distinguished psychiatrist Dr Anthony Clare, he admitted that he had great difficulty in telling truth from fiction. This perhaps was the single moment in Wynne's life when he was truly candid.

Glossary

Abwehr	German military intelligence service
AFSA	US Armed Forces Security Agency
BSC	British Security Coordination, New York
Compartmenting	Separation of data to prevent leakage
CPGB	Communist Party of Great Britain
DCI	Director of Central Intelligence
DDO	Deputy Director of Operations, CIA
DEA	US Drug Enforcement Agency
DST	French Security Service
GOC	General Officer Commanding
GRU	Soviet military intelligence service
HDE	Home Defence Security Executive
Meal ticket	Defector's information which renders him valuable to his host country
MI5	British Security Service
NACA	National Advisory Committee on Aeronautics
NSA	US National Security Agency
NSC	US National Security Council
PLO	Palestine Liberation Organisation
PRU	Provincial Reconnaissance Unit
RCMP	Royal Canadian Mounted Police
Rezident	Senior KGB officer in overseas country
SAC	Strategic Air Command
SAVAK	Iranian security and intelligence service
SAVAMA	Iranian Republican security service
SHAEF	Supreme Headquarters Allied Expeditionary Force
SIS	British Secret Intelligence Service
SOE	Special Operations Executive

Notes

Introduction

1 Principal among the historians who have criticised the historiographers are Professor Donald Cameron Watt and Christopher Andrew. The latter himself fell foul of his academic colleagues when he published *Inside the KGB* with Oleg Gordievsky without supporting documentation. It was noted that the book contained virtually no new research and depended heavily on either secondary sources or a single source without verification.

2 Harry Williamson appears in the Abwehr's Hamburg archives as Agent A3725, and has been identified by Ladislas Farago and David Kahn as 'Fritz Hansen'. His true identity was known, though not published by Gunter Peis in *Mirror of Deception* (Weidenfeld & Nicolson, 1977). Contrary to his wishes, his name was first made public in the *Sunday Express*, 24 June 1990.

CHAPTER I: Dusko Popov

1 For further details of Julius Hanau see *Secret War: The Full Story of SOE* (Hodder & Stoughton, 1991).

2 In his memoirs *Spy/CounterSpy* (Weidenfeld & Nicolson, 1974), Popov did not reveal Clement Hope's real name, but referred only to 'the chief of MI6 for the Balkans, and Spiradis was his cover name' (p. 28).

3 For further details of Arthur Owens see *MI5: British Security Service Operations 1909–45* (Bodley Head, 1981).

4 Georges Graf's post-war career includes a scrape with the counter-espionage authorities in France and a spell as a Czech consular official in Britain. He now lives in Czechoslovakia.

5 Ivan Spaniel's career as a double agent was short-lived, but his true name is mistakenly referred to as a cryptonym by Masterman in *The Double Cross System* (Yale University Press, 1972), p. 54.

6 Ralph Jarvis, SIS's Section V officer responsible for the whole of the Iberian Peninsula, is referred to by Popov as simply 'Colonel Jarvis, my local MI6 contact' (p. 75).

7 Friedle Gaertner's identity was disguised by Popov as 'Gerda Sullivan'. She was unamused to see his description of her (p. 78).

8 Masterman p. 74.

9 Ibid. p. 73.

10 Although Eric Glass was identified as the unwitting lynchpin of Plan MIDAS, he threatened a legal action for defamation when his name was published in *MI5: British Security Service Operations 1909–45*. Subsequent editions had his name deleted.

11 Contrary to an assertion made by Dr H. Montgomery Hyde (*Times* letters, 5 September 1982), this was not the very first operational use of microdots by the Abwehr. Reduction photography had previously been practised by CHARLIE, a photographer of German origin living in Liverpool who had been recruited by the Abwehr in 1938. The first recorded use of microdots by the Abwehr was in a letter from Lisbon received by RAINBOW in August 1941 shortly before Popov was given his questionnaire in microdot form (See Hinsley Vol. 4, p. 103).

12 Whether J. Edgar Hoover ever actually met Popov is open to doubt. See Thomas F. Troy's article 'The British Assault on J. Edgar Hoover' in the 1990 *International Journal of Intelligence & Counterintelligence* Vol. 3 No. 2, pp. 169–209.

13 There is a slight discrepancy regarding the date of this questionnaire's receipt by Popov. Masterman gives a date of April 1942 (p. 176), by which time Popov had returned to the US, but Popov suggests he received it in Brazil whence he departed in December 1941 (*Spy/CounterSpy*, p. 154).

14 Masterman pp. 176–77.

15 Eugn Sostaric's identity was concealed by Popov as 'Thomas Sardelic' (p. 195).

16 For further details of Alphons Timmerman see Hinsley, *British Intelligence in the Second World War* (HMSO, 1990), Vol. 4, p. 329.

17 For further details of Karl Muller see *The Branch: A History of the Metropolitan Police Special Branch 1883–1983* by Rupert Allason (Secker & Warburg, 1983), p. 49.

18 Popov refers to Stefan Zeis only as 'Jean' (p. 212).

19 GARBO's true name, Juan Pujol, was correctly identified for the first time in a newspaper article (*Mail on Sunday*, 3 June 1984). He subsequently co-authored *GARBO* with Nigel West (Weidenfeld & Nicolson, 1985).

20 Masterman p. 153.

21 JUNIOR's true identity had never been revealed, although he had been linked incorrectly to Erich Vermehren, who planned his own defection almost simultaneously.

22 Colonel Wren had previously been MI5's representative at BSC and the Defence Security Office at Trinidad.

23 The Marquis de Bona is Popov's 'Count Nicholas de Ruda' (p. 199).

CHAPTER II: Wulf Schmidt

1 Abenra (or Aabenraa) is in the county of South Jutland. When Harry was born in 1911 it had been in German hands since the Prussian War of 1854. A referendum in 1919, won narrowly by the Danes, returned the territory to Denmark.

2 For further details of Goesta Caroli, see *MI5: British Security Service Operations 1909–45*.

3 Harry cannot recall anything of RAINBOW. See Masterman p. 59.

4 *Game of the Foxes* (McKay & Co, NY, 1971) by Ladislas Farago.

5 *Hitler's Spies* (Hodder & Stoughton, 1978) by David Kahn.

6 Masterman p. 73.

7 Harry's favourite swearword, which appeared frequently in his messages, was '*Gotz von Berlichingen*', from Goethe's famous poem, which actually meant '*Lech mich am Arsch*'.

8 Kahn p. 350.

9 Ibid.

10 Ibid.

11 Hinsley Vol. 4, pp. 96–97.

12 Ibid.

13 Ibid.

14 Kahn p. 351.

15 Masterman p. 74.

16 Originally an RSS radio operator, Reed has contributed the anonymous Appendix 3, 'Technical Problems Affecting Radio Communications by the Double Cross Agents', in Hinsley Vol. 4, pp. 309–13.

17 Hinsley Vol. 4, pp. 331–32.

18 Sir Michael Howard's *British Intelligence in the Second World War*, Vol. 5, p. 11.

19 Hinsley Vol. 4, p. 333.

20 Masterman p. 78.

21 Ibid. p. 73.

22 Kahn p. 351.

23 Ibid.

24 Masterman pp. 52–53.

CHAPTER III: William Buckley

1 Felix Rodriguez in *Shadow Warrior* (Simon & Schuster, 1989), p. 193.

2 Tucker Gougelmann's PRUs comprised Viet Cong defectors deployed in small paramilitary units to identify and eliminate the Viet Cong's civilian infrastructure. It was a highly successful, if controversial, operation that attracted much criticism because of the ruthless nature of the PRU's mission. Gougelmann, a much-decorated former Marine, retired from the CIA in 1972 but was arrested in April 1975 by the North Vietnamese Army in Saigon a few days after the city had fallen. He had returned to help his Vietnamese family escape but was himself caught. His badly mutilated body was returned to the US two years later and interred with full military honours in the Arlington National Cemetery on 28 October 1977 in grave no. 685/3, section 11. Powers is buried in grave no. 685/2 (see p. 177).

3 For Agee's defence see *On The Run* (Lyle Stuart, 1987). He asserts correctly that he was not the first to publicise Welch's CIA rôle. He had previously been listed by an East German, Julius Mader, in his notoriously inaccurate *Who's Who in the CIA* (Berlin, 1968). In 1966 Peer de Silva, the CIA station chief in Vietnam, was badly injured when a Viet Cong car bomb detonated just outside his office in the US Embassy in Saigon, killing one of his secretaries.

4 In 1989 Mark Hessner succeeded Nahum Admony as head of Mossad.

5 See *Guards Without Frontiers* by Samuel M. Katz (Arms & Armour, 1990).

6 See *By Way of Deception* by Victor Ostrovsky and Claire Hoy (St Martin's, 1990), p. 324.

7 *Nest of Spies* by Amir Taheri (Hutchinson, 1988), p. 165.

8 Bob Woodward in *Veil* (Simon & Schuster, 1987), p. 396

9 Shackley is the author of *The Third Option: An American View of Counterinsurgency Operations* (Reader's Digest, 1981), p. 396. Before his retirement in 1979 his career in the CIA encompassed Berlin (1958–61); Miami (1962–65); Laos (1966–69); Vietnam (1969–72); Chief, East Asia Division; and finally Associate Deputy Director of Operations.

10 See *Inside the KGB* (André Deutsch, 1990).

11 Tower Commission Report, p. 106.

12 *Best Laid Plans* by David C. Martin and John Walcott (Harper & Row, 1988), p. 346.

13 Tower Commission Report, p. 178.

14 The Tower Commission deliberately avoids identifying Portugal as the European country used by the CIA as a transit point for the weapons.

15 Tower Commission Report, p. 194.

16 Southern Air Transport was identified by the US Army as the recipient of one thousand TOW missiles supplied from Redstone Arsenal, Alabama, on 13/14 February 1986.

17 Tom Milligan in *CIA Life: 10,000 Days with the Agency* (Foreign Intelligence Press, 1991), p. 215.

18 See *Casey* by Joseph Persico (Viking, 1990), p. 570.

19 Speculation about Waite's close involvement with Oliver North was reported by *USA Today* (15 December 1986) and appeared in *The Times* (Waite 'not told of Iran deal' by David Sapsted, 16 December 1986) with Waite's denial that he had known of 'arms dealings or anything like that'. However, on the following day, 17 December 1986, *The Times*' diplomatic correspondent confirmed in an item entitled 'Waite was aided by North over hostages' that 'a highly reliable source' had admitted that Waite had been provided with 'transport and security back-up during his missions', and that 'Colonel North arranged for Mr Waite to be dropped into the Lebanon by a US helicopter in the dead of night.' On 21 December John Witherow of the *Sunday Times* quoted Robert Oakley, identified as the former head of the State Department's Office for Combating Terrorism: 'North helped Waite by arranging planes, shelter and protection for him.'

CHAPTER IV: Anthony Blunt

1 Recollection of Lord Rothschild, 22 January 1987.

2 Hinsley's official history, *Security and Counter-intelligence*, Vol. 4,

implies that age was the reason for Kell's dismissal, stating that 'Kell was in his 67th year' (p. 10). It omits to mention that his replacement, Sir David Petrie, was only a year younger.

3 For further information on Willy Brandes see Robert Lamphere's *The FBI-KGB War* (Random House, 1986, p. 26) and John Costello's *Mask of Treachery* (Morrow, 1988, p. 282).

4 The paediatrician has requested anonymity.

5 That Driberg was Knight's source 'M8' is rejected by his biographer Francis Wheen who, by his own admission, cannot provide an alternative explanation for Driberg's sudden expulsion from the CPGB. Hinsley confirms that MI5 suffered 'the loss of one of its agents' inside the CPGB in 1940 following a leak (p. 285).

6 Belfrage, who died on 21 June 1990, had been named as a key KGB agent in 1945 by Elizabeth Bentley (*Out of Bondage* (Ivy Books, NY, 1988)). See Lamphere (p. 253) and Bentley (pp. 139–40).

7 See David Dallin's *Soviet Espionage* (Yale University Press, 1955) and *The Rote Kapelle* (University Publications of America, 1979).

8 When interviewed in East Berlin on 19 April 1991 Ursula Kuczynski stated she had only met Fuchs on five occasions in England.

9 The only non-classified open source reference to Weisband is in *The New KGB* by William Corson and Robert Crowley (Morrow, 1986) p. 216.

10 Pavel P. Mikhailov, Soviet Consul in New York 1941–46, was subsequently identified as Piotr P. Melkishev, a senior GRU officer (see *The Penkovsky Papers* (Wheatsheaf Books, 1988), p. 76). He later used the alias Fiodr P. Malin and was Colonel Stig Wennerstrom's controller when the latter was arrested and imprisoned in Sweden for espionage in 1963. David Dallin refers to him as Shinikov (p. 274) and Thomas Whiteside as Lemenov (*An Agent in Place* (Viking, 1966), p. 147).

11 Examples of this disinformation can be seen in Robert Lamphere's *The FBI-KGB War* (p. 84) and Peter Wright's *Spycatcher* (p. 180). Lamphere incorrectly stated that 'Gardner

could not break into any messages dated after . . . May 1945' (Ibid.).

12 Lamphere p. 85.

13 Boris Krotov, Third Secretary at the Soviet Embassy in London 1942–46, Second Secretary 1947.

14 The only non-classified open source reference to ALES is Thomas S. Powers' article in the *New York Review of Books*, 17 August 1989.

15 Jurgen Kuczynski, as leader of the exiled German Communist Party, put Fuchs in touch with his sister when the physicist volunteered to spy for the GRU. Interview, East Berlin, 19 April 1991.

16 Simon D. Kremer was to later to be confirmed as the GRU's *rezident* in London.

17 MI5 code-named the Soviet spy in the British Embassy in Washington HOMER, which probably was not the cryptonym which appeared in the Soviet signals traffic.

18 Interview with John Cairncross, Rome, 23 April 1981.

19 White Paper (Cmd 9577), 23 September 1955.

20 I. I. (Tim) Milne was the SIS Head of Station in Tokyo at the time of Philby's defection. He retired from SIS in October 1968.

21 See James Klugmann's *History of the Communist Party of Great Britain* (Lawrence & Wishart, 1968).

22 Michael Straight in *After Long Silence*, p. 102.

23 Anatoli Gromov (alias Gorsky, known to his agents as 'Henry'), Attaché then First Secretary in London 1940–44, was transferred to the USA in the summer of 1944 following Donald Maclean's appointment at the British Embassy in Washington. He returned to Moscow in December 1945 having been compromised by the defection of Gouzenko in Ottawa.

24 The allegation that Herbert Norman had been a KGB agent remains a matter of controversy in Canada. The most recent report on the subject by Professor Peyton V. Lyon (18 March 1990), commissioned by the Canadian Department of External Affairs,

contains many flaws of fact and interpretation, not the least of which is the author's assertion that Blunt incriminated Norman in order to obtain an immunity from prosecution. In fact Blunt named Norman *after* having received the immunity which was, by its nature, irrevocable.

25 According to Oleg I. Tsarev, interviewed in Moscow, 26 April 1991, Deutsch died during the war when his ship was sunk in the Atlantic, *en route* to the USA. The Cambridge Five's other illegal controller is a hitherto unknown 'illegal' named Ignace Reif.

26 See Flora Solomon's *Baku to Baker Street* (Collins, 1984).

27 See Anita Brookner's response to the disclosure that she had unwittingly pumped Phoebe Pool for information in *The Spectator*, 25 July 1987.

28 For Jenifer Hart's explanation see the *Sunday Times* 18 July 1983, and BBC TV's *Timewatch*, 19 July 1983.

29 Yuri Modin was willing to discuss his dealings with all the other Cambridge spies apart from Watson when interviewed in Moscow, 24 April 1991.

30 The most recent identification of ELLI, by Christopher Andrew and Oleg Gordievsky in *The KGB: The Inside Story* (Hodder & Stoughton, 1990), is singularly unconvincing, as ELLI was known to be a GRU source, while Long had been run by the KGB.

31 The death certificate for Nathaniel Rothschild shows that he died of a cut throat on 12 October 1923.

32 According to rumour, he met St John Hutchinson's daughter while he was defending Rothschild, who had been charged with manslaughter following the death of a cyclist in Cambridgeshire. Certainly his twenty-first celebrations had been cancelled unexpectedly, but no court record survives of Rothschild's prosecution in Cambridgeshire.

33 For a detailed account of this incident see Rothschild's *Meditations on a Broomstick* (Collins, 1977).

CHAPTER V: George Blake

1 *George Blake Superspy*, H. Montgomery Hyde, (Constable, 1987), p. 21.

2 Rebecca West in *The New Meaning of Treason*, (Viking, NY, 1964), p. 303.

3 E. H. Cookridge in *Shadow of a Spy* (Leslie Frewin, 1967), p. 55.

4 George Blake in *No Other Choice* (Jonathan Cape, 1990), p. 94.

5 Ibid. p. 143.

6 Ibid. p. 144.

7 Philip Deane, *Captive in Korea* (Hamish Hamilton, 1953), p. 163. Deane is in fact Greek and his true name is Gerassimos Gigantes. His most recent publication is *I Should Have Died* (Atheneum, 1977).

8 Blake p. 145.

9 Lord quoted by Cookridge, p. 112.

10 Cookridge p. 114.

11 Ibid.

12 Ibid.

13 *Soviet Defectors* by Vladislav Krasnov (Hoover Institution Press, 1986).

14 H. Montgomery Hyde, p. 39.

15 James Rusbridger in *The Intelligence Game* (Bodley Head, 1989), p. 43.

16 *KGB: The Inside Story* by Christopher Andrew and Oleg Gordievsky (Hodder & Stoughton, 1990), p. 404.

17 Ibid. p. 708.

18 Ibid. p. 403.

19 Ibid. p. 404.

20 Blake p. 17.

21 Ibid. p. 19.

22 Ibid. p. 160.

23 Ibid. p. 163.

24 Ibid. p. 165.

25 Philby in *My Silent War* (Grove Press, 1968), p. 162.

26 Andrew and Gordievsky, p. 173.

27 Ibid. p. 182.

28 CIA Clandestine Service History Series, 'The Berlin Tunnel Operation, 25 August 1967'.

29 Ibid.

30 *The Agency: The Rise and Decline of the CIA* by John Ranelagh (Simon & Schuster, 1986).

31 Ibid. p. 295.

32 Ibid. p. 187.

33 Ibid. p. 193.

34 See *New Lies for Old* (Bodley Head, 1984) by Anatoli Golitsyn, p. 287. General Rodin is also referred to by Peter Wright in *Spycatcher* (p. 363), but is not identified as Korovin, who is mentioned separately. Rodin/Korovin was subsequently identified by John Vassall in 1962 as a KGB officer to whom he had been introduced in Moscow in 1956, and had known as 'Grigori' thereafter in London. After 'Grigori's' departure Vassall had been handed on to 'Nikolai', whom he recognised as Sergei Kondrashev. Oddly, Andrew and Gordievsky incorrectly name Blake's controller as Yuri Modin (p. 362), and suggest that Blake's meeting in The Hague took place 'in the summer of 1956' whereas in fact it occurred in July 1953.

35 See *Mole* by William J. Hood (Norton, 1982).

36 The Smith case was investigated by Richard Harris Smith in the *International Journal of Intelligence and Counterintelligence* Vol. 3 No. 3, pp. 333–46. Some members of the West's counter-intelligence community believe Smith succumbed to blackmail and was recruited by the KGB as an agent. After his dismissal from the CIA Smith became an academic at the Hoover Institute at Stanford University and in 1967 wrote a bibliography of *The Okhrana – The Russian Department of Police*.

37 Blake p. 207.

38 Ibid. p. 208.

39 Ibid. p. 211. Blake is insistent that the only agents he betrayed were low-level sources, none of whom were executed. His own agents, recruited in Berlin, were, he says, 'plants' deliberately supplied by the KGB.

40 See Tom Bower's review, *Sunday Telegraph*, 16 September 1990.

41 See *Aquarium* by Viktor Suvorov (Hamish Hamilton, 1985).

42 Ibid. p. 3.

43 *The Blake Escape* by Michael Randle and Pat Pottle (Harrap, 1989).

44 *The Springing of George Blake* by Sean Bourke (Cassell, 1970).

45 *Report of the Inquiry into Prison Escapes and Security* Cmmd 3175 (HMSO, December 1966).

46 Bernard Porter's *Plots and Paranoia* (Unwin Hyman, 1989) p. 181.

47 James Rusbridger in *The Intelligence Game*, p. 53.

48 Harold Macmillan in the House of Commons, 4 May 1961.

49 Blake's suggestion that Brooke lied to the Commons and denied Lonsdale and Blake ever met is mischievous. On 7 May 1964 Alice Bacon MP asked in a Written Question: 'What instructions were given to the authorities in Wormwood Scrubs about the association of the two prisoners George Blake and Gordon Lonsdale?' The reply was: 'Lonsdale and Blake were in the same prison, Wormwood Scrubs, only from 3rd May, 1961, to 15th June, 1961. Throughout that period special precautions were taken in accordance with instructions given to the Governor to prevent communication between them.' Thus the Home Secretary avoided an unequivocal denial that the two had actually met.

50 Bourke pp. 58 and 97.

51 Ibid. p. 97.

52 Ibid. p. 60.

53 Ibid. p. 97.

54 Montgomery Hyde p. 63.

55 Ibid.

56 Ibid. p. 162.

57 Blake admitted having identified every SIS officer who had served in Moscow, including Terence O'Bryan Tear, Head of Station at the time of Blake's release from Korea, and his successor (Dame) Daphne Park. She was replaced in 1956 by the SIS officer who had previously held Blake's post in Section Y, whose cover was erroneously thought within SIS to be completely watertight.

CHAPTER VI: Francis Gary Powers

1 For a detailed account of the Popov case see *Mole* by William Hood (Norton, 1982). No exact date is given for Popov's disclosure relating to the U-2, but, since the meeting at which it was made is described as having taken place in Berlin, it must have occurred before Popov's transfer to Moscow in late November 1958 (p. 251).

2 Oswald has been identified as the KGB's source on the U-2 by Michael Beschloss in *Mayday* (Harper & Row, 1968), p. 236. Beschloss cites *Mole* (see note 1 above) for his claim, but then asserts, in contradiction to Hood's account, that the key meeting between Kisevalter and Popov took place 'in early 1959' (p. 236). David Charters in *Deception Operations* (Brassey's, 1990) also cites *Mole* as his source for suggesting that Popov's disclosure was 'early in 1958' (p. 338). Neither can be correct, as Popov was certainly under arrest long before Oswald ever reached the Soviet Union.

3 Oswald was reportedly hospitalised five days after his arrival in Moscow, when he slashed his wrists in his hotel on 21 October 1959, the Soviets having rejected his request for political asylum. If accurate, this would seem to imply that the KGB had not recognised Oswald's potential value. The only corroborated dates are those of Oswald's arrival in Moscow (16 October) and his visit to the US Embassy (31 October) to renounce his citizenship, when he mentioned having volunteered sensitive information. The exact date of Popov's arrest is unknown but there is some evidence to suggest that he was operating under KGB control as early as December

1958, when General Ivan Serov of the KGB was transferred to the GRU, presumably in response to some unprecedented incident (see *KGB* by John Barron (Reader's Digest), p. 344, and *Mole*, p. 309).

4 The exact number of U-2 flights over Soviet territory is unknown. Walter Laqueur suggests 'two hundred' (*A World of Secrets* (Basic Books, 1985), p. 144). Other sources claim a total of thirty, or maintain that the Powers flight on 1 May 1960 was the twentieth.

5 For further details of the GIDEON case see John Sawatsky's *For Services Rendered* (Doubleday, 1982), p. 34.

6 Hood p. 25.

7 According to Powers in *Operation Overflight* (Holt, Rinehart, 1970), the flight on 9 April returned to Incirlik and his mission was the first of its kind (p. 73); but there is evidence to suggest that it was not.

8 The Soviet version of events was published in *The Trial of the U2* (Translation World Publishers, 1960) and *Trial of the American U-2 Spy Pilot* (Soviet Booklet No. 76, September 1960).

9 These were training missions, not illicit overflights.

10 Frau Hellen Abel wrote to Donovan on 8 May 1961 from Eisenacherstrasse 22, Leipzig.

11 The Krogers, who now live in Moscow, are believed to have worked for Abel in New York as radio operators.

12 The Kroger case is uniquely well documented. The MI5 officer who conducted the investigation, Charles Elwell, wrote an account of it under the name Charles Elton in the *Police Journal*, Vol. XLIV No. 2, April-June 1971. Superintendent George C. Smith of Special Branch, who arrested Krogers, described the case in the Police College magazine 1964 and in his biography written by Norman Lucas entitled *Spycatcher*. Two of those arrested, Gordon Lonsdale and Harry Houghton, wrote their own versions in *Spy: Twenty Years of Secret Service* (Neville Spearman, 1965) and *Operation Portland: The Autobiography of a Spy* (Hart Davis, 1972). An unsuspecting colleague of the Krogers in the book trade, Fred Snelling, recalled them in *Rare Books and Rarer People* (Werner Shaw, 1982).

13 See *The Little Toy Dog* by William L. White (Dutton, 1962).

14 *Board of Inquiry Report to DCI*, 27 February 1962.

15 Ibid.

16 *Operation Overflight* by F. Gary Powers (Holt, Rinehart & Wilson, 1970).

CHAPTER VII: Greville Wynne

1 Piotr Deriabin and Frank Gibney, *The Penkovsky Papers*, (Doubleday, 1966).

2 *The Man From Moscow* (Hutchinson, 1967). Wynne's ghost-writer, John Gilbert, had previously published four novels: *The Buff Envelope* (Peter Davies, 1958) in which the heroine was named Vicki (see p. 185 above); *Zigzag* (Peter Davies, 1959), a story about a shell-shock victim laced with racist remarks about 'wogs'; *After The Storm* (Peter Davies, 1960); *The Fly Paper* (Arthur Barker, 1961).

3 'The Spy Who Deserted Me' by Philippa Kennedy, *Daily Express*, 27 March 1985.

4 Ibid.

5 Correspondence to the author from Sir Fitzroy Maclean.

6 *The Man From Odessa* (Robert Hale, 1981).

7 *The Man From Moscow*, p. 62.

8 *The Friends: Britain's Postwar Secret Intelligence Operations* (Weidenfeld & Nicolson, 1988).

9 *The Man From Odessa*, p. 40.

10 Ibid. p. 206.

11 *After the War – What then Soldier?* Author's collection.

12 Ibid. p. 85.

13 Ibid. p. 86.

14 Ibid. p. 79.

15 Ibid. p. 79.

16 Ibid. p. 80.

17 Ibid. p. 78.

18 Ibid. p. 78.

19 Ibid. p. 55.

20 Ibid. p. 64.

21 Ibid. p. 98.

22 Ibid. p. 154.

23 Although Wynne identifies Pavlov as 'a high ranking officer in the KGB' (p. 125) and later as 'actually the KGB's top man in Britain' (p. 158), he was no such thing. The KGB *rezident* in London during that period was Nikolai B. Korovin and his deputy was Nikolai P. Karpekov. The claim that Anatoli G. Pavlov was a KGB officer is unsubstantiated.

24 *The Man From Odessa*, p. 148.

25 The *Possev* arrest list is analysed by Professor Vladimir Krasnov in his *Soviet Defectors* (Hoover Institute, California, 1985).

26 *Games of Intelligence* (Weidenfeld, 1989).

27 *The Aquarium* by Viktor Suvorov (pseud.) (Hamish Hamilton, 1985).

28 *The Man From Odessa* p. 10.

29 Ibid. p. 139.

30 Ibid. p. 139.

31 Ibid. p. 112.

32 Ibid. p. 113.

33 Wynne's reference to Kuznov's 'lifelong friend' (p. 156) seems remarkably cavalier, considering his stated belief that 'the friend who helped Kuznov get out is still working at the same job' (p. 158). If true, this would appear to contradict Wynne's earlier assurance that the lives of the Soviet citizens who played a part in Kuznov's escape 'cannot be endangered by my disclosures' (p. 9).

34 Ibid. p. 156.

35 Ibid. p. 155.

36 Ibid. p. 146.
37 Ibid. p. 144.
38 Ibid. p. 222.
39 Ibid. p. 144.
40 Ibid. p. 164.
41 *The Man From Moscow*, p. 21.
42 *The Man From Odessa*, p. 116.
43 Ibid. p. 154.
44 Ibid. p. 203.
45 Ibid. p. 202.
46 Ibid. p. 202.
47 Ibid. p. 202.
48 Affidavit sworn by Greville Wynne, August 1989.
49 *The Man From Odessa*, p. 208.
50 Ibid. p. 208.
51 Ibid. p. 209.
52 Ibid. p. 210.
53 Ibid. p. 197.
54 Ibid. p. 197.
55 Ibid. p. 223.
56 *Thirteen Days* by Robert Kennedy (W. W. Norton, 1969).
57 *The Man From Moscow*, p. 78.
58 Ibid. p. 78.
59 *The Man From Odessa*, p. 196.
60 Ibid. p. 196.
61 Ibid. p. 196.
62 Ibid. p. 189.
63 Ibid. p. 190.
64 See Peter Wright's *Spycatcher* (Viking Books, NY, 1987), p. 202.

65 *The Man From Odessa*, p. 195.

66 *Penkovsky: Facts and Fancy* by Viktor Kutuzov (Novosti, 1966).

67 Ibid. p. 84.

68 Ibid. p. 33.

69 *The Man From Moscow*, p. 130.

70 *The Rote Kapelle* (University Publications of America, 1979), p. 383. King's career between July 1947 and his resignation from the Foreign Service in July 1969 took in Romania, Austria, Aden and France.

71 See Gordon Brook-Shepherd's *The Storm Birds* (Weidenfeld, 1988), p. 157, in which he alleges that Penkovsky and Wynne were arrested on the same day, on 2 November 1962. All other evidence indicates that Penkovsky was arrested first, and at least by 22 October, when one of his CIA contacts was detained briefly in Moscow. Wynne was still in Austria on this date, and was not arrested in Budapest until 2 November. Curiously, Brook-Shepherd's obviously inaccurate version of events is described by Oleg Gordievsky as 'the most reliable account' (*KGB: The Inside Story*, p. 715).

72 *Penkovsky: Facts and Fancy*, p. 58. This chronology has been confirmed most recently by Wynne's KGB interrogator, Nikolai Chistiakov, who states that Penkovsky's flat was searched for the first time on 20 October 1962, and that he was 'secretly arrested' two days later. (*Sunday Telegraph*, 5 May 1991).

73 'The Spy Who Deserted Me' by Philippa Kennedy, *Daily Express*, 27 March 1985.

74 *The Man From Odessa*, pp. 251–54.

Index

Index

Index

GAIL SHEEHY

Gorbachev

Once or twice in a century, a great leader emerges to change the course of history. Mikhail Gorbachev has accomplished the unthinkable – and transformed the world.

Yet little is known about the man.

Gail Sheehy, author of *Passages*, draws on a year and a half of research in the USSR to portray the architect of its second revolution. Given unparalleled access, she interviews Gorbachev's childhood neighbours, university friends and those who knew him as an *apparatchik* in the provinces; traces the U-turns and compromises of principle he has had to make on his path to ultimate power; and analyses the pivotal role of Raisa, the woman he fondly calls 'my general'. This is the first major biography of Russia's greatest statesman.

MARK AARONS & JOHN LOFTUS

Ratlines

The Vatican's Nazi Connection

In 1944, inside the Vatican, a secret cabal of right-wing priests established a network for smuggling Nazis out of Europe. In the name of intelligence, the group allowed fugitive war criminals to escape from justice and gave Soviet Intelligence their greatest Cold War triumph – for many Nazis were later recruited as agents and 'freedom fighters' by the intelligence agencies of Australia, Great Britain, Canada, Italy, West Germany and the US.

Ratlines is a shocking litany of disaster, duplicity and betrayal which reveals a Vatican deeply compromised by its nefariousness and thoroughly infiltrated and manipulated by communists *and* fascists.

GEOFFREY HOSKING

The Awakening of the Soviet Union

'The vital imperative which faces mankind is the priority of all human values, a world without violence and wars, diversity of social progress, dialogue and co-operation for the sake of development and the preservation of civilisation, and movement towards a new world order' Mikhail Gorbachev

'The most useful and reliable guide to the chaos of the current Soviet Union' *The Economist*

'Geoffrey Hosking's book is based on his Reith lectures . . . They were excellent radio pieces and make even better reading . . . Like all good historians, he anticipated an acceleration of history. He could hardly have imagined it would move exponentially' *Sunday Times*

'One of the best accounts available of life in Gorbachev's Soviet Union' *Sunday Correspondent*

'Concise, comprehensive and admirably clear, this book is an excellent starting point for a reader anxious to understand contemporary events in the Soviet Union. It reflects the combination of hope and foreboding with which the author regards the USSR's future' *Daily Telegraph*

TOM BOWER

Maxwell: The Outsider

Larger Than Life, Larger Than Legend

Robert Maxwell continues to make news even after his sensational and mysterious death. This book, which Maxwell tried to ban, now asks – and answers – the unresolved questions which remain. Completely revised and updated, it reveals:

- the truth behind Maxwell's extraordinary links with the KGB, the Kremlin and Eastern Europe
- the notorious 'Mirrorgate' affair and the reality of Maxwell's close relationship with the Israeli power elite
- his history of shady dealings which shocked the City
- his fatal greed in the USA which devastated his life's ambition
- the conspiracy of public and private companies that intentionally concealed a staggering £3 billion of debts
- and the sensational truth behind Robert Maxwell's death